D0758650

OXFORD READINGS IN PHILOSOPHY

THE CONCEPT OF GOD

Also published in this series

The Concept of Evidence, edited by Peter Achinstein
The Philosophy of Law, edited by Ronald M. Dworkin
Moral Concepts, edited by Joel Feinberg
Theories of Ethics, edited by Philippa Foot
The Philosophy of History, edited by Patrick Gardiner
The Philosophy of Mind, edited by Jonathan Glover
Knowledge and Belief, edited by A. Phillips Griffiths
Scientific Revolutions, edited by Ian Hacking
Philosophy and Economic Theory, edited by Frank Hahn and Martin Hollis
Divine Commands and Morality, edited by Paul Helm
Hegel, edited by Michael Inwood
The Philosophy of Linguistics, edited by Jerrold J. Katz
Reference and Modality, edited by Leonard Linsky
The Philosophy of Religion, edited by Basil Mitchell
Aesthetics, edited by Harold Osborne
The Theory of Meaning, edited by G. H. R. Parkinson
The Philosophy of Education, edited by R. S. Peters
Political Philosophy, edited by Anthony Quinton
Practical Reasoning, edited by Joseph Raz
The Philosophy of Social Explanation, edited by Alan Ryan
The Philosophy of Language, edited by J. R. Searle
Semantic Syntax, edited by Pieter A. M. Seuren
Applied Ethics, edited by Peter Singer
Philosophical Logic, edited by P. F. Strawson
Locke on Human Understanding, edited by I. C. Tipton
Theories of Rights, edited by Jeremy Waldron
Kant on Pure Reason, edited by Ralph C. S. Walker
Free Will, edited by Gary Watson
The Philosophy of Action, edited by Alan R. White
Leibniz: Metaphysics and Philosophy of Science, edited by R. S. Woolhouse

Other volumes are in preparation

THE CONCEPT OF GOD

EDITED BY
THOMAS V. MORRIS

OXFORD UNIVERSITY PRESS
1987

Oxford University Press, Walton Street, Oxford OX2 6DP
Oxford New York Toronto Melbourne Auckland
Delhi Bombay Calcutta Madras Karachi
Petaling Jaya Singapore Hong Kong Tokyo
Nairobi Dar es Salaam Cape Town
Associated companies in Beirut Berlin Ibadan Nicosia

OXFORD *is a trade mark of Oxford University Press*

Published in the United States
by Oxford University Press, New York

British Library Cataloguing in Publication Data
The Concept of God.—(Oxford readings in Philosophy)
1. God 2. Philosophical theology
I. Morris, Thomas V.
211'.01 BT102
ISBN 0–19–875077–3
ISBN 0–19–875076–5 Pbk

Library of Congress Cataloging in Publication Data
The Concept of God.
(Oxford readings in philosophy)
Bibliography: p.
Includes index.
1. God. I. Morris, Thomas V. II. Series.
BT102.A1C66 1987 212 86–31118
ISBN 0–19–875077–3
ISBN 0–19–875076–5 (pbk.)

Set by Hope Services, Abingdon
Printed in Great Britain
at the University Printing House, Oxford
by David Stanford
Printer to the University

CONTENTS

INTRODUCTION

The past twenty years have been a remarkable time for the philosophy of religion. The sheer number of prominent philosophers who recently have devoted their energies to a careful examination of traditional religious topics is in itself quite noteworthy, given the rather inhospitable climate for matters of religion prevailing amongst leading members of the profession throughout most of this century. What is of real importance, however, is the degree of disciplined creativity, the novel perspectives and rigorous analysis which have been brought to bear on a wide range of time-honoured religious issues during these two decades. Much of the recent work has been broadly epistemological in scope, dealing with traditional arguments for and against the existence of God, as well as with related issues concerning the rationality of religious belief; and a great deal of progress has been made on these issues. We now have a much better understanding of ontological arguments, cosmological arguments, design arguments, the problem of evil, and the epistemic dynamics of claims grounded in religious experience than philosophers in the past have had. Certainly, many issues remain unresolved; but we have made a great deal of progress in coming to ascertain precisely what the crucial issues are in these matters of religious epistemology, as well as in coming to appreciate both their intricacy and their general philosophical interest.

It is by no means the case, however, that all the interesting and successful philosophical work done on religious topics of late has been epistemological in nature. A considerable amount of attention has been devoted to an examination of fundamental religious concepts, including, centrally, the concept of God. This work in what has come to be known as philosophical theology is not, of course, altogether independent of the epistemological questions concerning religion. The question of whether, for example, some traditional conception of God is coherent can be critical for assessing the overall epistemic status of a particular brand of theism. Likewise, all arguments concerning the existence of God are arguments concerning the exemplification of some more or less precisely defined conception of deity. So there are many close connections between the conceptual and epistemological questions falling within the province of the philosophy of religion. However, it seems in general that the conceptual explorations constituting contemporary philosophical theology have been pursued as much for their own intrinsic interest and for their deep metaphysical implications as for their possible epistemic pay-off. And this has been to good effect, for recent work in philosophical theology has shed a great deal of light on both the nature and implications of a good many traditional theistic affirmations.

In the present volume, I have brought together a sample of some of this recent work centring on the concept of God. Not all of the topics relevant to the concept of God which have been discussed lately are covered here. Nor is the work of all leading contributors to the current development of the field represented. Omissions on both these counts have been unavoidable, but are mitigated to some extent, I hope, by the references included in the Select Bibliography at the end of this book. I shall have something more to say about my principles of selection, something relevant to the use of this volume in teaching, at the end of this brief introductory essay. I have attempted here to provide, within the justified constraints of this series, a collection of essays which will be suitable for acquainting students with the sorts of issue and method to be found in contemporary philosophical theology, as well as for helping to orientate new teachers and researchers to at least some of the prominent problems and results of its recent literature.

I

The descriptive phrase 'the concept of God' is a bit like such phrases as 'the ontological argument' and 'the cosmological argument'. Upon examination, we find that what is referred to with the definite article as '*the* ontological argument' or '*the* cosmological argument' is usually either a family of distinct but interestingly related arguments, or a general type of argument distinguishable by some distinctive sort of main premiss and form of inference, or else is either some favoured member of such a family or instance of such a type which may be no more uniquely deserving of the title than any other. Somewhat analogously, in the history of religions there have been a great many differing *conceptions* of deity, but nothing uniquely answering to the definite description 'the concept of God'. Even if we attempt to specify the scope of our interest as 'the Western, Judaeo-Christian concept of God', the same sort of point can be made. It seems that there has been no single, determinate concept of God shared by all Jews and Christians, or even by Jewish and Christian theologians, or, for that matter, by all Christian theologians throughout the centuries. Some have ascribed timelessness to God. Others have thought of God as temporal. Some have claimed that, by definition, God is a being without limits of any kind. Others have conceived of God as limited in various respects.

Some theologians maintain that the concept of God is the concept of a most perfect being. Some, again, say that by the word 'God' they *mean* just 'the creator of the universe'. Others insist that the concept of God in Judaeo-Christian thought is that of the Lord of Israel, or alternatively that the concept of God in Christian theology is that of an almighty, triune creator, redeemer, and sustainer of all—Father, Son, and Holy Spirit. So it is clear that 'the concept of God' is no more a properly definite description than is, say, 'the argument for design', or 'the problem of evil'. Yet, no less than the latter, it is also a useful and proper characterization of a subject of philosophical inquiry. By entitling this volume *The Concept of God*, I thus do not presume to indicate the existence of a degree of conceptual unity which is not, as a matter of fact, to be found within the subject-matter of philosophical theology. Nor do I make any controversial assumptions concerning the concept of a concept, the notion of conceptual content, or even concerning the basic semantic functions of the word 'God' in standard English. The appropriateness of our title, and, correspondingly, of its delimitation of our subject matter, is not hostage to such hotly disputed topics.

There is, as a matter of fact, a significant measure of widespread agreement on what are best thought of as broadly conceptual issues concerning God in contemporary philosophical theology. For instance, a good many philosophers nowadays think of deity or divinity as a role, or office, or ontological status which a particular individual will have, or fail to have, depending upon what other properties that individual has. On this way of thinking, deity is something like a second-order attribute, much like the attribute of worship-worthiness. An individual who has the second order property of worship-worthiness will have it in virtue of having other, first-order properties, such as the property of being good, or the property of being holy. More precisely, from this point of view as standardly explicated, deity will be a higher-order property, perhaps a third-or-more-order property, in virtue of depending upon or containing second-order properties such as worship-worthiness, as well as first-order properties such as goodness. In any case, deity or divinity—the property of being God—is commonly understood along these lines in such a way as to support conceptual truths about God, propositions which are necessarily true, and can in some sense be known *a priori*. Consider, for example, the proposition that

(G1) God is good

From this sort of common perspective, (G1) is thought of as a proposition which is necessary *de dicto* in virtue of specifying a condition of deity, a requisite or necessary condition for holding the divine office, or for having the ontological status of being God. It is thought of as a partial explication of an adequate concept of God, in much the same way that the proposition that a triangle is a plane figure is a partial explication of the concept of triangularity. No individual can count as literally divine on this view unless that individual is good, in some specific sense. And in like manner, philosophers who think in this way about deity typically affirm the necessity *de dicto* and the *a priori* status of such other propositions as

(G2) God is omnipotent

and

(G3) God is omniscient

which, of course, are thereby taken to express no more than the conceptual claims that nothing can count as God without being omnipotent, and that nothing likewise can be divine without exemplifying omniscience.

On this quite common way of thinking about deity, a philosophical examination of the concept of God must involve two distinguishable though not wholly separable tasks: (i) a consideration of what array of attributes is best thought of as distinctive of deity, or requisite for being God, and (ii) an exploration into the proper analysis of each of those attributes. The first task can consist in asking such question as whether God is best conceived of as a maximally perfect being, a being having some unsurpassably great set of properties it is intrinsically better to have than to lack, and whether omnipotence, omniscience, and incorporeality can all be requisites of deity. The second sort of task involves, for example, the attempt to arrive at an intuitively adequate and logically consistent characterization of the precise scope of power or knowledge to be ascribed to God. The interrelation of these tasks is obvious. The question of whether a particular array of attributes can be constitutive of deity, or can be thought in any way to characterize God, will turn in part on a consideration of whether precise analyses of those attributes show them to be compossible, or mutually consistent. And it is often the case that theists will deliberately tailor the analysis of one divine attribute in such a way as to allow it to be consistent with others they take to be distinctive of deity. This can appear to critics to be a suspect procedure but, as we shall have occasion to note shortly, can be an entirely proper method of developing a conception of God.

I do not mean to give the false impression that there is anything close to unanimity amongst philosophers concerning the treatment of 'God' as something like a role or title term supportive of conceptual truths. There are those who treat the word 'God' as more like a non-connotative proper name. For such philosophers, the consideration of propositions such as (G1)–(G3) is an *a posteriori* matter. They may view traditional Western theism as committed to goodness, omnipotence, and omniscience, among others, as properties of God, and may even themselves take such attributes to be essential properties of God, properties exemplified necessarily by God; but they do not consider these questions to be, in the sense indicated, *conceptual* issues. In practice, however, much of the work done on divine attributes by such philosophers is indistinguishable from work done by their more conceptualist colleagues. They also ask questions both about the array of attributes to be ascribed to God and about the ways in which individual divine attributes are to be understood.

There is no denying that there exists a great deal of disagreement among philosophers concerning the nature of God. Recent writers have differed over such matters as the precise scope of God's power, the exact range of his knowledge, the nature of his relation to the physical world, and the modalities of his various attributes. Some of these disagreements can seem to be so basic and highly ramified as to indicate a sort of fundamental conceptual disarray at the heart of contemporary philosophical theology. Take, for example, the differences between those who conceive of God as impassable, immutable, atemporal and metaphysically simple, and those who reject such claims outright, thinking of God rather as a ceaselessly changing, perfectly responsive temporal agent continually interacting with created, temporal beings. An onlooker can begin to wonder whether disagreements so deep and many can be disagreements about one and the same subject-matter. Are temporalists and atemporalists just differing over the nature of some one being, or over the proper explication of some single concept they both have in common? If so, how could it be that one side of the dispute has got matters so wrong? It can begin to seem as if there is in fact no common ground between such disputing parties. But this would be a false appearance.

When we inspect the nature of these disputes as they have been carried on during the past twenty years, we find something quite interesting. Beneath the many deep differences that divide philosophers on the nature of God, a single unifying consideration seems to have been operative in much of the work that has been done, a consideration sufficient to constitute a unity of subject-matter and to provide, to some extent, a commonality of procedure for the disputants. In one way or another, most recent contributors to the literature on divine attributes have worked in the broad tradition of perfect being theology. That is to say, their overall conception of God has been that of a maximally perfect or greatest possible being. The consideration of what such perfection involves has been the guiding force in their thinking about God. The substantial differences which have arisen over the divine attributes have to a significant extent merely registered differences in what perfection has been thought to require.

Consider again the dispute between the temporalists and the atemporalists. Typically, atemporalists, those who ascribe timelessness to God, will justify their view by arguing that, intuitively, it is better or more perfect not to be bound by time than to be so bound, and so the logic of perfection requires us to characterize God as an atemporal being. A variant on this is to claim that perfection requires metaphysical simplicity, and to derive timelessness from simplicity as one of its entailments. In either case, the notion of perfection is operative, and is applied by means of an intuition concerning what property it would be intrinsically better to have than to lack. Temporalists usually respond to this sort of argument by challenging the key intuition in one way or another.

Some temporalists simply lack the intuition that it would be better or more perfect for God not to be bound by time, and so themselves claim to have no ground for thinking perfection requires timelessness. Often they will go on to attempt to impugn the intuitive status of this belief on the part of the atemporalist by suggesting that the intuition arises only in connection with, and because of, the highly metaphorical and misleading description of temporality as a state of being 'bound by time'. Other temporalists will agree with the intuition that it would be better not to be bound by time, *if that were possible* for a personal agent such as God is thought to be. They just deny that the notion of a timelessly existing personal agent is a coherent or intelligible one. What is important for our purposes to see is that both sides of this fundamental dispute most often agree that the notion of perfection should govern our articulation of a conception of deity. Both are working within the tradition of perfect being theology, and their dispute takes place within the broad unity of that perspective. It is evident, then, how their subject matter can be taken ultimately to be the same.

In principle, there are indefinitely many methods possible for thinking about God, for constructing an idea of God. One possible method would consist in merely consulting the data of purported divine revelations and confining what is thought about God to what is contained therein. But this is problematic in many ways. For example, purported revelations are to be found which conflict. We must somehow separate the wheat from the chaff. How is this to be done? Another method which might be favoured by empirically minded theologians would consist in constructing a concept of God as an explanatory hypothesis intended to account for the existence and structural features of our world. Only such properties would be ascribed to God as would have a functional role in such an explanation. But this would result in a quite minimal and unsatisfying conception of deity.

Many other methods are possible, and this poses a problem for philosophical theology. In fact it may be that the most important, and most neglected, problem for philosophical theology is the problem of method: is it possible to select rationally a best method for thinking about God? The interminable and apparently intractable nature of many disputes in philosophical theology presses this question upon us. Although I shall not argue it here, I believe, as I have suggested elsewhere, that perfect being theology provides a method which ought to govern our thinking about God, our articulation of a philosophically adequate conception of God. It can be argued that perfect being theology, as it is standardly deployed, is unique in providing a method of thinking about God which is both intuitively plausible and capable of integrating and guiding our application of any other intuitively plausible methods.[1] This is not true of any other method. So if such an argument can be made out, perfect being theology ought to be pursued.

In light of this, it is very interesting to note the prevalence of perfect being theology in contemporary philosophical theology. Throughout most of the past twenty years, the issue of method has

[1] This is suggested in my book *Anselmian Explorations* (Notre Dame, 1986), Ch. 1, and is argued more fully in 'Perfect Being Theology', a paper from which some of the material in this section derives, and which at the time of writing is scheduled to be delivered to a Symposium at the Central Division meetings of the American Philosophical Association during the Spring of 1987, and to be published in *Noûs* (1987).

hardly been raised at all. Most philosophers who employ the methods of perfect being theology have never attempted to justify their course. Yet, I believe, their instincts have been right. And their adoption of this way of thinking about God has contributed greatly to the degree of fundamental unity which can be found in philosophical theology.

It is well known that empirically based methods are in a strict sense open-textured, under-determining a precise conception of God. The documents of the Bible, for example, do not give us by explicit statement or strict implication a precise array of well-defined divine attributes. Various detailed accounts of divinity, mutually exclusive analyses of omnipotence, omniscience, and so forth, are equally compatible with the data of the Bible. Of course, not just any conception of God is compatible with the data of just any empirical, experiential, or revelational method of constructing a concept of God. The point is rather that such methods clearly under-determine a precise, well-articulated concept of God.

Some philosophers seem to think of perfect being theology, in contrast, as providing a wholly *a priori* method of thinking about God which self-evidently will entail a fully adequate, exactly defined conception of deity free of open texture, or of any hint of under-determination. But this it cannot do. Recall that, in the tradition of Anselm, the operative conception of God for perfect being theology is that of a greatest possible or maximally perfect being. What this means is that God will be conceived of as having some unsurpassable array of compossible great-making properties, properties it is intrinsically better to have than to lack. What precisely those properties are thought to be will be a function of our intuitions concerning what properties are great-making properties, as well as concerning when an array of such properties is compossibly exemplified, and, if so, whether it is or is not surpassable in value. It is a well-known and often lamented fact that philosophical intuitions differ. And even those who are relatively sanguine about the trustworthiness of such intuitions must admit that they provide, at best, defeasible epistemic warrant. This, together with the fact that none of us has a comprehensive arsenal of intuitions ready to be applied to every question which can be raised about divine attributes, amply allows for a phenomenon of open texture and under-determination within the parameters of perfect being theology.

Thus, within the theoretical unity provided by this operative concept, and accompanying method, of perfect being theology, there is significant opportunity for disagreement over quite important matters, such as those disputed by temporalists and atemporalists. For the perfect being theologian, the concept of perfection is the pre-eminent philosophical control on his thinking about God. Typically, it will guide his assessment of purported divine revelations, his interpretations of any texts or experiences he might believe to convey actual revelations, and his philosophical analyses of the several divine attributes. Because of the open texture of perfection intuitions, several differing analyses of the nature of, for example, divine goodness are possible, analyses which may be judged on the basis of how well they comport with other attributes perfection requires, such as omnipotence. But, again, there will be under-determination concerning the precise understanding of omnipotence, from the perspective of perfection intuitions alone. So there is clearly room within the rubric of perfect being theology for differences to arise concerning what attribute should be understood in light of which other attributes, and so on. It seems that a perfect being theologian can be fully justified in tailoring his analyses of the several divine attributes ascribed to God to comport with his overall conception of perfection, and to cohere with each other. The differences which arise in the application of such a procedure account to some degree for the diversity of claims made about God by many of those working in contemporary philosophical theology.

II

In recent years, numerous philosophers have talked about God with a degree of confidence which, interestingly, is not to be found amongst many professional theologians. Some prominent professors of theology have subscribed to a characterization of God as in every way utterly transcendent. They have gone on to hold that God and his creatures, such as human beings, can have literally no properties in common, since they are of such different ontological status. Indeed, some of them have ventured to add, none of our human concepts applies to God at all.

It is no surprise that this sort of attitude would engender little confidence concerning the enterprise of philosophical theology. But this sort of view clearly is radically unacceptable. For if, *per impossibile*, God and humans, for example, shared no properties in common owing to their difference in ontological status, they would have to share at least the following property: the property of having properties not shared by some being with a different ontological status. Likewise, if no human concepts applied to God, at least one human concept would apply to him—the concept of being such as to escape characterization by human concepts. These may appear to some to be artificial or contrived objections, but they do in fact suffice to show this precise view of deity to be logically self-defeating and thus incoherent. Furthermore, careful reflection will reveal that, even if this sort of view were qualified and buttressed in such a way as to circumvent this sort of objection, it still would be such that no one could possibly have any evidence, argument, or rational justification of any kind for thinking it true.

Nonetheless, merely making this sort of point does not alone suffice to banish all worries we might have concerning the otherness of God as he is thought of in classical theism. In what sense can properties of personal agency, purposes, intentions, beliefs, and attitudes be ascribed to a being who is also said to be incorporeal, eternal, and infinite? If God is so different from us in metaphysical status, it is *prima facie* problematic how such ordinary properties as that of being knowledgeable or that of being powerful can be thought to apply to him. For if that aspect of deity we characterize as power and that aspect we refer to as knowledge are so very different from the power and knowledge enjoyed by human beings, it can appear that even to use such predicates in this unusual context is to twist language beyond what it can bear.

This issue is so important for our handling of the concept of God that a paper which treats it directly has been selected as the first reading in this volume. All the other readings deal with a single divine attribute or with a closely related cluster of attributes. William P. Alston's 'Functionalism and Theological Language' is a very general consideration of the predication issue. Alston argues that a tremendous degree of metaphysical difference between Creator and creature is compatible with a univocal use of language for both. He draws upon the functionalist characterization of properties well-known in the philosophy of mind and applies it fruitfully to this issue.

A number of the philosophers whose work is represented in this volume treat the various divine attributes such as omnipotence, omniscience, and goodness as essential properties of God, properties God could not possibly have failed to exemplify in any world in which he exists. Some standing in the Anselmian tradition think it a conceptual requirement that all the distinctively divine attributes be exemplified as essential properties. Many others dubious of conceptual claims here nevertheless endorse the strong modal status of the core divine attributes. Most who are deeply influenced by Anselm go on to say that God exists necessarily, in every possible world, and so that it is with the strongest necessity that the attributes distinctive of deity are exemplified. They are exemplified in every possible world.

The claim that God's existence is necessary has been a very controversial one. In 'Divine Necessity', Robert M. Adams attempts to defend the sense of the claim against a number of the most common worries philosophers have raised. His article points out that many of the best-known objections to modally exalted claims for deity depend on unsatisfactory understandings of modality. At the end of his clear and instructive essay, Adams concludes by making some highly suggestive remarks about modal epistemology from a theistic perspective.

Given the transcendence and necessity often claimed for God, the question looms large as to what his relation could be to the contingent, created, physical world. Traditional theism has highlighted the metaphysical distance between God and his world, but this is a perspective Robert Oakes asks us to reconsider in his fascinating paper 'Does Traditional Theism Entail Pantheism?'. Oakes explores the intimate nature of the world's metaphysical dependence on God according to traditional theism, and suggests that what is most reasonable on this view is to characterize God's creatures as aspects or modifications of God—a conclusion which would be quite surprising to most of the great theistic philosophers in the Judaeo-Christian tradition. To arrive at his conclusions, Oakes focuses on the notions of creation and conservation used for centuries to explicate the relation between God and the world.

In 'God's Body', William J. Wainwright further considers the relation of God to physical reality. The vast majority of philosophically sophisticated theists throughout history have argued that God can neither be identical with any physical object nor even be said in any sense to have a physical body. Wainwright begins by canvassing and evaluating the standard arguments against God's being a body. Most of these he finds unconvincing, but a couple are viewed as persuasive. Next he considers the weaker claim that God *has* a body, and reviews a series of classical arguments to the contrary. After trying out a number of models of embodiment which seem clearly incompatible with many of the commitments of classical theism, Wainwright makes the surprising suggestion that a peculiarly platonic conception of the body–soul relation in human embodiment can be used to model a divine embodiment in the world in such a way as to comport with most classical theistic concerns about the nature of deity. Throughout, the paper is an exemplary exercise in philosophical theology—Wainwright takes a set of properties, incorporeality and non-embodiment, strongly associated with deity in traditional Western religious thought, carefully lays out the possible lines of reasoning supporting this association, and by his novel suggestion indirectly highlights the open texture to be found even in perfect being theology. One unstated moral of his paper is that in thinking about God we must be careful about what we take for granted. Instructively, he relates the results of his argument to such diverse theological traditions as ancient Hindu thought and contemporary process theology, further encouraging a breadth of perspective in our thinking about God.

At the very core of the Judaeo-Christian tradition is the claim that God is good. This has been not only one of the most important tenets of theism throughout the centuries, but also one of the most problematic, in light of the amount of pain and suffering to be found in our world. Many philosophers have thought that a perfectly good, omnipotent and omniscient God could create only the best possible universe, that such a being would have to be a universal maximizer of value in everything he did. Serious problems then arise for theism from the *prima facie* difficulty in thinking the actual universe to be the best possible. In his essay 'Must God Create the Best?', Robert M. Adams challenges these assumptions about what divine goodness entails, and suggests a very different way of thinking about how God's goodness is manifest in his creating of a world. The change in thinking which Adams recommends has profound implications for theism which philosophers have hardly yet begun to explore.

My paper, 'Duty and Divine Goodness', investigates a very different set of issues concerning how God's goodness is conceived. I examine an apparent logical difficulty arising from three very common theistic commitments: (i) the belief that God is necessarily good (that it is impossible that God do evil), (ii) a conception of divine goodness as involving *moral* goodness, and (iii) a libertarian conception of moral freedom. If God is necessarily good, it appears that he cannot have the freedom required by libertarianism for being a moral agent at all, and so it is problematic how divine goodness is to be understood. In order to deal with this problem, I suggest a new way of understanding the use of moral categories to conceptualize God's goodness.

One of the divine attributes which has been most fascinating to philosophers over the past decade or two is that of omnipotence. The description of God as all-powerful is deceptively simple, for the attempt to provide a precise and intuitively adequate definition of omnipotence has been exceedingly difficult. In 'The Definition of Omnipotence', Anthony Kenny confronts some of these difficulties in a very clear manner, and proposes a way of explicating the concept which he believes will avoid some of the problems that have attended the efforts of others. With great brevity and in a very straightforward way, Kenny introduces us to the sorts of problems tackled in much greater detail by Thomas P. Flint and Alfred J. Freddoso in 'Maximal Power'. Taking into account the vast literature and complex disagreements which have arisen from the effort to define 'omnipotence', Flint and Freddoso isolate five conditions of philosophical adequacy for an explication of what they term 'maximal power', the sort of power to be ascribed to God. Their discussion touches on nearly all of the philosophically interesting problems, and provides a useful framework for thinking about the issues in greater depth.

Parallel in deceptive simplicity to the claim that God is all-powerful is the traditional claim that God is all-knowing. On close examination, it is hard to find any more agreement over the exact range of God's knowledge than over the precise scope of his power. That it is maximal is not in dispute, but what such maximality can involve is the issue. The most notorious problem concerning God's knowledge is the widely discussed problem of foreknowledge and free will. Many philosophers have suggested, and many theologians have worried, that if God knows everything concerning events which are future to us, that somehow indicates that we are not free with respect to whether any of those events will or will not come about. And if there is an incompatibility between foreknowledge and free will, it is altogether general: since, on any plausible theistic view, God has existed from all eternity and has always enjoyed complete foreknowledge, there has never been a human act outside the sweep of his vision. If foreknowledge is incompatible with our future acts exemplifying true freedom, it is incompatible with any human acts ever being free.

Some theists have appeared willing to give up the belief that human beings are ever free in a robust libertarian sense, although they often do so at great expense to their theologies elsewhere. Others have reasoned from the conviction that we are free to the conclusion that complete foreknowledge is not contained within the scope of omniscience. In his paper 'On Ockham's Way Out', Alvin Plantinga attempts to avoid both these stratagems, and to square complete foreknowledge with the reality of human freedom. Plantinga broaches some deep and difficult issues concerning power and subjunctive conditionals in this essay, issues which philosophers have only recently begun to explore with the degree of thoroughness needed.

The paper 'On the Compossibility of the Divine Attributes', by David Blumenfeld, raises a different set of problems for defining the scope of omniscience, although the intent of the paper is much broader than this. Blumenfeld seeks to unveil what he considers a contradiction in the idea of God as an absolutely perfect being. Briefly, Blumenfeld argues that a perfect being must be both omniscient and omnipotent, but that an omnipotent being could not be omniscient, for an omnipotent being would not be vulnerable to the sorts of experience necessary for fully grasping such concepts as those of fear, frustration, and despair. The contention is that, given a very modest form of concept empiricism, an all-powerful being could not know what it is like to be fearful, despairing, and so forth, and so could not know all there is to be known. He could not be all-knowing, or omniscient. Whatever judgement is rendered about the cogency of Blumenfeld's arguments and the success of his overall case, his essay clearly raises numerous thought-provoking questions about the idea of perfection, as well as about the scope of divine knowledge.

'Eternity', by Eleonore Stump and Norman Kretzmann, addresses with a great deal of originality and philosophical sensitivity one of the most controversial issues in philosophical theology, an issue already mentioned as paradigmatic of fundamental philosophical disputes over the concept of God: the issue of whether God's mode of existence should be conceived of as involving everlasting temporal duration, or rather a form of timeless eternity, such as that favoured by Boethius and many other theists of the past. Stump and Kretzmann argue for the Boethian conception of eternity, defending it against numerous objections and explicating it in a most interesting way.

It is roughly the same sort of perspective which is explored and defended in William E. Mann's concise essay 'Simplicity and Immutability in God'. Mann focuses on what he calls the 'doctrine of divine simplicity', the important medieval thesis that God, as absolutely perfect, must have no parts of any kind, that the divine being must admit of no spatial, temporal, or metaphysical composition whatsoever. Mann relates divine simplicity to the more widely discussed attributes of eternity and immutability, and responds to various problems the resultant view of deity is generally thought to face. As in a number of the other selections, historically important work on the concept of God is brought into contact here with some of the best of recent philosophical techniques and results.

III

A few words should be said about the overall composition of this collection relevant to its use in teaching, in addition to what has already been said about individual papers. The essays included here reflect some of the diversities of interest and commonalities of approach to be found in the philosophical literature on the concept of God, or on the divine attributes, within the past twenty years. I have attempted to cover in this volume most of the major issues which have generated significant philosophical discussion, and most of the central tenets of classical theism. The organization of the selections is such that they can be read with profit, I think, by a beginning student or novice to the field in roughly the order in which they are printed. Any section which contains a more difficult or complex piece also contains a piece which will be more accessible to the beginner. For example, in the omnipotence section, the Kenny selection can helpfully be used as a preparation for the paper by Flint and Freddoso. In the omniscience section, the Blumenfeld paper may be more accessible to the beginner than some later sections of the paper by Plantinga. Likewise, the Mann article is a bit easier for the novice than is some of the more difficult material in the essay by Stump and Kretzmann. In every section, there is some place for the beginner to begin.

It cannot be emphasized enough that this is only a sample of the recent work, which continues to grow and deepen in philosophical perspective. It is my hope that the availability of a volume such as this will contribute in some small way, however indirect, to the future of that growth.

*

I would like to express my appreciation to the National Endowment for the Humanities (USA) for awarding me a Fellowship for Independent Study and Research which provided the time during which this project was completed.

September 1986 T. V. M.

I

THE ATTRIBUTES AND EXISTENCE OF GOD: SOME GENERAL CONCERNS

I

FUNCTIONALISM AND THEOLOGICAL LANGUAGE

WILLIAM P. ALSTON

I

THOUGHTFUL theists have long felt a tension between the radical 'otherness' of God and the fact that we speak of God in terms drawn from our talk of creatures. If God is radically other than creatures, how can we properly think and speak of Him as acting, loving, knowing, and purposing? Wouldn't that imply that God shares features with creatures and hence is not 'wholly other'?

To be sure, whether there is a problem here, and if so just what problem, depends both on the precise way(s) in which God is 'other', and on the way in which the creaturely terms are used. Let's take a brief look at both issues.

The respects in which God has been thought to differ from creatures can be roughly arranged in a scale of increasingly radical 'otherness'. Without aspiring to range over all possible creatures, including angels, let's just think of the ways in which one or another thinker has deemed God to be different from human beings:

(A) Incorporeality
(B) Infinity. This can be divided into:
   B_1. The unlimited realization of each 'perfection'.
   B_2. The exemplification of all perfections, every thing else equal it is better to be than not to be.
(C) Timelessness
(D) Absolute simplicity. No composition of any sort.
(E) Not *a* being. (God is rather 'Being-itself'.)

Reprinted with permission from, *American Philosophical Quarterly*, Vol. 22, No. 3, July 1985, 221–230.

Even if (D) and (E) rule out any commonality of properties between God and man, it may still be, as I shall be arguing in this paper, that (A)–(C) do not.

As for the other side of the problem, let's first note the impossibility of avoiding *all* creaturely terms in thinking and speaking of God. We can avoid the crudest anthropomorphisms, speaking of God's hands, arms, and other bodily parts. But we cannot so easily avoid psychological and agential terms ('know', 'love', 'forgive', 'make') that are taken from our talk about ourselves. Suppose that we do carry out so heroic a renunciation and restrict ourselves to speaking of God in such terms as 'being itself', 'ground of being', 'supreme unity', and the like. Even so, we would not be avoiding all terms that apply to creatures, for example, 'being' and 'unity'. The notion of a 'ground' is presumably derived from the notion of *causality*, or perhaps the notion of a *necessary condition*, and both these terms apply to creatures. So long as we say anything at all, we will be using terms that apply to creatures, or terms derivative therefrom. Hence, so far as the aim at avoiding creaturely language is concerned, we may as well retain the more concrete mentalistic and agential concepts that are so central to the religious life.

But of course there are various ways in which creaturely terms can be used in speaking of God; and some of these may be ruled out by a certain form of otherness, and not others. These ways include:

(1) Straight univocity. Ordinary terms are used in the same ordinary senses of God and human beings.

(2) Modified univocity. Meanings can be defined or otherwise established such that terms can be used with those meanings of both God and human beings.

(3) Special literal meanings. Terms can be given, or otherwise take on, special technical senses in which they apply only to God.

(4) Analogy. Terms for creatures can be given analogical extensions so as to be applicable to God.

(5) Metaphor. Terms that apply literally to creatures can be metaphorically applied to God.

(6) Symbol. Ditto for 'symbol', in one or another meaning of that term.

The most radical partisans of otherness, from Dionysius through Aquinas to Tillich, plump for something in the (4)–(6) range and explicitly reject (1). The possibility of (3) has been almost wholly ignored, and (2) has not fared much better.

I can use this background to explain what I will do in this paper. First I shall be concentrating on the psychological terms we apply to God—'know', 'will', 'intend', 'love', and so on. I do not suppose it needs stressing that these are quite central to the way God is thought of in theistic religion. As creator, governor, and redeemer of the world God acts in the light of his perfect knowledge to carry out his purposes and intentions, and as an expression of his love for his creation. As is implicit in this last sentence, the divine psychology comes into our religious dealings with God as an essential background to divine action. God impinges on our lives primarily as agent, as one who does things—creates, guides, enjoins, punishes, redeems, and speaks. But action is an outgrowth of knowledge, purpose, and intention; unless we could credit these to God we would not be able to think of him as acting in these ways or in any other ways.

Second, I am going to work with a conception of God that involves modes of otherness (A)–(C), but stops short of a doctrine of absolute simplicity and does not deny that God is in any sense a being. There is no opportunity here to defend that choice; I will only say that I find the arguments for (D) and (E) quite unconvincing, and that this particular packaging has been a common one. Third, I shall seek to show that these modes of otherness are compatible with a degree of univocity in divine–human predication. I shall not go so far as to defend (1), though my position will be compatible with that strong a claim. I shall be arguing that, even if God differs from creatures as radically as this, we can still identify a common core of meaning in terms for human and divine psychological states, and that we can, at least, introduce terms to carry that meaning. If ordinary terms already carry just that meaning, so much the better. But whether or not that is the case, it will at least be possible to speak univocally, in an abstract fashion, of divine and human knowledge and purpose.

As my title indicates, I am going to exhibit this divine–human commonality by exploiting a functionalist account of human psychological concepts. But before getting into the details of that, I want to give a more general characterization of the sort of view of which my functionalist account is one version.

The most general idea behind the argument of this paper is that the common possession of abstract features is compatible with as great a difference as you like in the way in which these features are realized. A meeting and a train of thought can both be 'orderly', even though what it is for the one to be orderly is enormously different from what it is for the other to be orderly. A new computer and a new acquaintance can both be 'intriguing' in a single sense of the term, even though what makes the one intriguing is very different from what makes the other intriguing. This general point suggests the possibility that the radical otherness of God might manifest itself in the *way* in which common abstract features are realized in the divine being, rather than in the absence of common features. What it is for God to *make something* is radically different from what it is for a human being to make something; but that does not rule out an abstract feature in common, for example, that *by the exercise of agency something comes into existence.* It is something like the way in which a man and a wasp may both be *trying to reach a goal*, even though what it is for the one to try is enormously different from what it is for the other to try. Many theistic thinkers have moved too quickly from radical otherness to the impossibility of any univocity, neglecting this possibility that the otherness may come from the way in which common features are realized.[1]

More specifically, I shall be suggesting that there are abstract

[1] The general thrust of the preceding paragraph is reminiscent of St Thomas's distinction between the property signified by a term and the mode of signifying (or the mode signified). Thomas says that for certain predicates that are applied both to God and to man, e.g. 'good', the property signified is common but the mode of signifying is not (*Summa Theologiae* Iae, xiii, 3; *Summa Contra Gentiles*, i, 30). That naturally suggests an elaboration in terms of underlying common abstract features that are realized in quite different ways. But neither Thomas nor the Thomistic tradition has seized the opportunity to locate an area of univocal predication.

common properties that underlie the enormous differences between divine and human psychological states. By extricating and specifying these properties, we can form terms that apply univocally to God and man.

II

The tools I shall use to exhibit this commonality are drawn from the movement in contemporary philosophy of mind called 'functionalism'. Functionalism has been propounded as a theory of the meaning of psychological terms in ordinary language and as a theory of the nature of psychological states and processes, whatever we mean by our ordinary terms for them.[2] Since we are concerned here with meanings of terms, I shall restrict attention to the former version. The basic idea, the source of the name, is that the concept[3] of a belief, desire, or intention is the concept of a particular *function* in the psychological economy, a particular 'job' done by the psyche. A belief is a structure that performs that job, and what psychological state it is—that it is a belief and a belief with that particular content—is determined by what that job is. In saying of a subject, S, that S believes that it will rain tomorrow, what we are attributing to S is a structure that performs this function. Our ordinary psychological terms carry no implications as to the intrinsic nature of the structure, its neurophysiological or soul-stuff character. No such information is embedded in our common-sense psychological conceptual scheme. Thus, on this view, psychological concepts are functional in the same way as many concepts of artefacts, for example, the concept of a loudspeaker. A loudspeaker is something the function of which is to convert electronic signals to sound. Its composition, its internal mechanism, and its external appearance can vary widely so long as it has that function. In thinking of something as a loudspeaker, we are thinking of it *in terms of* its function.

If this basic insight is to be exploited, we will have to specify the

[2] The latter version may be accompanied by proposals as to how psychological terms should be given meaning for theoretical purpose.

[3] I shall use 'The concept of *x* is . . .' interchangeably with 'The term '*x*' means . . .'.

defining functions of various kinds of psychological states. One of the guiding principles of functionalism is that the basic function of the psyche is the regulation of behaviour. The point of having desires, aversions, likes and dislikes, interests and attitudes, is that they set goals for behaviour; and the point of having knowledge, beliefs, memories, perceptions, is that they provide us with the information we need to get around in our environment in the pursuit of those goals. In seeking to exploit these commonplaces in the analysis of psychological concepts, functionalism is following the lead of analytical behaviourism, one of its ancestors. Analytical behaviourism sought to construe a belief or a desire as a disposition to behave in a certain way, given certain conditions. Thus a belief that it is raining might be thought of as a set of dispositions that includes, for example, the disposition to carry an umbrella if one goes out. Behaviourism failed because it was committed to the thesis that each *individual* psychological state determines a set of dispositions to behaviour. Human beings just are not wired that simply. Whether I will carry an umbrella if I go out is determined not just by whether I believe that it is raining, but rather by that factor in conjunction with my desire to keep dry, my preferences with respect to alternative ways of keeping dry, my beliefs about the other consequences of carrying an umbrella, and so on. Even if I believe that it is raining I might not carry an umbrella, if I am wearing a raincoat and hat and I believe that is sufficient, or if I do not object to getting wet, or if I believe that I will project an unwanted image by carrying an umbrella. What I do is a function not just of a single psychological state but rather of the total psychological 'field' at the moment.

Functionalism, as an improved version of behaviourism, seeks to preserve the basic insight that the function of the psyche is the guidance of behaviour, while avoiding the simple-minded idea that each psychological state determines behavioural dispositions all by itself. It tries to bring this off by thinking of a belief, for example, as, indeed, related to potential behaviour, but only through the mediation of other psychological states. A belief that it is raining is, *inter alia*, a disposition to carry an umbrella if one is going outside, provided one has such-and-such other beliefs, desires, aversions, attitudes, etc. The concept of a belief is (in part) the concept of a certain way in which a state combines with other states and processes to determine behaviour.[4] And since other psychological states have to be mentioned anyway, there is no bar to bringing purely intra-psychic transactions into the picture. Functionalism recognizes that a belief has the function of combining with other beliefs to produce inferentially still other beliefs, the function of combining with desires and aversions and other beliefs to produce other desires and aversions (as when my belief that I can't get a wanted object without earning money gives rise to a derivative desire to earn money), and the function of combining with desires to produce affective reactions (as when my belief that I have not been accepted to medical school combines with my desire to go to medical school to produce disappointment), as well as the function of combining with other psychological states to influence behaviour. Clearly a complete analysis of a psychological concept along functionalist lines would be an enormously complicated affair and perhaps beyond human power to achieve.[5]

Most contemporary formulations of functionalism are even wider than we have yet suggested. A typical recent statement is the following. 'Functionalism is the doctrine that pain (for example) is identical to a certain functional state, a state definable in terms of its causal relations to inputs, outputs, and other mental states.[6]

[4] When the matter is put in this way, in terms of the *determination* of behaviour, it looks as if functionalism is committed to psychological determinism, and to the denial of free will in any sense in which it is incompatible with determinism. But the theory need not be stated in those terms. We could hold that one's current psychological state, at most, renders certain lines of behaviour more probable than others, and still state functionalism in terms of these probabilistic relationships.

[5] For important formulations of functionalism, see N. Block, 'Troubles with Functionalism', in C. W. Savage (ed.), *Perception and Cognition: Issues in the Foundations of Psychology* (Minneapolis, 1978), and 'Are Absent Qualia Impossible?', *Philosophical Review* 89 (1980), pp. 257–74; D. Lewis, 'Psychophysical and Theoretical Identifications', *Australasian Journal of Philosophy* 50 (1972), pp. 249–58; and 'Mad Pain and Martian Pain', in N. Block (ed.), *Readings in the Philosophy of Psychology* (Cambridge, Mass., 1980); H. Putnam, *Philosophical Papers*, vol. 2, *Mind, Language and Reality* (Cambridge, 1981), chs. 18–21; S. Shoemaker, 'Some Varieties of Functionalism', *Philosophical Topics* 12 (1981); and R. van Gulick, 'Functionalism, Information, and Content', *Nature and System* 2 (1980), pp. 139–62.

[6] Block, 'Are Absent Qualia Impossible?', p. 257. The reference to 'inputs' and 'outputs' reflects the computer orientation of functionalism, of which more below. The 'output' on which we have been concentrating is behaviour.

This brings into the picture the way in which sensory inputs create or affect psychological states, as well as the way the latter interact in the guidance of behaviour. Because of the focus of this paper, we will not be concerned about 'inputs' or any other influences on the genesis of psychological states. Since we are looking for concepts that could be applied to a timeless deity (as will appear in due course), such concepts will have nothing to say about how a state originates. And even apart from timelessness, a being of perfect, unlimited knowledge, power, and goodness will not acquire his knowledge via any sort of process. He will have it just by virtue of being what he is. Hence in this essay I shall restrict even human functionalist concepts to those that specify the ways in which a given kind of psychological state combines with another to affect behavioural output and other psychological states.

Behaviourism was a reductive theory, one that aspired to show that each psychological concept could be explained in purely non-psychological terms—physical antecedent conditions, physical behavioural response, plus the overall dispositional structure. But since functionalism does not take psychological states individually to determine behavioural dispositions, it cannot aspire to reduce or eliminate psychological concepts one by one. A functional definition of any given psychological term will include many other psychological terms. If any such reduction is to be effected, it will have to be a wholesale affair.[7] For our purposes we are not interested in functionalism as a reductive theory. For that matter, the use to which I am going to put functionalism does not even require that any (much less every) psychological concept has to do solely with functional role. Critics of functionalism have contended that a belief cannot be completely characterized in functional terms, since that leaves out the distinctive 'intentionality', the 'about-ness', characteristic of the mind. And it has also been contended that feelings and sensations cannot be adequately characterized in terms of functional role, since that leaves out their distinctive 'qualitative' or 'phenomenal' character. For our purposes it doesn't matter whether those criticisms are justified; it doesn't matter whether a concept of a functional

[7] For a suggestion as to how this can be done, see Lewis, 'Psychophysical and Theoretical Identifications'.

role does the whole job. As will appear in the sequel, it will be enough if our concept of a given type of psychological state is, *in part*, the concept of a functional role.

III

With this background we are in a position to bring out how functionalism can help us to reconcile a degree of univocity with the radical otherness of the divine. The crucial point is one that was just now made in passing, viz., that a *functional* concept of X is non-committal as to the intrinsic nature, character, composition or structure of X. In conceiving of a Ø in functional terms we are simply thinking of a Ø in terms of its function (or some of its functions), in terms of the job(s) it is fitted to do. So long as something has that function it will count as a Ø, whatever sort of thing it is otherwise, whatever it is like in itself. One of the main sources of functionalism in the philosophy of mind is the attempt to use our knowledge of computers to throw light on the mind and mental functioning, and, conversely, to understand the sense in which mental terms can be used to characterize the activities of computers. Functionalism is well fitted to bring out a sense in which it might well be true that mental terms (or some of them) apply univocally to human beings and to computers. For if the concept of recalling that *p* or the concept of perceiving that *p* is a concept of a certain *function*, then this same concept might well apply to beings as different in their composition, nature, and structure as a human organism and a computer.[8] Since in saying that S recalled that *p* we are, on the functionalist interpretation, not committing ourselves as to whether a neurophysiological, an electronic, or a purely spiritual process was involved, the concept might apply in the same sense to systems of all those sorts. This point is often put by saying that a given functional property or state can have different, even radically different, 'realizations'.

The application to theological predication should be obvious, in its main lines. The same functional concept of knowledge that

[8] I am by no means endorsing the view that psychological terms apply univocally to human beings and computers. I am merely indicating one application that has been made of the feature of functional concepts under discussion.

p, or of purpose to bring about R, could be applicable to God and to man, even though the realization of that function is radically different, even though what it is to know that *p* is radically different in the two cases. We can preserve the point that the divine life is wholly mysterious to us, that we can form no notion of what it is like to be God, to know or to purpose as God does, while still thinking of God in terms that we understand because they apply to us.

But of course the obviousness of the application is no guarantee that it will work. Even if functional psychological terms apply univocally to man and computer, to man and beast, and even to man and angel, there could still be Creator–creature differences that make common functions impossible. So we will have to get down to the details.

Whether any functional properties can be common to God and man, and if so which, depends on what divine–human differences there are. It will be recalled that we are working with a conception of God as differing from human beings in three main respects: incorporeality, timelessness, and infinity. We shall consider them in turn.

Can an immaterial spiritual being perform (some of) the same psychological functions as an embodied human being? Are functional psychological concepts neutral as between physical and non-physical realizations, as well as between different sorts of physical realizations? It would seem so.[9] If a functional concept really is non-committal as to what kind of mechanism, structure, or agency carries out the function, then it should be non-committal as to whether this is any kind of physical agency, as well as to what kind of physical agency it is if physical. To be sure, if human psychological functioning is, in large part, the guidance of behaviour, then behaviour guidance will figure heavily in human psychological concepts. The concept of the belief that it is raining will be, in considerable part, the concept of some state that joins with psychological states of various other kinds in certain ways to produce tendencies to behaviour. If such concepts are to apply to

[9] A prominent functionalist without dualist or theological sympathies, Hilary Putnam, has stressed this conceptual possibility (*Mind, Language and Reality*, p. 436).

God, then God will have to be capable of behaviour, and it might be thought that this is impossible without a body. If God has no body to move, how can he *do* anything, in the same sense in which an embodied human being does things? But this is not an insuperable difficulty. The core concept of human action is not *movement of one's own body*, but rather *bringing about a change in the world—directly or indirectly—by an act of will, decision, or intention*. That concept can be intelligibly applied to a purely spiritual deity. It is just that we will have to think of God as bringing about changes in the 'external' world directly by an act of will—not indirectly through moving his body, as in our case.[10]

Timelessness, like immateriality, may seem to inhibit the application of functional concepts. How can an atemporal being *carry out* or *perform* a function, something that, like all activities, requires a temporal duration? This consideration does show that we shall have to abandon the term 'function' in its strictest sense; but that does not mean that we shall have to give up the project of applying to God what functionalism calls 'functional concepts'. We have already noted that functionalists broaden out the strict notion of a function into the view that a functional concept of a state, S, is the concept of the causal relations in which S stands to inputs, outputs, and other states. Now if causality is thought to require temporal succession, such concepts too will be inapplicable to a timeless being. Rather than get into an arugment over that, I will loosen the requirements one more notch and say that a functional concept of S is a concept of *law-like connections* in which S stands with other states and with outputs.[11] Some such connections involve temporal sequence (as with causal laws of the 'Lighting the fuse produces an explosion' type) and some do not. For an example of the latter type, consider: 'If S wants X more than anything else and realizes that doing A is necessary for getting X, and believes that doing A is possible, then S will intend to do A.' This is a 'law of co-existence'. It tells us what intention S has now if S's current beliefs, desires, etc., are related *now* as specified. Of

[10] For a detailed exposition of the point, see my 'Can We Speak Literally of God?', in A. D. Steuer and J. W. McClendon, Jr. (eds.), *Is God GOD?* (Nashville, 1981).

[11] See above for the explanation of why 'input' has been omitted.

course a human being would normally have arrived at these desires, beliefs, etc., by some kind of process, which would often have included some process of deliberation, but this particular law-like statement doesn't get into any of that. It simply specifies what intention a subject will have at a given time, provided it has the other psychological states specified at that time. There is no reason why such regularities should not enter into a functional psychological concept, and a concept wholly made up of such regularities could apply to a timeless being.

To be sure, common-sense concepts of human psychological states are not made up wholly of such 'laws of co-existence', but also include 'laws of temporal succession', such as: 'If S considers whether it is the case that *p*, and in the course of this consideration brings to consciousness his beliefs that *If q then p* and *q*, then S will come to believe that *p*.' And this suffices to show that our ordinary concepts of human psychological states cannot be applied in their entirety to a timeless being. But I have already disavowed any intention to show that any of the psychological terms we commonly apply to creatures can, in precisely the same sense, be applied to God. I am only seeking to show that terms for psychological functions can be devised that apply in just the same sense to God and to creature. What the above considerations show is that we could form functional psychological concepts that are made up wholly of laws of co-existence, and that could apply univocally to creatures and to a timeless Creator. Or at least these considerations indicate that the timelessness of the Creator is no bar to this.

IV

In considering the infinity of God we will have to further restrict the range of functional psychological concepts that are applicable to God. We are understanding 'infinity' here as the absence of any imperfections and the possession of all perfections. Thus among the modes of divine infinity will be omnipotence, omniscience, and perfect goodness.

Let's begin by considering the sort of behaviour guidance principle that functionalists take to be partly constitutive of the concepts of beliefs and wants. Here is the most simple-minded version.

(1) If S wants that *p* and believes that doing A will bring it about that *p*, then S will do A.

This will not do. The antecedent might be true and yet S not do A, and this for a number of reasons.

(A) S may want something else more than she wants *p*.
(B) S may have a stronger aversion to doing A or to something she believes to be a consequence or accompaniment of *p*.
(C) S may believe that doing B would also lead to *p* and may prefer doing B to doing A.
(D) S may have scruples against doing A.
(E) S may not have the capacity or opportunity to do A.
(F) S may be prevented from carrying out an intention to do A by some emotional upset.

A natural way of taking account of these complexities is to change (1) to:

(2) If S wants that *p* and believes that doing A will bring about *p*, then S has a *tendency* to do A.

Having a tendency to do A is a state that will lead to doing A, given ability and opportunity, provided it is not opposed by stronger tendencies. At a given moment the 'motivational field' will contain a number of competing tendencies, and what is actually done will depend on which of these tendencies is the strongest.[12]

Now let's consider whether this kind of law-like connection could be partly constitutive of any divine psychological state, and if not what modifications would be required. The first point that may strike the reader is the inappropriateness of attributing wants to the deity. And so it is, if 'want' is taken to imply lack or deficiency. However, even if this is true of the most common

[12] Again, this may seem to rule out free will. However, if we wish we can include the will as one source of tendencies, and hold that whenever a subject makes a strong enough effort of will, the tendency so engendered will be stronger than any other tendency.

psychological sense of the term (and I doubt that it is), it is easy to modify that sense so as to avoid that implication. What we need for our purposes, and for purposes of human psychology, is a sense in which a want is any 'goal-setting' state. This sense is sufficiently characterized by (2). Anyone in whom a belief that A *will lead to p* increases the tendency to do A, thereby has a want for *p* in this sense.

In this broad sense 'want' ranges over a vast diversity of goal-setting human psychological states—aversions, likes, interests, attitudes, internalized moral standards, and so on. It is an important question for human motivation whether all 'wants', in the broad sense, operate according to the same dynamic laws. But be this as it may, it is noteworthy for our present concerns that there is no such diversity in the divine psyche. God is subject to no biological cravings, rooted in the needs for survival. Since God is perfectly good, he wants nothing that runs contrary to what he sees to be best, and so there is no discrepancy between what he wants and what he recognizes to be right and good. He does not pursue goals in sudden gusts of passion or uncontrollable longing. And so on. This means that a lot of the complexity of human motivation drops out. 'Recognizing that it is good that *p*' would be a better term for the 'goal-setting' state in the divine psyche.

Here is another simplification. In human motivation we can think of the various current action tendencies as interacting to produce a winner, an intention to do something right away. Whether this intention to do A actually issues in doing A will depend on the current state of S's abilities, and on co-operation from the environment. But God's abilities are always in perfect condition, and he needs no such co-operation. Therefore there can never be a gap between divine intention and action. But then is there any point in inserting intention as an intermediary between the field of tendencies and action? Can't we just say that what God sees to be best (or what he chooses between incompatible equal goods) he *does*? So it would seem.

I have been talking as if God apprehends or recognizes the comparative goodness of various possible states of affairs and acts accordingly, actualizing those that are good enough to warrant it. This presupposes that the values are independent of God's will, that he *recognizes* them to be as they are. But many theologians have protested against this, on the ground that it limits God's sovereignty by assuming a realm of values that exists and is what it is independently of his creative activity. The 'voluntarists' who put forward this argument think of values as themselves being created by an act of the divine will. Hence God's will is not guided by his apprehension of values, at least not primordially. I will not try to decide between these two powerful theological traditions in this paper. Instead I will point out that a functionalist account of the divine psychology can accommodate either, though the precise form taken by the account will be correspondingly different. On a voluntarist view there will either be a single primordial act of will that sets up values and standards, after which action is guided by apprehensions of the values so constituted; or else many divine decisions are constitutive of value. However, on either version there will still be many divine acts that are guided by the values so constituted. Whereas, on the opposite view, 'intellectualism' as we might call it, all divine volition and action is guided by divine apprehension of the inherent value qualities of alternative possibilities. Thus the main bearing of these differences on functionalism stems from the fact that for voluntarism, but not for intellectualism, there is at least one action that is not guided by apprehensions of value. Nevertheless, the general account of the function of cognition and wants in the guidance of behaviour will be the same on both views.

Turning now to the cognitive side of behaviour guidance, there are problems about the application of 'belief' to God, somewhat analogous to the problems about 'want'. 'Belief' in the sense in which it is contrasted with knowledge, 'mere belief', does not apply to God. Since God is a perfect cognizer, he has no beliefs that do not count as knowledge. But even if we are thinking of a wider sense of 'belief', in which when S believes that *p*, S may or may not know that *p*, the whole point of having that sense is that a subject *may* believe that *p* without knowing that *p*. Since that possibility is lacking for God, the term 'belief' loses its point in application to him. Therefore we will speak most felicitously about the divine motivation if we simply substitute 'know' for 'believe' wherever cognition enters in.

Where does this leave us with respect to the cognitive guidance of behaviour in the divine psychology? To turn the question around, what behaviour guidance principles figure in concepts of divine cognitive states? First of all, as we have seen, evaluative apprehensions play a crucial role on an intellectualist construal and a lesser role on a voluntarist construal. Second, does God's knowledge of the existing situation exercise any guiding role? Here we must take account of another theological controversy, this time over whether God determines every detail of creation. Those who hold that he does will not recognize any action of God, with respect to the created world, other than His creation of that world in all its details. There is nothing else for him to do. *We* may think of God as reacting to successive stages of the world as they unfold, but that is because we are, illegitimately, thinking of God as moving through time, responding to successive phases of the world process as it unfolds. If God is timeless, he decides on and constitutes the entire affair in one act of will—the beginning of the universe and all of its successive stages, including anything that looks to us like *ad hoc* responses of God at a particular time. From this perspective, God's knowledge of how things are in the world plays no guiding role in his behaviour, which wholly consists of the one complex act of determining every detail of the world. That act is not guided by an awareness of how things are in the world, since apart from the completed act there is no way in which things are. Cognitive guidance of behaviour is limited to evaluative apprehension.

Suppose, on the other hand, that God does not determine every detail of creation. He voluntarily abstains from determining the choices of free agents like human beings. This means that there will be certain aspects of creation that he does not know about just by knowing his own creative acts. With respect to the choices of free agents and states of affairs affected by them, he will have to 'look and see' how things came out in order to know what they are. If he is timeless he does not have to '*wait* and see'; all of his knowledge and activity is comprised in one 'eternal now'. Nevertheless, his activity *vis-à-vis* the world is divided into (*a*) original creation *ex nihilo*, and (*b*) activity directed to states of affairs that, in part, are what they are independently of divine fiat.

Creative activity of this latter sort *will* be guided by his knowledge of these states of affairs.

Next, let's turn to another sort of regularity that enters into concepts of human cognitive states, viz., that based on inferential relations. One of the functions that makes a belief that *p* the state it is, is its tendency to enter with other beliefs into inferences that generate further beliefs. Thus the belief that Jim is Sam's only blood-related uncle tends to give rise to the belief that Sam's parents have only one brother between them; it also tends to combine with the beliefs that Jim is childless and that Sam has no aunt to produce the belief that Sam has no first cousins.

Now a timeless deity will not carry out inferences, since this requires a temporal duration. Indeed, an omniscient deity will not *derive* any of its knowledge from inference, or even from an atemporal analogue of inference; for any true proposition, *p*, such a deity will automatically know that *p* without needing to base it on something else he knows. So inferential regularities cannot be even partly constitutive of concepts that apply to God. But suitable analogues of such regularities may be available. It will still be true that, whatever God knows, he knows all the logical consequences thereof, knows that all probabilistic consequences thereof are probable, knows that all contradictories thereof are false, and so on. That is, there is a certain structure to divine knowledge that corresponds to logical relationships, and corresponds much more closely than any body of human knowledge.

The discussion of this section indicates that the divine psyche is much simpler than the human psyche in the variety of its constituents. Assuming God to be atemporal, it involves no processes or activities, no sequences of events. There are no beliefs as distinct from knowledge, and hence no distinction of degrees of firmness of belief. Propositional knowledge is all intuitive, the simple recognition that *p*. There is no distinction between wants, cravings, longings, and the sense that something ought to be done. There is only one kind of goal-setting state, which could perhaps best be characterized as the recognition that something is good or right. There are no bursts of passion or emotional upsets to interfere with rational motivational processes. There is no point in distinguishing between a present intention to do A and doing A intentionally. Though God may not be as simple as St Thomas supposed, it is true that much of the complexity of human psychological functioning drops out. The complexity of human psychology is largely due to our limitations: to the fallibility of our cognition, the internal opposition to rational decision making, the limitations of our capacities, and the relative irrationality of our intellectual processes.

V

Where do all these differences leave our project of identifying psychological commonalities in God and human beings? We have discovered a vast reduction in the number of distinct types of divine psychological states, in comparison with the human estate. But that is quite compatible with important commonalities in states of those types. How does the matter stand in that regard? Let's see just how divine psychological states could be functionally construed, adopting a non-voluntarist position for the sake of illustration. As for the cognitive side, a divine recognition that it would be good that *p* can be construed, in part, as a state that will give rise to the action of bringing about *p* unless God recognizes something logically incompatible with *p* as a greater or equal good.[13] On the cognitive side, God's knowledge that *p* can be construed as a state that (*a*) will carry with it the knowledge of everything logically entailed by *p* and exclude the knowledge of anything contradictory to *p*, and (*b*) gives rise to action that is appropriate to *p*, given what God sees to be good.[14] Do functional concepts like this apply to human beings?

They do not apply just as they stand, because of the human limitations we have just noted. A human being does not know, or believe, everything entailed by what she knows or believes, nor does she fail to believe everything logically incompatible with what she believes. A human being does not always (or even usually) do what she recognizes to be the best thing to do in the circumstances,

[13] If God apprehended something incompatible to be equally good, he still might bring about *p*, but he would not necessarily do so.

[14] As we saw earlier, (*b*) is applicable only if God does not determine every detail of the created world.

even assuming that she correctly assesses the circumstances. But these differences do not prevent a significant commonality in functional psychological states. This commonality can best be brought out by constructing tendency versions of the law-like generalizations imbedded in the functional concepts just articulated, and attributing them to human beings. Thus we can ascribe to a human being a *tendency* to believe whatever is entailed by what she knows or believes, and a tendency to reject what is incompatible with what she knows or believes. And we can regard these tendencies as partly constitutive of the concepts of belief and knowledge. Likewise, we can say of a human being that she will tend to do what she can to bring about what she recognizes to be best in a given situation, and we can take this tendency to be partly constitutive of the concept of recognizing something to be best. We can then formulate the divine regularities in tendency terms also. Thus it will be true of God also that if he recognizes that it is good that *p* he will tend to bring about *p* in so far as he can, unless he recognizes something incompatible with *p* to be a greater good.[15] These tendency statements about God constitute a limiting case in which the qualifications are vacuous, since God can do anything he chooses to do, and since God is not subject to non-rational interferences in carrying out what he recognizes to be good. Nevertheless, they are true of God.

I take it that this brings out a significant commonality of meaning between psychological terms applicable to God and to man. Even though there is no carry-over of the complete package from one side of the divide to the other, there is a core of meaning in common. And the distinctive features on the divine side simply consist in the dropping out of creaturely limitations. Thus a functional approach to psychological concepts makes it possible to start with human psychological concepts and create psychological concepts that literally apply to God, thus generating theological statements that unproblematically possess truth values.[16] This

[15] The 'or equal' (see note 13 and text above) drops out when the generalization is in terms of a tendency. God will still have a tendency to bring about *p* even if something incompatible is equally good, and even if that other alternative is chosen.

[16] Or at least the predicates present no bar to the attribution of truth values.

saves us from the morass of an unqualified pan-symbolism, and makes possible a modicum of unquestionably cognitive discourse about God.[17]

[17] This paper has profited from comments by Jonathan Bennett.

2

DIVINE NECESSITY

ROBERT MERRIHEW ADAMS

THE subject of this paper is the doctrine of divine necessity, the belief that God's existence is necessary in the strongest possible sense—that it is not merely causally or physically or hypothetically, but logically or metaphysically or absolutely necessary. When I use 'necessary' (and its modal relatives) below, I shall normally be using it in this strong sense (and them in corresponding senses). I will not attempt to prove here that God's existence is necessary, nor even that God exists, though some theoretical advantages of theistic belief will be noted in the course of discussion. Nor will I try to explain exactly *how* God's existence can be necessary. I believe the most plausible form of the doctrine of divine necessity is the Thomistic view that God's existence follows necessarily from his essence, but that we do not understand God's essence well enough to see how his existence follows from it. What I will attempt is to refute two principal objections to the doctrine of divine necessity—two influential reasons for thinking that the existence of God, or indeed of any concrete being, could not be necessary.[1]

I

Many philosophers have believed that the proposition that a certain thing or kind of thing exists is simply not of the right *form* to

Reprinted from, *The Journal of Philosophy*, Vol. 80, No. 11 (November 1983), pp. 741–746, by permission of the Managing Editor and the author.

[1] I have treated this subject before. The two objections roughly correspond to the second and third discussed in my 'Has It Been Proved that All Real Existence Is Contingent?' *American Philosophical Quarterly*, 8 (3) (July 1971), pp. 284–91. I do not substantially disagree with what I said there, but what is said here is different and, I hope, goes deeper.

be a necessary truth. They think that necessity cannot be understood except as consisting in *analyticity*, and that existential propositions cannot be analytic. It has become notorious that the notion of analyticity itself is difficult to analyse; but for present purposes it seems fair to say that an analytic truth must be of one of the following three sorts.

(1) It may be a (broadly speaking) conditional proposition of the form $\ulcorner p \supset q \urcorner$ or $\ulcorner (x)(Fx \supset \phi x) \urcorner$, where q is a correct analysis or partial analysis of p, or ϕ of F. As has often been noted, such conditional propositions do not say that anything exists.

(2) A proposition that follows formally from such conditional analyses will also be analytic, but will still not say that any particular thing or kind of thing exists.

(3) Theorems of formal logic are usually counted as analytic, but they too will not say that any particular thing or kind of thing exists.

It would be very questionable to use in this context a system of logic that would not be valid in an empty domain and in which '$(\exists x)(Fx \vee \sim Fx)$', for example, is a theorem; but even in such a system it will not be a theorem that there exists a thing of any particular sort (that is, of any sort to which a thing could fail to belong). So in none of these three ways could it be analytic that a certain particular thing or kind of thing exists.

I am prepared to grant that existential propositions cannot be analytic in any of these ways, but I do not see any good reason to believe that all necessary truths must be analytic. Philosophical work in the past generation has given us cause to doubt the identification of necessity with analyticity. There are in the first place the well-known difficulties in understanding the notion of analyticity itself; and in the second place it has come to seem clear to many of us that there are necessary truths *de re* that are not exactly analytic. What I wish to emphasize here, however, is an even more fundamental point. The identification of necessity with analyticity has retained its grip on so many philosophers because it has seemed to them to provide the only possible explanation of the meaning of 'necessary'. But in fact it provides no explanation at all of the meaning of 'necessary', and should never have been thought to provide one.

To see this, it will be helpful to begin with an account of necessity that is even older than the one in terms of analyticity. A necessary truth, it has been said, is one whose negation implies a contradiction. Let us think about this, beginning with the limiting case of a proposition *p* whose negation *is* a formal contradiction. Such a proposition is, no doubt, necessary; and the fact that its negation is a contradiction gives us reason to believe that *p* is necessary. For a contradiction can't be true, and hence a proposition whose negation is a contradiction can't be false. But this does not explain what 'necessary' means here. A contradiction *can't* be true; that is, it is necessarily false. And when we say that a contradiction is *necessarily* false, surely we are saying more than just that it is a contradiction. This 'more' is precisely what we want explained, but it is not explained by saying that a necessary truth is one whose negation implies a contradiction.

The plot thickens when we think about a necessary truth *q* whose negation is not a contradiction but *implies* a contradiction. Semantically understood, 'implies a contradiction' presumably means '*can't* be true unless a contradiction is'. But 'can't' here involves the very notion of necessity that we are trying to analyse; 'can't be' means 'necessarily is not'. Thus the use of 'implies a contradiction', semantically understood, in the analysis of necessity renders the analysis viciously circular. Suppose, then, that we give a syntactic or purely formalistic account of implication, so that what we mean when we say that not-*q* (the negation of *q*) implies a contradiction is that it stands in a certain formal relation to a contradiction. This relation, I grant, gives us reason to believe that not-*q* can't be true and, hence, that *q* is necessarily true. But this again cannot explain what 'necessary' means here. We say that not-*q* can't be true; that is, it is necessarily false. And when we say this, we surely mean more than just that not-*q* stands in this formal relation to a contradiction. We mean that something else is true about not-*q* because it stands in this relation to a contradiction. Indeed, our belief that this 'something else' is true of propositions that stand in this formal relation to a contradiction, but is not true of all propositions that stand in certain other formal relations to a contradiction, is presumably what would guide us, in our syntactic analysis, to interpret implication in terms of certain formal relations and not others. Involved in this something else is precisely the notion of necessity that we want explained. It is not explained by saying that a necessary truth is one whose negation implies a contradiction.

Consideration of the identification of necessity with analyticity will lead to a similar conclusion. Of the three sorts of analytic truths mentioned above, let us begin with theorems of formal logic. No doubt all the theorems of a good or valid or semantically satisfactory system of formal logic are indeed necessary truths. But it would be circular to appeal to this fact to explain what we mean by 'necessary' here; for what makes a system of formal logic good or valid or semantically satisfactory is, at least in part, the necessary truth of all its theorems (or of all substitution instances of its theorems).

Perhaps it will be objected to me here that the notion of a valid or semantically satisfactory logical system need not presuppose the notion of *necessary* truth—that it is enough for the validity of a logical system if all its theorems and all their substitution instances are in fact true, provided that the theorems contain no non-logical constants. On this view the analyticity (and hence necessity) of truths of logic is to be understood in terms of their being true solely by virtue of their logical form, and being true solely by virtue of their logical form is to be understood in terms of the actual (not necessary) truth of all propositions that have that logical form. We might find it difficult to understand the notion of logical form without presupposing the notion of logical necessity; but quite apart from that, this view will not be plausible if there are any logical forms all of whose substitution instances are true, but not in every case necessarily true. And it is not obvious that there are no such 'contingently valid' logical forms, as we might call them. Consider, for example, the proposition that something exists. If we may express it as '$(\exists x)(x = x)$', it is the only proposition of its logical form; and it is certainly true. Yet a number of philosophers have been convinced that it is a contingent truth. I am not convinced of that, but I think it would be ridiculous to argue that it must be a necessary truth *because* it is both actually true and the only proposition of its logical form (and hence is of a logical form all of whose substitution instances are true). So it seems to me implausible to suppose that the meaning of 'necessary truth' is to be understood in terms of the actual truth of all instances of a logical form.

Indeed, it should not require elaborate argument to show that no such analysis is plausible. For when we say that all the instances of a certain logical form are *necessarily* true, we surely mean more than that they *all are* true. We mean that they can't be false.

Turning from theorems of formal logic, let us consider another sort of analytic truth. 'All husbands are married' is an analytic truth if anything is. It is analytic because 'married' is a correct partial analysis of 'husband'—'married man' being a correct complete analysis of 'husband'. But this does not explain what we mean by 'necessary' when we say it is a necessary truth that all husbands are married. For in the first place it is not clear that we can understand the notion of a *correct analysis* without presupposing the notion of necessity. When asked what we mean by saying that 'married man' is a correct analysis of 'husband', our first response is likely to be that we mean that by 'husband' we *mean* 'married man'. But this is not an adequate explanation. For there is surely a sense in which by 'God' we *mean* 'the Creator of the universe'; yet 'God (if He exists) is the Creator of the universe' is not an analytic truth—or at any rate not a necessary truth—since God could have chosen not to create any universe. In order to maintain that 'All husbands are married' is analytic (and necessary) because by 'husband' we mean 'married man', we will therefore have to distinguish the sense in which by 'husband' we *mean* 'married man' from the sense in which by 'God' we *mean* 'the Creator of the universe'. The former sense will imply a *necessary* equivalence, and the latter won't; but I don't see how to distinguish the two senses without presupposing the notion of necessity that concerns us (or the corresponding notion of possibility). This argument (which is a variation on W. V. Quine's argument about analyticity)[2] would need more discussion if I were going to rely heavily on it; but that is not my intention.

[2] *From a Logical Point of View*, 2nd edn. (New York, 1963), pp. 20–46.

My main argument is of a kind that should be familiar by now. Suppose we could understand the notion of a correct analysis without presupposing the notion of necessity (or any of that family of modal notions). In that case, it seems to me, when we say that 'All husbands are married men' is a necessary truth, we are saying more than just that it expresses a correct analysis. We are saying that it *can't* be false, in the same sense in which we say that theorems of a valid formal logic can't be false. This is a property that correct analyses have in common with theorems of a valid formal logic. As a common property, it must be distinct both from the property of expressing a correct analysis and from the property of being a theorem of a valid formal logic. And we could not plausibly claim to have explained what necessity is by saying it is the disjunctive property of expressing a correct analysis *or* being a theorem of a valid formal logic. For why should that disjunctive property possess an importance not possessed by, say, the disjunctive property of being a theorem of formal logic *or* asserted by Woody Allen? Presumably because correct analyses and theorems of valid formal logics have something in common *besides* the disjunctive property—namely their necessity, the fact that they can't be false.

If the foregoing arguments are correct, the meaning of 'necessary' cannot be explained in terms of analyticity. Of course it does not follow that there are any necessary truths that are not analytic. But the principal ground for believing that all necessary truths must be analytic is exploded. And I think it is plausible to suppose that there are necessary truths that do not belong to any of the three types of analytic truth identified above. Not to mention necessities *de re*, let us consider.

(T) Everything green has some spatial property

This seems to be a necessary truth, and is not a theorem of anything we would ordinarily recognize as formal logic. It is more controversial whether 'has some spatial property' is a correct partial analysis of 'green'; but I think it is not. For I do not think there is a satisfactory complete analysis of 'green' of which 'has some spatial property' is a part. This point can be backed up by the following observation. In the case of 'husband', which has 'married man' as a satisfactory complete analysis and 'married' as a correct partial analysis, we can easily say what would be otherwise like a husband but not married: an unmarried man. But if we ask what would be otherwise like a green thing but with no spatial property, there is nothing to say, except that it is obvious that there cannot be any such thing. This suggests that the impossibility of separating greenness from spatiality is not rooted in any composition of the concept of green out of spatiality plus something else—and hence that the necessary truth of (T) cannot be explained as based on correct *analysis*. Perhaps some will complain that I am insisting here on an unreasonably strict interpretation of 'analysis' and 'analytic'. It is enough for the analyticity of (T), they may say, if (T) is true 'solely by virtue of the meanings of its terms'. But this criterion, cut loose from any precise conception of analysis, is so vague as to be useless for any serious argument (not to mention that it may presuppose the notion of necessity). In particular, I defy anyone to show that existential propositions cannot be true solely by virtue of the meanings of their terms.

Now of course I have not proved that the existence of God, or of any other particular being or kind of being, is necessary. What I think can be shown by such arguments as I have been presenting is that we are not likely to get a satisfying analysis of necessity, from which it will follow that such existence cannot be necessary. That is because we are not likely to get a satisfying analysis of necessity at all. I think we have a good enough grasp on the notion to go on using it, unanalysed; but we do not understand the nature of necessity as well as we would like to. Such understanding as we have does not rule out necessity for existential propositions. Aquinas's supposition that God's existence follows necessarily from his essence although we do not see how it does is quite compatible with the state of our knowledge of the nature of necessity.

II

Another objection to the doctrine of divine necessity is that if God exists his existence is too real to be necessary. Many philosophers believe that absolute necessity is 'logical' or 'conceptual' in such a way as to be confined to a mental or abstract realm, and that it cannot escape from this playground of the logicians to determine the real world in any way. On this view, necessary truths cannot be 'about the world', and cannot explain any real existence or real event, but can only reveal features of, or relations among, abstract or mental objects such as concepts or meanings. They cannot govern reality, but can only determine how we ought to think or speak about reality.

If, on the other hand, it is a necessary truth that God exists, this must be a necessary truth that explains a real existence (God's); indeed it provides the ultimate explanation of all real existence, since God is the creator of everything else that really exists. Thus if God's existence follows from his essence in such a way as to be necessary, his essence is no mere logicians' plaything but a supremely powerful cause. This is a scandal for the view that necessary truths cannot determine or explain reality.

This view is extremely questionable, however. It is not, I think, the first view that would suggest itself to common sense. If we think about the role that elaborate mathematical calculations play in scientists' predictions and explanations of, say, the movements of the planets or the behaviour of a rocket, it seems commonsensical to say that the necessary truths of mathematics that enter into those calculations also contribute something to the determination of the real events and form part of the explanation of them. The doctrine that necessary truths cannot determine or explain reality is also not the only view that has commended itself to philosophers. The extremely influential Aristotelian conception of a 'formal cause', for example, can be understood as the conception of a cause that governs the action of a real thing by a logical or quasi-logical necessity. It is far from obvious that necessary truths cannot cause or explain any real existence or real event; why should we believe that they can't?

I suspect that the most influential ground for the belief that necessary truths are not 'about the world' is epistemological. This motive is clearly articulated by A. J. Ayer, when he writes that if we admit that some necessary truths are about the world,

> we shall be obliged to admit that there are some truths about the world which we can know independently of experience; that there are some properties which we can ascribe to all objects, even though we cannot conceivably observe that all objects have them. And we shall have to accept it as a mysterious inexplicable fact that our thought has this power to reveal to us authoritatively the nature of objects which we have never observed.[3]

The main assumptions of this argument seem to be, first, that if necessary truths are about the world, we can sometimes know that they apply to objects that we have not experienced; and second, that if we know something about an object, there must be some explanation of how it comes to pass that our beliefs agree with the object. Both of these assumptions are plausible. Ayer seems to make a third assumption, with which I will disagree, that the only way in which agreement of our beliefs with a real object can be explained is through experience of that object. (Ayer mentions as an alternative, but only to dismiss it, 'the Kantian explanation'—presumably that our mind imposes necessary truths on the world.[4]) From these three assumptions it follows that necessary truths are not about the world.

Before we draw this conclusion, however, we should ask whether our knowledge of necessary truths is any more explicable on the view that they reveal only features or relations of abstract or mental objects such as concepts or meanings. I think it is not. For if necessary truths reveal features or relations of thoughts, they reveal features or relations of thoughts that we have not yet thought, as well as ofthose that we have thought. If I know that *modus ponens* is a valid argument form, I know that it will be valid for thoughts that I think tomorrow as well as for those I have thought today. If this is a knowledge of properties and relations of the thoughts involved, the question how I can know properties and relations of thoughts I have not yet experienced seems as pressing as the question how I could know properties and relations of

[3] *Language, Truth and Logic*, 2nd edn. (New York, n.d.), p. 73.

[4] Ibid., p. 73. Induction is another way in which beliefs are extended beyond experience. It would not be plausible, however, to say that the beliefs that concern us here are based on induction from experience—and there may also be comparable problems in explaining why our inductive processes are reliable with regard to future events that have not influenced them.

objects outside my mind that I had not yet experienced. The retreat to abstract or mental objects does not help to explain what we want explained.

The prospects for explanation are not any better if we accept an idea that Ayer espouses in *Language, Truth and Logic*. He says that necessary truths (which he regards as all analytic) 'simply record our determination to use words in a certain fashion', so that 'we cannot deny them without infringing the conventions which are presupposed by our very denial, and so falling into self-contradiction' (p. 84). I grant that there is no special problem about how we can know the determinations, intentions, or conventions that we have adopted for the use of words. But that is not all that we know in knowing necessary truths that will govern our thoughts tomorrow. We also know what follows (necessarily) from our determinations and which intentions would (necessarily) be inconsistent with other intentions, tomorrow as well as today. We know, in Ayer's words, what 'we *cannot* deny . . . without infringing' our conventions or determinations. And we are still without an explanation of how we can know these properties of thoughts we have not yet experienced.

Given that we know things about our future thoughts which we have not learned from experience of them, it is reasonable to suppose that we have a faculty for recognizing such truths non-empirically. We would expect a theory of natural selection to provide the most promising naturalistic explanation of our possessing such a faculty. True belief is in general conducive to survival; hence individuals with a hereditary ability to recognize truths will have survived and passed on their hereditary ability to their descendants. This does indeed provide a possible explanation of our having the perceptual ability to recognize truths about our physical environment. Perhaps it also gives an acceptable explanation of our possessing the power to recognize simple truths of arithmetic. The ability to count, add, subtract, and multiply small numbers correctly has survival value. We may well suppose that under the conditions prevailing during the formative periods of human evolution, humanoids that usually or systematically made gross errors about such things would have been less likely to survive and reproduce themselves. (Be it noted, however, that this argument seems to assume that the *truth* of arithmetical propositions makes a difference to what happens in the world. This assumption seems to fit better with the view that necessary truths can determine reality than with the contrary opinion.) But there are aspects of our knowledge of necessary truths for which this evolutionary explanation is less satisfying. That is particularly true of the knowledge of modality which most concerns us in this discussion. During the formative periods of human evolution, what survival value was there in recognizing necessary truths as necessary, rather than merely as true? Very little, I should think. Logical or absolute necessity as such is a philosophoumenon which would hardly have helped the primitive hunter or gatherer in finding food or shelter; nor does it seem in any way important to the building of a viable primitive society. Those of us who think we have some faculty for recognizing truth on many of the issues discussed in this paper can hardly believe that such a faculty was of much use to our evolving ancestors; nor is there any obvious way in which such a faculty, and its reliability, are inevitable by-products of faculties that did have survival value.

The prospects for explanation of our knowledge of necessary truth may actually be brighter on the view that necessary truths can determine and explain reality. For then we may be able to appeal to an explanation in terms of formal cause. For example, we might suppose that it is simply the nature of the human mind, or perhaps of mind as such, to be able to recognize necessary truths. Then the explanation (and indeed the cause) of our recognizing necessary truths as such would be that this recognition follows necessarily from the nature of our minds, together with the fact that the truths in question are necessary.

I do not believe the explanation I have just sketched. We are too easily mistaken about necessary truths and too often unable to recognize them. And there is too much reason to believe that other mechanisms or causal processes are involved in our knowing them. But I do seriously entertain the hypothesis that there is a mind to whose nature it simply pertains to be able to recognize necessary truths. Indeed I am inclined to believe that such a mind belongs to God.

And that opens the way for another explanation of our

knowledge of necessary truths, an explanation in terms of divine illumination. Suppose that necessary truths do determine and explain facts about the real world. If God of his very nature knows the necessary truths, and if he has created us, he could have constructed us in such a way that we would at least commonly recognize necessary truths as necessary. In this way there would be a causal connection between what is necessarily true about real objects and our believing it to be necessarily true about them. It would not be an incredible accident or an inexplicable mystery that our beliefs agreed with the objects in this.

This theory is not new. It is Augustinian, and something like it was widely accepted in the medieval and early modern periods. I think it provides the best explanation available to us for our knowledge of necessary truths. I also think that that fact constitutes an argument for the existence of God. Not a demonstration; it is a mistake to expect conclusive demonstrations in such matters. But it is a theoretical advantage of theistic belief that it provides attractive explanations of things otherwise hard to explain.

It is worth noting that this is not the only point in the philosophy of logic at which Augustinian theism provides an attractive explanation. Another is the ontological status of the objects of logic and mathematics. To many of us both of the following views seem extremely plausible.

(1) Possibilities and necessary truths are discovered, not made, by our thought. They would still be there if none of us humans ever thought of them.

(2) Possibilities and necessary truths cannot be there except in so far as they, or the ideas involved in them, are thought by some mind.

The first of these views seems to require Platonism; the second is a repudiation of it. Yet they can both be held together if we suppose that there is a non-human mind that eternally and necessarily exists and thinks all the possibilities and necessary truths. Such is the mind of God, according to Augustinian theism. I would not claim that such theism provides the only conceivable way of combining these two theses; but it does provide one way, and I think the most attractive.[5]

There are many things that I have not explained, and indeed do not know how to explain, about the necessity of God's existence and the necessity of his knowledge of necessary truths. But I hope I have given some reason to believe that the doctrine of divine necessity does not saddle us with problems about either the nature or the knowledge of necessity which could be avoided, or solved more advantageously, on views incompatible with divine necessity.[6]

[5] One readily available classic text in which this point is exploited as the basis for an argument for the existence of God is Leibniz's *Monadology*, sections 43 and 44. Alvin Plantinga makes similar use of it at the conclusion of his recent Presidential address to the Western Division of the American Philosophical Association. My general indebtedness to the philosophy of Leibniz in the second part of this paper is great.

[6] This paper was presented in an American Philosophical Association symposium of the same title, 29 December 1983. Thomas P. Flint served as commentator.

I am indebted to a number of colleagues and students, and especially to Marilyn McCord Adams, for helpful discussion of these topics.

II

GOD AND THE PHYSICAL WORLD

3

DOES TRADITIONAL THEISM ENTAIL PANTHEISM?

ROBERT OAKES

I

WHILE philosophical theists of note often differ dramatically on just what constitutes a proper account of Hell–Berdyaev,[1] for example, views the time-honoured eschatology of retribution-for-the-wicked as an extraordinarily loathsome assault upon the religious sensibility—it seems that *this* much is unimpeachable: a (if not *the*) core component of *any* intuitively promising explication of the concept of Hell is the idea of *separation from God.* Intriguingly, however, it would seem to be nothing less than an *entailment* of theistic orthodoxy that all of us *are*, in a straightforwardly metaphysical sense, 'separated from God'. For traditional theism gives every indication of being wedded to the view that God is *metaphysically distinct* from his creation, i.e., 'God is *separate from and independent of the world*'.[2] Alternatively expressed, 'The Judaeo-Christian idea of God is theistic because God has created the world and so affects it, *yet is decidedly distinct from it.*'[3]

Thus, allowing that there seems to be an entirely proper sense in which God (if existent) is 'immanent' in his creation hence indwelling *in us*—one need only consider the centrality of the notion of the Holy Ghost in Christianity and that of the Shekinah (or 'Divine Presence') in Judaism—the Creator, strictly speaking,

Reprinted with permission from, *American Philosophical Quarterly*, Vol. 20, No. 1, Jan. 1983, pp. 105–112.

[1] Nicholas Berdayaev, *The Destiny of Man* (New York, 1960), pp. 266–83.

[2] William L. Rowe, *Philosophy of Religion* (Belmont, 1978), p. 11 (Rowe's italics).

[3] William H. Capitan, *Philosophy of Religion* (Indianapolis, 1972), p. 5 (my italics).

has been proclaimed with confident authority to be *wholly other*[4] than his creation. Accordingly, it is entailed that we (as creatures) most certainly do not—in any straightforwardly metaphysical sense—dwell *in God*. Consequently, and, I should think, somewhat ironically, this insistence upon an unbridgeable metaphysical bifurcation between God and the cosmos (God's 'creation') clearly entails that we are all existing in a condition of separation from God, i.e., that nothing within the domain of God's creation has the ontological distinction of being an *aspect* of God. Hence, it entails that each of us is existing in a condition of (what I suggest can perspicuously be termed) *Metaphysical Hell*. Surely, however 'close' to God some person may be or become—and notwithstanding that 'unity' or 'spiritual absorption into God' seems to constitute a central phenomenological feature of theistic mystical experience—the view that God and the world are 'decidedly distinct' from each other places each of us in Metaphysical Hell by virtue of entailing that contingent objects, while assuredly *products* of God, are in no proper sense *aspects* of God. Rather, it would seem to be a *presupposition* of theistic orthodoxy that it is incompatible with any version of 'pantheism', and thus precludes the legitimacy of characterizing created things as aspects of modifications of God.

II

In what follows, I hope to show that there is strong or sufficient—albeit not conclusive—reason for maintaining that traditional theism is *not* incompatible with the view that contingent things are aspects or modifications of God. More strongly and more interestingly (since the bare *consistency* of the latter view with traditional theism would clearly be insufficient to guarantee the *reasonableness* of its being adopted by traditional theists), I intend to establish that there is sufficient reason for holding that a doctrine which constitutes an absolutely essential or non-negotiable element of traditional theistic metaphysics is such that it is

[4] An expression immortalized by Rudolph Otto in his now classic book *The Idea of the Holy* (Oxford, 1968).

incompatible with its being *false* that contingent objects are aspects or modifications of God. Thus, I hope to show that traditional theists have ample justification for embracing the view that every one of *us* is an aspect or modification of God. If I am right about this, there is ample justification for holding that traditional theism itself is sufficient to deliver us from Metaphysical Hell.

It might, plausibly enough, be responded here that the distinctness of God from the cosmos is *also* an absolutely essential or non-negotiable element of traditional theistic metaphysics, and, consequently, that it is *a priori* clear or obvious that no traditional theist could justifiably believe that contingent or created things are aspects or modifications of God. I know of no conclusive way of putting this objection to rest, since it seems to me that the question of what is—as opposed to what is not—a constitutive or 'un-give-up-able' part of traditional theistic metaphysics may well be inherently unresolvable. Hence, my one response to this objection is this: the doctrine which I shall argue justifies the traditional theist in holding to a version of pantheism is such that there cannot be the slightest *rational doubt* that it constitutes a non-negotiable element of theistic belief: i.e., it is entirely uncontroversial that, *minus* the doctrine in question, theistic belief would no longer be identifiable as *theistic* belief. However, it is *not* entirely uncontroversial that the doctrine of God's-distinctness-from-the-cosmos is one without which theistic belief would no longer be identifiable as such. For it was St Paul himself, a classical theist of surpassing significance in so far as the shaping of Christian theism is concerned, who said (Acts 17: 28) the following in speaking of God to the men at Athens: 'In him we live and move and have our being.' Now while it *may* be permissible to construe this oft-cited dictum of St Paul's in a manner which does not imply any version of pantheism, and *a fortiori* does not imply that each of us is an aspect or modification of the one unlimited being, clearly there is room for rational doubt that such is the case.

Another preliminary objection to my thesis that ought to be addressed here can be formulated along the following lines: *process* theists such as Professor Hartshorne have argued that 'God' could not properly be taken to refer to anything less than the 'all-inclusive reality'.[5] Am I not, then, simply arguing for a version of process theism, or, perhaps more precisely, that there is strong reason for maintaining that traditional theism is reducible to process theism? It seems to me that any such objection to our present project is far too facile. For as anyone familiar with process (or 'neoclassical') theism is well aware, there is considerably *more* at issue between that doctrine and traditional theism than the question of whether contingent objects can properly be viewed as aspects or modifications of God. However, it seems to me that the crucial point to be driven in responding to this objection is as follows: since I propose to provide sufficient reason for holding that (what is *clearly*) an essential or non-negotiable element of traditional theism entails that every contingent thing is an aspect or modification of God, I propose thereby to provide sufficient reason for regarding that version of pantheism as worthy of a place within the corpus of *traditional* theistic metaphysics. Hence, that each of us constitutes an aspect or modification of God is, I hope to establish, a proposition that the traditional theist—hence the theist who finds process theism to be unpalatable on a number of other grounds—has ample justification for accepting.

These preliminary objections to my thesis—which I believe have properly been coped with (if not entirely laid to rest)—are, of course, not *exhaustive* of the objections which can be raised against it. Towards the completion of this paper, I shall discuss and respond to what many might consider to be three serious obstacles to the reasonableness of believing an entailment of traditional theism to be that each of us is an aspect or modification of God, and, thus, to the reasonableness of believing that traditional theism yields us an exit from Metaphysical Hell. First, however, we must proceed with the task of providing a positive defence of our thesis.

III

Outstanding philosophical theists within the classical tradition have, with unanimity, been unequivocal in emphasizing that every

[5] Charles Hartshorne, *A Natural Theology For Our Time* (La Salle, 1969), p. 9.

element of the cosmos (as well, of course, as the cosmos taken as a whole) is such that God is its *conserver* as well as its creator. (In what follows, I shall often refer to this as 'the conservation doctrine'.) I do not think it possible to overstate the clear centrality of the conservation doctrine to traditional theistic metaphysics. Indeed, it is entirely unproblematic that, *minus* this doctrine, theistic belief reduces (at best) to *deistic* belief. As noted by Father Copleston in his discussion of Aquinas on God and creation,

> Aquinas' conception of creation is not deistic . . . . Every finite thing depends existentially on God at every moment of its existence, and if the divine conserving activity were withdrawn, it would at once cease to exist.[6]

Aquinas thereby reflects what is non-negotiably or unimpeachably central to theistic belief as such. To be absolutely secure on this point, let us appeal as concisely as we can to some representative and outstanding philosophical theists. We will see that this is useful not simply to validate the point that the conservation doctrine is absolutely integral to traditional theism, but also in providing us with some reasonable grasp of what it *means* to claim that God conserves the existence of all 'finite things' at every moment of their existence.

To begin with Aquinas himself, he observed that 'The conservation of things by God is not a new action, but a continuation of that action whereby He gives being . . .'.[7] Using natural imagery, Duns Scotus mused on the dependence of all created things upon God's conserving power by noting 'that every creature depends upon God for its being, in the way the air depends upon the sun for its illumination'.[8] Moving up through the centuries, we find Descartes to be in complete agreement with his medieval predecessors:

> It is . . . perfectly clear and evident . . . that, in order to be conserved in each moment in which it endures, a substance has need of the same power and action as would be necessary to produce and create it anew, supposing

[6] F. C. Copleston, *Aquinas* (Harmondsworth, 1955), p. 142.

[7] *Summa Theologiae*, pt. i, q. 104, art. 1, ad. 4.

[8] Quoted in James F. Ross, 'Creation', *Journal of Philosophy* 77 (1980), p. 620.

it did not yet exist, so that the light of nature shows us clearly that the distinction between creation and conservation is solely a distinction of the reason.[9]

As is Leibniz, who finds conservation by God to be such that 'one can perhaps not explain it better than by saying . . . that it is a continued creation.'[10] Likewise, Berkeley states the following in a letter to Samuel Johnson:

the divine conservation of things is equipollent to, and in fact, the same thing with a continued repeated creation; in a word, that conservation and creation differ only in *terminus a quo*.[11]

We need not, of course, confine our attention to philosophical theists of past centuries in order to illustrate the centrality of the conservation doctrine to traditional theism. For example, in speaking of an ordinary tree, George Mavrodes has observed:

If Christian theology is correct, one of the characteristics which this tree has is that it is an entity whose existence is continuously dependent upon the activity of God.[12]

It seems clear that any additional citations would be otiose. Rather, I think it can be taken as unproblematic that a constitutive (hence 'un-give-up-able') element of theistic orthodoxy is the doctrine that God conserves the existence of all contingent objects at every moment of their existence, and that such conservation is to be viewed as an extension, continuation, or repetition of the activity of divine creation. Clearly, this marks a very significant way in which God (if existent) acts upon the world. Indeed, it would be difficult to conceive of a *more* significant way in which God (if existent) acts upon the world, i.e., it would be difficult to conceive of some sort of providential activity that God might exercise upon the domain of created objects that is more

[9] *The Philosophical Works of Descartes*, tr. E. S. Haldane and G. R. T. Ross (London, 1968), p. 168.

[10] *Theodicy*, edited and introduced by Diogenes Allen (Indianapolis, 1966), p. 43.

[11] Letter to Samuel Johnson, 25 November, 1729. Cf. Berkeley's *Principles, Dialogues, and Philosophical Correspondence*, ed. Colin Murray Turbayne (Indianapolis, 1965), p. 225.

[12] George I. Mavrodes, *Belief in God* (New York, 1970), p. 70.

significant or fundamental than the activity whereby he ensures its very perdurance.

IV

We need now to focus just a bit upon a point of major significance to the defence of our thesis: namely, the unequivocally *modal* character of the conservation doctrine. Specifically, it is readily seen that, according to that doctrine, it is not simply the case—though of course it *is* the case—that the domain of God's creation *would* not perdure in the absence of God's conserving power. Rather, as noted by St Augustine, God's conserving power is such that, in its absence, 'the world *could* not stand, not even for the wink of an eye'.[13] Similarly, Aquinas observed that the dependence of every creature upon God is such 'that it *could* not subsist for a moment'[14] in the absence of divine conservation. Maimonides expressed this point with admirable elegance and precision in noting that, since it is God who continually endows the world

> with permanence and continued existence, it would be *impossible* that He who continually endows with permanence should disappear and that which is continually endowed by Him and has no permanence except in virtue of this endowment should remain.[15]

Accordingly, if we consider the case of a vibrating bell, it has been noted that—given the soundness of theistic belief—its dependence 'upon the sustaining activity of God' for its existence 'at all temporal points' of its existence 'is *even closer than* the dependence of the sound wave upon the bell'.[16] Surely, however, just as there is no possible world which includes the existence of something that becomes hot without undergoing molecular motion, there is no possible world which includes the existence of a bell that emits sound waves without vibrating. Hence, an entailment of theistic

[13] Quoted in Ross, 'Creation', p. 620 (my italics).

[14] *Summa Theologiae*, i, q. 104, a. 1 (my italics).

[15] Moses Maimonides, *The Guide of the Perplexed*, tr. with notes Shlomo Pines, and with an introductory essay by Leo Strauss (Chicago, 1963), vol. i, p. 171 (my italics).

[16] Ibid., p. 69 (my italics).

metaphysics is that there could not *conceivably* be a contingent object which exhibits temporal extension in the absence of God's conserving power.[17]

This being clear, we must now direct our efforts to establishing just how it ensures the reasonableness of believing an entailment of traditional theism to be that everything within the domain of God's creation is an aspect or modification of God, and, consequently, the reasonableness of believing that traditional theism yields us an exit from Metaphysical Hell.

V

It seems clear that the procedure requisite for illuminating and resolving the issue before us is to examine paradigm cases of conservation relations which (*a*) involve—since God (if existent) is the Supreme Mind or Supreme Person—rational or 'minded' entities, i.e., *persons*, as the conserving agents, and (*b*) are such that—to ensure conformity with the modal character of the conservation doctrine—it is a *necessary* truth that the items conserved depend, at every moment of their existence, upon some (broadly speaking) mentalistic conserving activity/power of their conserving agents. What I think becomes clear in the course of such an examination is that the items so conserved are necessarily such that they are aspects or modifications of their conserving agents; further, *that* they enjoy this ontological status gives every indication of being *entailed* by its being a necessary truth that they depend for their perdurance upon such conserving activity.

To begin with, let us consider the handy or familiar examples afforded by the intentional, emotional, and perceptual states of human persons. Clearly, it is a necessary truth that the existence of such things as thoughts, beliefs, feelings, and sensa depend—at every moment of their existence—upon the (broadly speaking) mentalistic conserving activity of such persons. For it clearly is *inconceivable* that there should be a time at which there exists a thought without a thinker, a belief without a believer, grief without a griever, or a colour sensation without a perceiver.

[17] Ross makes virtually the identical point in 'Creation', pp. 620, 623.

Notice, however, that intentional, emotional, and perceptual states are necessarily such that they are aspects or modifications of their conserving agents. Surely, it is implausible to ascribe this to happenstance: rather, does it not seem clear that their existence as aspects or modifications of their conserving agents is an *entailment* (or *function*) of its being a necessary truth that they depend for their existence—at every moment at which they exist—upon the relevant conserving activity of such agents?

I think we can shed some even brighter light on this point by considering Berkeley's metaphysic of 'theocentric mentalism'. (Whether or not Berkeley's world view is true or even reasonable need not, of course, concern us here.) This constitutes a particularly rich example since—*however* the predicate 'perceives' is to be construed when applied to God[18]—it remains clear that God's 'perceptual' activity is a kind of *conserving* activity. That is, it confers perdurance upon those assemblages of sense impressions that constitute perceptual objects or 'unthinking things', thus guaranteeing the persistence of any such object through time, and, consequently, at all of those moments when it is not being perceived by some 'finite spirit'.

This being clear, it is important to note that *Berkeley's* conservation doctrine is an enormously instructive analogue to the conservation doctrine indigenous to traditional theism as such, since it is *also* modal in character: it is, for Berkeley, a *necessary truth* that unthinking things are 'mind-dependent'—dependent upon the conserving activity of mind—at every moment of their existence. Surely, a central feature of Berkeley's doctrine is his rejection of the very *conceivability* of there existing unthinking things which exemplify 'absolute external existence'.[19] We need only note his contention that 'the absolute existence of unthinking things are words without a meaning, or which include a contradiction' (p. 51). Hence, Berkeley regards it as *impossible* that there

[18] It seems to me that George Pitcher has done an admirable job in exposing the untenability of the standard view whereby Berkeley is taken to regard God as a 'cosmic observer' of sensible objects. See his book *Berkeley* (London, 1977), pp. 166–79.

[19] *The Works of George Berkeley*, eds. A. Luce and T. Jessop (Edinburgh, 1947–58), vol. 2, p. 251. Subsequent quotations from Berkeley are documented in the text by page number from this source.

should exist any such thing as material substance 'because the notion of it is inconsistent . . . because it is repugnant that there should be a notion of it' (p. 232). Now, if anything seems clear, it is that unthinking things or perceptual objects—on Berkeley's doctrine—constitute aspects of modifications of Infinite Spirit. Indeed, Berkeley's polemic is patently incompatible with the view that sensible objects are *metaphysically distinct* from God; on the contrary, Berkeley notes very firmly that objects of that sort 'cannot exist otherwise than in a mind or spirit' (p. 212). In short, sensible objects—in contra-distinction to finite spirits and Infinite Spirit—do not enjoy the ontological status of *substances*: rather, they are 'passive' entities or things which are *ontologically parasitical*[20] upon (active beings or) spirits. In the final analysis, then, sensible objects are such that Infinite Spirit is their one and only 'substratum'.

In this regard, it seems to me that the following passage from the *Dialogues* is of central significance: 'As sure, therefore, as the sensible world really exists, so sure is there an infinite omnipresent spirit who contains and supports it' (p. 212). One cannot but be struck by Berkeley's use of the word 'contains' here, and there is every reason to take it with the utmost seriousness. He is not a philosopher who is careless about wording, and, consequently, I think it would be a serious mistake not to interpret his use of 'contains' in a very straightforward or strict sense. God *contains* the sensible world—indeed, how could it be otherwise, given that perceptual objects have only the 'ideas' of Infinite Spirit as constituents?—and, thus, sensible objects are *aspects* or *modifications* of God. (I take this to be a self-evident entailment of the view that sensible objects are—as they are, for Berkeley—*included* within the being of Infinite Spirit.) Hence, we have seen that,

[20] I owe this happy expression to Philip Quinn, who, in turn, credits Roderick Chisholm with its invention. Cf. Philip Quinn, 'Divine Conservation and Spinozistic Pantheism', *Religious Studies* 15 (1979), pp. 289–302. Quinn's paper constitutes a response to my 'Classical Theism and Pantheism: A Victory for Process Theism?' *Religious Studies* 13 (1977), pp. 167–73. This latter paper contains a very sketchy or embryonic version of the thesis presently being defended. I am grateful to Professor Quinn for his many helpful criticisms of, and suggestions concerning, my former paper—both in his article and in subsequent correspondence.

according to Berkeley's theocentric immaterialism, it is a necessary truth that sensible objects are conserved in existence by the activity of mind—specifically, of course, by the 'perceptual' activity of Infinite Spirit—and are necessarily such that they are aspects or modifications of their conserving agent. However, does it not seem clear—as clear as it seemed to be in our cases involving the intentional, emotional, and perceptual states of human persons—that Berkeleyan sensible objects are (necessarily) aspects or modifications of God *by virtue* of its being a necessary truth that their existence at every moment is conserved by Infinite Spirit?[21]

In our final effort to establish the reasonableness of answering Yes to this question, let us consider briefly a theory about the ontological status of aesthetic objects. The theory in question[22] is that works of art are perceiver-dependent in the sense that their existence at any time is a function of certain cognitive and/or affective states on the part of perceivers. (Once again, whether or not this theory is true or even reasonable need not concern us here.) According to this view, works of art are necessarily or essentially such that their existence is 'mind-dependent'. Consequently, aesthetic objects—on this view—have virtually the same sort of existence that is accorded by Berkeley to sensible objects as such, the one difference being that (single) works of art exist intermittently rather than continuously. For proponents of this theory, then, it is inconceivable that a work of art should exist unperceived, i.e., it is necessarily the case that a work of art is *conserved* in existence at every moment at which it exists by the cognitive and/or affective responses of some perceiver(s).

However, is it not also the case that an acceptance of this theory

[21] In para. 149 of the *Principles* (Luce–Jessop edn., p. 109), Berkeley reveals his firm adherence to the traditional conservation doctrine. Accordingly, he maintains that *we*—i.e., 'finite spirits'—have as much a dependence upon the conserving activity of God as do sensible things. In fact, he uses and italicizes the very words of St Paul, claiming that it is in God '*in whom we live, and move, and have our being*'. Hence, I would argue that Berkeley has no stronger basis for regarding *sensible things* as aspects or modifications of God (which he clearly does since God, according to him, '*contains*' the sensible world) than he has for regarding *finite spirits* as aspects or modifications of God.

[22] Cf. Joseph Margolis, 'The Mode of Existence of a Work of Art', *Review of Metaphysics* 12 (1958), pp. 26–34. Incidentally, Margolis assured me in recent discussion that he no longer subscribes to this view.

commits one to the position that works of art are necessarily such that they exist as aspects or modifications of their relevant or respective perceivers? Note that it is necessarily the case, given this theory, that truths about aesthetic objects are one and all analysable into truths about perceivers, i.e., analysable into truths which involve reference to certain cognitive and/or affective states of perceivers. Such, it seems clear, is incompatible with aesthetic objects being metaphysically distinct from persons. Accordingly, the doctrine that aesthetic objects are necessarily mind-dependent gives every indication of *entailing* that, necessarily, they exist as aspects or modifications of perceivers, or, alternatively, that they could not conceivably exist other than as 'phases' in the cognitive and/or affective lives of their conserving agents.

It seems to me that our foregoing discussion yields us very solid (albeit not conclusive) justification for holding that, for any object *x* and conserving agent *C*,

> It is a necessary truth that the existence of *x* depends—at every moment of its existence—upon some mentalistic conserving activity/power of *C*

entails

> It is a necessary truth that *x* exists as an aspect or modification of *C*

Consequently, I suggest that our analysis has yielded us sufficient justification for maintaining that traditional theistic metaphysics (by virtue of the modal character of the conservation doctrine) entails that, necessarily, everything which owes its existence to God is such that it exists as an *aspect* or *modification* of God. Hence, I believe we have established that there is ample justification for believing an entailment of traditional theistic metaphysics to be that, necessarily, human persons are such that *they* exist as aspects or modifications of God. If that is correct, however, it is reasonable to believe an entailment of traditional theistic metaphysics to be that, necessarily, none of us exists in a condition of separation from God since it is obvious that aspects or modifications of individuals are not metaphysically distinct from the individuals of which they *are* the aspects or modifications. *A fortiori*, it is obvious that anything which exists as an aspect or modification of God is not metaphysically distinct from God. Hence, I believe we have been successful in our effort to establish the reasonableness of believing that traditional theism—appearances to the contrary—yields each of us an exit from Metaphysical Hell.

VI

Finally—and briefly—I want to anticipate and respond to three objections to our thesis. Let us call them (1) *The objection from Divine Perfection*, (2) *The objection from Divine Incorporeality*, and (3) *The objection from Divine Simplicity*. According to theistic orthodoxy, perfection, incorporeality, and simplicity are among the undeniably essential attributes of God. (It is often held that the latter two attributes are logically equivalent—i.e., entail each other—and, in turn, that *both* of them are entailed by the attribute of perfection.) Hence, let us agree that God could not conceivably have (existed and) lacked any of these attributes. Consequently, it might well be maintained that my thesis is thereby unacceptable. The relevant objections (with responses) can be set out as follows:

(1) God is in no way deficient or lacking in perfection. However, if each of us were an aspect or modification of God, it follows that God *would* be lacking in perfection. For since each of *us* is lacking in perfection (some of us are positively *evil*), then, if each of us were an aspect or modification of God, certain aspects or modifications of *God* would be lacking in perfection: therefore, there is a sense in which *God* would be lacking in perfection. *Response:* This objection succeeds only on the condition that any property which can truly be predicated of an aspect or modification of some individual can truly be predicated of that individual as such. Clearly, however, this is mistaken. My eyes are brown and some of my beliefs are tenuous, but I am neither brown nor tenuous. Hence, that God is (essentially) perfect is in no way incompatible with our existing as aspects or modifications of God.

(2) As an essentially and exclusively spiritual being, God is in no sense corporeal. However, if persons and other contingent objects were aspects or modifications of God, it follows that God *would* be—in just that respect—corporeal. *Response:* The modal character

of the conservation doctrine guarantees, I submit, that (if God exists) nothing which owes its existence to God (these, presumably, being all concrete individuals with the exception of God himself) is corporeal in any ontologically *significant* sense of 'corporeal'. Surely, it is logically odd to maintain that objects which *can*not exist mind-independently—i.e., *can*not enjoy 'absolute external existence'—could be characterized as 'corporeal' in anything but a very Pickwickian sense. However, we have seen that, according to traditional theistic metaphysics, it is *necessarily* the case that everything which owes its existence to God depends for its existence upon God's conserving activity at every moment of its existence; hence, nothing could *conceivably* be such that it both owes its existence to God and manages to perdure in the absence of God's conserving activity.

This being so, if the cosmos—as insisted by traditional theism—owes its existence to God, no concrete individual is such that it constitutes (strictly speaking) a *corporeal substance*. Rather, the modal character of the conservation doctrine serves to ensure, as I have elaborated elsewhere,[23] that the Berkeleyan intuition concerning the incompatibility of theism with 'material realism' ought to be regarded as entirely sound. Hence, the modal character of the conservation doctrine is sufficient to defeat the objection that God would fail to be incorporeal in every respect if everything which owed its existence to him constituted one of his aspects or modifications. Rather, while both persons and 'unthinking things' would then be aspects or modifications of God, no things of either sort could properly be construed as corporeal substances. Consequently, it becomes eminently reasonable to regard traditional theism as entailing that human persons and 'unthinking things' are to be analysed along Berkeleyan lines, i.e., as—respectively—finite spirits and assemblages of the contents of divine consciousness.

(3) God is in no sense composite or divisible into parts; such is clearly incompatible with the (essential) simplicity of his nature. However, if human persons and the rest of God's creation were aspects or modifications of God, it follows that God *would* be

[23] Robert Oakes, 'God and Physical Objects', *International Journal for Philosophy of Religion* 9 (1978), pp. 16–29.

composite or divisible into parts.[24] *Response:* It seems clear that—largely due to the plausibility of viewing incorporeality and simplicity as logically equivalent properties—our response to the previous objection gives us a solid foothold here. For it seems clear that neither finite spirits nor assemblages of 'God's ideas' could legitimately be construed (strictly speaking) as *parts* of God, or things into which God was *divisible*, i.e., it would seem to be self-evidently misguided to suppose that incorporeal entities such as God's ideas or finite spirits could in any way *compose* the divine nature. Hence, it is implausible to suppose that God's simplicity would be vitiated if every such entity constituted one of his aspects or modifications.

In conclusion, then, I suggest we have established that the foregoing objections—taken collectively as well as singly—lack the force requisite to overturn the reasonableness of believing that traditional theism yields each of us an exit from Metaphysical Hell.

[24] As Copleston puts it (*Aquinas*, p. 146), 'the idea of finite things being internal modifications of the divine nature . . . would obviously be entirely incompatible with Aquinas' conviction concerning the divine simplicity'.

4

GOD'S BODY

WILLIAM J. WAINWRIGHT

THE belief that God has a body is by no means uncommon in the history of religious thought, nor is that belief confined to the primitive and unsophisticated. The Manichaeans, Tertullian, certain Egyptian anchorites, and the Mormons have all maintained that God has (or is) some particular body. Rāmānuja and, more recently, Charles Hartshorne have suggested that the *world* is God's body. There are two reasons why these views deserve more attention than they usually receive.

(1) Aquinas argued[1] that the root of the belief in God's corporeality is our inability to imagine God without using corporeal images. Be this as it may, there are other more respectable reasons for the belief. One may be convinced on philosophical grounds that all minds are, or must be, embodied and that, therefore, any divine minds which exist must also be embodied. Or one may be convinced of the truth of materialism—that all real substances are bodies. (Tertullian was heavily influenced by Stoic materialism. The Mormon apologist Orson Pratt offers philosophical support for materialism and then proceeds to argue that if God is real, He is material.) Both of these positions have had a long history and are not to be dismissed lightly.

(2) In view of the renewed interest in Indian religious thought and the increasing importance of process theology, any important position held both by a thinker of Rāmānuja's stature and by such a prominent process philosopher as Hartshorne deserves serious consideration.

Reprinted with permission from, *Journal of the American Academy of Religion*, Vol. XLII, No. 3, Sept. 1974, 470–481.

[1] St Thomas Aquinas, *On the Truth of the Catholic Faith*, vol. 1, tr. Anton C. Pegis (Garden City, 1955), ch. 20, nos. 33, 37.

In section I, I will examine the thesis that God is a body. In section II, I will consider the view that God has *a* (particular) body, and in sections III and IV, I will discuss the notion that the world is God's body.

I

In this section, I will consider some of the more important arguments which have been employed to show that God is not a body or material object.

(1) 1. God is omnipresent. Therefore,
2. If God is a body, God is an omnipresent body. (From 1)
3. An omnipresent body would permeate other bodies (for an omnipresent body would fill all space).
4. One body cannot permeate another body. (Two bodies can't occupy the same place at the same time.) Therefore,
5. God is not a body. (From 2, 3 and 4)[2]

This argument is inconclusive, for it fails to dispose of all the positions which a theistic materialist may adopt. Thus, Orson Pratt[3] identified God with a collection of divine but material particles which are diffused through space. Even though it is not the case that every place is occupied by one of these particles (and hence there is room for other things), God may be said to be omnipresent because the *collection* of divine particles permeates the whole cosmos.

(2) 1. Any body is finite and can, therefore, be transcended by our intellect and imagination.
2. God cannot be transcended by either our intellect or our imagination. (Our intellect and imagination can think of or imagine nothing greater than God.) Therefore,
3. God is not a body.[4]

This argument is not entirely satisfactory. When it is asserted

[2] For this argument see, e.g., Saint John of Damascus, *Writings*, Frederic Chase, Jr. (Washington, DC, 1958), p. 171.

[3] *The Absurdities of Immaterialism* (Liverpool, 1849).

[4] Aquinas, *On the Truth of the Catholic Faith*, ch. 20, no. 5.

that God cannot be transcended by our intellect and imagination, what is meant is that nothing more perfect than God can be thought or imagined. 1 can be understood in four ways:

1a. All bodies are spatially circumscribed and, therefore, for any body you please, one can always think of or imagine a body which exceeds that body in size.
1b. All bodies are spatially circumscribed and, therefore, for any body you please, we can always think of or imagine something which exceeds that body in perfection.
1c. All bodies are limited and imperfect and, therefore, for any body you please, we can always think of or imagine a body which exceeds that body in size.
1d. All bodies are limited and imperfect and, therefore, for any body you please we can always think of or imagine something which exceeds that body in perfection.

If 1 is understood as 1a or 1c, the argument fails because it equivocates. The relation between the antecedent and consequent of 1b and 1c is quite unclear. It is best to interpret 1 as 1d, but the argument remains incomplete in the absence of reasons for supposing that bodies are imperfect.

(3) 1. God is the most noble of beings.
2. It is impossible for a body to be the most noble of beings. Therefore,
3. It is impossible that God should be a body.[5]

1 is an essential part of theism. Various reasons can be provided for the second premiss. The relative imperfection of bodies may be regarded as a consequence of other properties which they possess, for example, their contingency, corruptibility, or passibility. Aquinas argues that bodies are less perfect than the souls which animate (some of) them and can, therefore, be only relatively perfect. Whatever one thinks of this last argument, Aquinas is correct in supposing that if there is some kind of non-material thing which is more perfect than all classes of material things, God cannot be regarded as a material object. (If, on the other hand,

[5] Aquinas, *Summa Theologiae*, pt. i, q. 3, art. 1.

material objects are the only beings which there *can* be, then no possible beings are nobler than material objects and 2 is false.)

(4) An argument of Alvin Plantinga[6] may be adapted to our purposes.

1. If anything is a body, it is necessary that it is that body. (Being identical with a particular body is never an accidental feature of a being which has it.)
2. There is no (actual or possible) body with which God is necessarily identical. (For it is logically possible that God exist and that no bodies exist.) Therefore,
3. God is not a body.

It should be noted that the second premiss would be rejected by those (e.g., Orson Pratt) who believe that *to exist* (*as a substance*) and *to be an actual body* are logically equivalent.

(5) 1. Bodies are potential in various respects (e.g. they are potentially divisible).
2. Since God is fully actual, He is potential in no respect. Therefore,
3. God is not a body.[7]

While the second premiss is firmly embedded in classical theology, it would be rejected by many contemporary theists. If (as these theists believe) God is in time, acting upon and reacting to other things, then He is potential in at least some respects.

(6) 1. Bodies can be moved by other agents.
2. God cannot be moved by other agents. Therefore,
3. God is not a body.[8]

For any body you please it is, I think, logically possible that it be

[6] 'World and Essence', *Philosophical Review* 79 (1970).

[7] Aquinas, *Summa Theologiae* pt. i, q. 3, art. 1.

[8] Aquinas, *On the Truth of the Catholic Faith*, ch. 20, no. 4. A related argument is presented in *Summa Theologiae*, pt. i, q. 3, art. 1, and in *On the Truth of the Catholic Faith*, ch. 20, no., 8, viz. God is a first mover. A first mover moves without being moved. No body moves without being moved. Ergo. The sort of motion envisaged in all of these arguments appears to be local motion.

moved even though it may in fact never be moved.[9] Furthermore, our concept of God is such that no being which was moved by another would be called 'God'. This argument appears, then, to be sound.

(7) Bodies are spatio-temporal objects, i.e., they have spatio-temporal dimensions and they can be spatio-temporally located. Bodies are complex. A body can be moved and destroyed, i.e., it is logically possible that any body be moved or destroyed. Bodies are engaged in the nexus of finite causes, i.e., they act upon, and are acted upon by, finite causes. Bodies are contingent, i.e., they do not exist necessarily, and their existence and behaviour is only intelligible upon the supposition that something else has caused them to be and to behave as they do.

If classical theology is correct, none of these properties can be ascribed to God. Some contemporary theists have insisted that God is complex or temporal or contingent or actively engaged in the causal nexus; but no contemporary theist has, to my knowledge, suggested that God is either movable or destructible, or that he requires a cause if his existence and behaviour are to be intelligible. It follows, therefore, that God is not a body. (If some of the features on our list are necessary properties of bodies and if it is necessary that God lack those features, then God *can't* be a body. I would suggest that destructibility and contingency are features of this sort.)

Summary: (1) is a weak argument and (2) requires further support. Since (3) and (4) are sound only if materialism is false, they cannot be successfully employed against theists like Tertullian and Pratt. (5) employs a premiss which would be unacceptable to many contemporary theists. (6) is included in (7). (6) and (7) are sound, and probably the most generally persuasive of those arguments which we have considered in this section.

[9] One might argue that an infinite body is possible(?) and that an infinite body could not be moved. But while a body of this type could not (as a whole) be moved from place to place, its parts could presumably be moved from place to place. The 'enforced' local motion of God's parts is no more compatible with divinity than the 'enforced' local motion of God as a whole.

II

Even if God is not a body, it may still be the case that God *has* a body. In this section, I will examine arguments directed against the thesis that God has some particular body, and in the next section, I will discuss the thesis that the world is God's body.

(1) If God has a body, then presumably he acts by means of his body in a way similar to the way in which we act through our bodies. That is, God acts by moving his body at some one place and (in virtue of laws which connect movements of his body and other events) thereby brings about effects at other places. But to suppose that God acts in this way involves two difficulties. (*a*) Even if we suppose that there are regular or law-like connections between the movements of God's body and all other events, it nevertheless appears to be the case that God is acting directly at only one place and indirectly at all other places. We are not forced to abandon the doctrine of God's omnipresent causal activity, but we are forced to abandon the notion that God's connection with any one place is no more direct or indirect than his connection with any other place. (*b*) As Swinburne has pointed out,[10] if God always acts through the instrumentality of his body, he cannot be the ground of all causal laws and regularities. He cannot be the ground of all causal laws and regularities because he cannot be the ground of those laws and regularities which make his own activity possible. (The notion that, by means of his body, God causes or brings about those regularities which govern the movements of his body and the connection of those movements with other things *seems*, at least, to be incoherent. Before bodily activity is possible, certain laws and regularities must obtain. These are prior to that activity and cannot, therefore, be explained by it.)

(2)(*a*) The possession of a body has often been thought to be an imperfection. Thus, in the *Phaedo*, Plato argues that the passions, desires, sicknesses, pleasures, and pains of the body distract us from the pursuit of the good, and that reliance upon the senses interferes with the quest for knowledge, both because of the

[10] R. G. Swinburne, 'The Argument From Design', *Philosophy* 43 (1968).

inaccuracy of the senses and the uncertainty of the inferences based upon the information which they provide, and because objects to which the senses provide access are not those objects which are truly knowable. In 83C Plato further suggests that a preoccupation with bodily goods and evils inevitably leads us to suppose that the objects of the invisible world are less real and less valuable than the objects of the visible world—a blindness of the soul which, as Hackforth says,[11] involves moral defect as well as intellectual error. According to Augustine, the body of fallen man is not only subject to pain, disease, and death, but it has also ceased to be perfectly subject to the motions of our soul.

If one cannot possess a body without being subject to these evils, then no perfect being possesses a body and, hence, God does not possess a body.

Unfortunately for the argument, these ills do not appear to be inevitable. The ills to which Augustine refers are a consequence of the Fall. Neither Adam's body nor the bodies of resurrected humanity will be subject to them. Furthermore, later Platonists 'believed in astral or celestial bodies which, like the glorified body for which Christians hope, were perfectly conformed and subordinate to spirit'.[12] Whatever we may think of these doctrines, it is clear that the ills in question are not logically necessary consequences of embodiment. Hence, that God has a body does not entail that God is subject to those ills.

(2)(*b*) Even if we were to argue (see argument (3) in section I) that bodies are less noble than immaterial substances, it would not follow that embodied beings are less noble than disembodied beings. One might indeed suppose that, since being incorporeal (in one respect) and corporeal (in another) is midway between being incorporeal and being corporeal, it is less valuable than the first and more valuable than the second; but it is perhaps equally plausible to argue that an intermediate state of this sort is more perfect than either of the extremes because it combines the perfections of both.

(2)(*c*) Being embodied (in a particular body) involves appre-

[11] R. Hackforth, *Plato's Phaedo* (Indianapolis, 1955), p. 95.

[12] A. H. Armstrong, 'St Augustine and Christian Platonism', in *Augustine: A Collection of Critical Essays*, ed. R. A. Markus (Garden City, 1972).

hending things from a special point of view and occupying a position from which the effects of one's activity radiate outwards in space. (See the first argument of this section.) It is not clear that these things are imperfections, but if they are imperfections it is reasonable to suppose that a perfect being will not have a particular body.

(3) With suitable modifications the fifth, sixth, and seventh arguments of section I can be employed to support the conclusion that God has no body. We normally suppose that what is true of someone's body is true of him. (Thus, I can truly say that I am five feet and ten inches tall, that I am located in Milwaukee, that I am struck [when my body is struck] and so on.) Hence, if all bodies are potential in certain respects, if they are complex, movable, contingent, have spatio-temporal dimensions and are spatio-temporally located, if they act and are acted upon, and if God has a body, then presumably God is potential in some respects, complex, movable, etc. Given that God is fully actual, simple, an unmoved mover, necessary, a-spatial, atemporal, and impassible, it follows that God has no body.

The assumption on which this argument rests will be called into question in section IV. For the moment, let us merely notice that even in those cases in which we hesitate to infer from 'my body is Ø' to 'I am Ø', we are willing to infer to 'some part (aspect) of me is Ø'. Thus, I may be reluctant to move from 'my body will be destroyed' to 'I will be destroyed', but I will be quite willing to infer that 'some part of me will be destroyed'. The point of this observation is the following. Even if we are not warranted in moving from, for example, 'God's body is destructible (contingent, etc.)' to 'God is destructible (contingent, etc.)', we would still be warranted in concluding 'some part of God is destructible (contingent, etc.)'—a conclusion which would be anathema to any classical theologian.

(4) According to orthodox Christian theology, there is a peculiiar sense in which God does have a (particular) body, viz. the body of Jesus. The Logos, who is the second member of the trinity and one of the three 'subjects' in which the divine nature inheres, has assumed a human nature and in so doing has assumed a human body. Is the Logos an embodied being? In so far as he is a human

being, the Logos is an embodied being, but in so far as he is God, the Logos is not an embodied being, i.e., the divine subject plus the human nature which it has assumed is an embodied being, while the divine subject plus the divine nature which belongs to it, essentially, is not an embodied being.[13] The fact that the body of Jesus is extended, spatially circumscribed, contingent, destructible, etc., does not imply that God (a divine subject in its divine nature) is extended, spatially circumscribed, contingent, destructible, etc. In short, Christians believe that the Incarnation on the one hand, and God's immateriality and freedom from physical limitations on the other, are compatible. Whether this attempted resolution of an apparent incompatibility is successful or not is, of course, a moot point.

III

I will now consider the view that the world is God's body. It should be noticed that there is an ambiguity in this thesis. God's body may be identified with the world in its entirety or it may be identified with the physical or material aspect of the world. The first and more popular of the two positions is the one adopted by Rāmānuja and Hartshorne. Though I will concentrate on the first position, most of the remarks that follow will apply to either view.

(1) The view cannot be dismissed on the grounds that the world (or its physical aspect) has no nervous system, no system of digestion and reproduction, and that it is in other ways very much unlike the bodies of those living beings with which we are familiar. As William James says, 'the particular features of *our* body are adaptations to a habitat so different from God's that if God have [sic] a physical body at all, it must be utterly different from ours in structure.'[14]

(2) There is a more serious difficulty. If the world (or its material aspect) is literally God's body, then it must *be* a body. Is the world a physical object? Because of the systematic and law-like connection of its members, the world can be regarded for some

[13] The divine subject has a body, but a subject *sans* nature is not a being and so is neither an embodied being nor a disembodied being.

[14] *A Pluralistic Universe* (New York, 1947), p. 152.

purposes as a single object. But if the world has a non-material aspect (soul, mind, intelligence), it is not clear that it can be regarded as a physical object, and if it is not a physical object it would seem that it cannot literally be God's body.[15] The physical aspect of the cosmos can more plausibly be regarded as a body, though we should notice that we do not normally think of all physical systems as bodies. Thus, we do not normally think of the solar system as a body or physical object.

I will not insist upon this objection, though I think it important, but will merely note that anyone who wishes to defend the view that the world is literally God's body must be prepared to defend the view that the cosmos as a whole is (in some sense) a physical object. This defence, to my knowledge, is seldom forthcoming.

(3)(*a*) Is the thesis which we are considering compatible with God's perfection? In the previous section we saw that the fact (if it is a fact) that bodies are less noble than souls is not sufficient to establish the proposition that embodiment is less perfect than disembodiment.

(3)(*b*) There is, nevertheless, a special problem connected with the view that the *world* is God's body. It is natural to suppose that if God is perfect, His body must be perfect. The world, however, appears to be infected with various evils and imperfections, the most obvious of which are suffering and moral wickedness. It would seem to follow that the world cannot be God's body.[16] This problem is a genuine one. I would only point out that it may be no more severe than the problem which confronts the more orthodox theist who must respond to the charge that if God is perfect, his creation must be perfect and that, since the world is imperfect, it cannot be God's handiwork. Both problems are versions of the

[15] Are all bodies physical objects? One might think here of the 'subtle bodies' of Indian thought. Cf. H. H. Price's discussion of image bodies in 'Two Conceptions of the Next World', *Essays in the Philosophy of Religion* (New York, 1972). Image bodies are extended and like 'our physical body in outward appearance'. They enjoy a certain publicity, for they appear to others, but they 'need not have an internal mechanism (thus, they have a face but not necessarily a skull) and are not in physical space' (p. 112). That the world as a whole is an image body seems even less plausible than that the world is a physical object.

[16] Does the same problem affect the view that the physical aspect of the world is God's body? The defects or evils of the physical aspect of the world are at least less obvious.

problem of evil, and can be handled in similar ways. (One might suppose that the problem is less acute for orthodox theists. If the world is God's body, its imperfections can be directly predicated of God himself, whereas the imperfections of God's work cannot be directly predicated of God himself. (That, for example, God's work contains suffering does not imply that God contains suffering.) On the other hand, imperfections in God's work do seem to imply that God is imperfect or at least limited in certain respects. Whether a (perhaps unavoidably) imperfect body is less obviously compatible with God's perfection than a (perhaps unavoidably) imperfect bit of workmanship is, I think, a moot point.)

(3)(*c*) At one point[17] Aquinas appears to argue that if God were the soul of the world, he would be a part of a totality which was greater than he, and this is impossible.

Although one might deny that wholes are always more perfect than their parts, it is not clear that this denial will strengthen the position of those who believe that the world is God's body. If God alone is more perfect than the complex which consists of God plus his body, then it would seem that, with respect to God at least, embodiment is less perfect than disembodiment, in which case the view that the world is God's body would appear to be incompatible with his perfection.

There is, however, another way of meeting Aquinas's objection. Those who adopt the view that we are examining in this section use 'God' somewhat ambiguously. 'God' may refer to the ruling and guiding intelligence which directs the movements of the cosmos, or it may refer to the whole which is composed of this ruling intelligence plus the cosmos. (Just as, on certain views, 'man' can be used either for the body–soul complex or for the soul alone. One may also compare the ambiguous use of 'Brahman' in Rāmānuja's school. 'Brahman' sometimes refers to Īśvara—the ruling and guiding principle of the cosmos—and sometimes to the complex consisting of Īśvara, souls, and 'matter'.) In so far as 'God' is used to refer to the whole which consists of the divine soul plus the divine body, Aquinas's objection fails. God, in this sense,

[17] Aquinas, *On the Truth of the Catholic Faith*, ch. 27, nos. 4, 5.

is not part of any larger complex which is more perfect than He is.

(4) The argument which was employed in section II (3) can also be used here. The world as a whole (and its physical aspect) is potential in various respects. It is complex, contingent,[18] has spatio-temporal spread (though no spatio-temporal location). It acts (upon God)[19] and is acted upon (by God). The world cannot, as a whole, be moved but it can change. Furthermore, its parts can be moved locally. Given that what is true of a person's body is true of the person himself (or at least of some part of him) and given that the world (or its physical aspect) is God's body, it follows that God (or some part of him) is potential in various respects, complex, etc.

(5) None of the standard ways in which the mind–body relationship is construed provides an appropriate analogy of the God–world relationship.[20]

(5)(*a*) Some believe that mind and (some part or aspect of) body are identical. God is not related to the world in this way because God is not identical with the world. If the world can be regarded as a physical object (which is doubtful), the arguments introduced in section I may be used to show that God is not the world. (If God is not a physical object and if the world is a physical object, then God and the world are not identical.) But in any case, unless the world or one of its aspects is omnipotent and omniscient, a living and conscious moral agent, God, cannot be identified with the world or one of its aspects. Again, the contingency, passibility, mutability, and complexity of the cosmos and its parts would prohibit a classical theist from making the identification.

(5)(*b*) According to mind–body parallelism, mental and physical events occur in two parallel series. Events in one series (for example, a feeling of pain) correspond to events in the other (the appropriate physiological events), but there is no causal interaction between them. If God is related to the world in this fashion, then God neither acts upon nor is acted upon by the world. The first of

[18] Hartshorne argues that it is necessary that a world occur, though no member of the world is necessary. Hence, on Hartshorne's view, the existence of the world is not contingent though its parts are contingent.

[19] At least according to the process theologians and some others.

[20] Or the relationship between God and the physical aspect of the world, though I will ignore this in what follows.

these consequences would be unacceptable to a classical theist. Both would be unacceptable to a neo-classical theist.

(5)(*c*) Epiphenomenalists maintain that physical events in the brain and nervous system causally produce mental events (as well as physical events), but that mental events themselves have no causal efficacy. The supposition that God is related to the world in a similar way is incompatible with God's sovereignty and independence, and with the claim that God acts upon the world.

(5)(*d*) Mind–body interactionism would seem to provide a more appropriate model of the God–world relationship, but it is objectionable on two counts. According to classical theism, God acts upon the world but the world does not act upon God. Furthermore, by allowing a certain independence to mind and body, the model fails to provide for the radical dependence of the world upon God which is so essential to classical theism.

IV

The argument of section III entitles us to conclude that the God of classical theism cannot stand in a relation to the world like that in which the mind or soul is usually supposed to stand to the body. At this point there are at least two moves which can be made.

(1) There is another account of the soul–body relation which provides a more appropriate model for the God–world relation—the 'Platonic'.[21] In the *Phaedo*, Cebes suggests that the soul may create its own body (or bodies) as a tailor weaves his own coats. In later Platonism, the soul creates or produces or emanates its own body.[22] This body (or the lower self *cum* body) is an image or expression of the soul (or higher self) on a lower level.[23] Furthermore, Plotinus argues that the (higher parts of the) soul are necessary, immutable, and impeccable.[24] While the later Neo-Platonists refused to follow Plotinus on this point, they did agree

[21] The view which I will describe is a pastiche drawn from various Platonic sources. I am not pretending to offer an accurate account of the views of Plato or of any individual Platonist.

[22] Armstrong, 'St Augustine and Christian Platonism', p. 7.

[23] Ibid., p. 5. Cf. Armstrong's account in *The Cambridge History of Later Greek and Early Medieval Philosophy*, ed. A. H. Armstrong (New York, 1967).

[24] Ibid., p. 7.

that the body cannot act upon the soul.[25] Rāmānuja also believes that the defects and imperfections of the body do not affect the soul, and, interestingly enough for our purposes, he goes on to argue that just

> as the defects or deficiencies of the body do not affect the soul, so . . . the defects of the latter [the world] cannot . . . affect the nature of Brahman. Thus, though Brahman has a body, He is partless . . . and absolutely devoid of any *karma*. . . . He is . . . wholly unaffected by all faults and remains pure and perfect in Himself.[26]

What accounts for these views? (i) They can be partially explained by the belief that the body is a mere adjunct of the soul, a tool or instrument which it employs, a cloak which the soul may put on or off. If body is related to soul in this way and if (as Platonists maintain) a man is essentially his soul, the inference from 'my body is Ø' to 'I am Ø' (or 'some part of me is Ø') loses its force. (It has no more force than the inference from 'my hammer (coat) is Ø' to 'I am Ø' or 'some part of me is Ø'.) (ii) The Neo-Platonic position reflects the belief that soul surrounds and engulfs a body which is both weaker and less valuable than it—a mere shadow or image of soul.

By supposing that God is related to the world as a 'Platonic' soul is related to its body, we avoid the most serious objections presented in section III. If the Platonists are correct, the inference from 'the body of x is Ø' to '(some part of) x is Ø' is illegitimate. Hence, from the fact that the world is God's body and exhibits various defects and limitations, it does not follow that God or some part of him does so. Furthermore, the 'Platonic' account of the soul–body relationship provides a model for the God–world relationship which is not subject to the difficulties considered in section III(5). Just as, on a Platonic view, the body depends upon but does not affect the soul, so the world depends upon but does

[25] Ibid., p. 34.

[26] S. Dasgupta, *A History of Indian Philosophy*, vol. 3 (New York, 1952), pp. 200–1. There appears, however, to be a significant difference between the Neo-Platonic view and that of Rāmānuja's school. According to the former, the body does not act upon the soul even when the soul perceives. According to the latter, the body does appear to play a causal role in, for example, the production of the soul's knowledge, although the imperfections of the body do not affect the soul.

not affect God. God's sovereignty and independence are preserved.

One final point. In Plotinus, the most significant division is not the one between soul and body but the one between the higher soul and the (lower) soul–body complex which includes our natural appetites and urges, and the senses. (This distinction resembles the Indian distinction between the Atman on the one hand, and the psycho-physical organism on the other.) If the world is not a body (physical object), the relation between the higher self and the soul–body complex might provide a more accurate analogy of the God–world relation than the relation between soul and body.

(2) Charles Hartshorne is also able to meet the most serious objections presented in section III.

(2)(*a*) According to Hartshorne, it is necessary that the world exists, and since its existence is necessary, the world is neither destructible nor requires a cause. It follows that God cannot be said to exist contingently or to be destructible or to require a cause on the ground that his body exhibits those features. On the other hand, while the world is a mutable, complex, spatio-temporal entity which includes contingent contents. Hartshorne does not object to ascribing change, complexity, temporality, and spatiality to God, and to including contingent contents within God's life. In short, he accepts the inference from 'God's body is Ø' to 'God—or some part of Him—is Ø' but he is not disturbed by its consequences.

(2)(*b*) Hartshorne's view of the mind–body relationship resembles that of the interactionists in crucial respects. (Our soul is constituted by occasions in which the mental pole predominates, while our body is constituted by occasions in which the physical pole predominates. The occasions which make up our soul prehend those occasions which make up our body and vice versa. Hence the two sets of occasions causally interact.) In section III, we concluded that interactionism provided an objectionable model because it failed to preserve God's independence *of* the world, and allowed too much independence *to* the world. Neither of these features would be regarded as objectionable by Hartshorne, for he insists that God and the world do interact, and wishes to ascribe a certain independence to both of the parties to this transaction.

(3) What conclusions can we draw from these considerations?

The 'Platonic' model enables us to speak of the God–world relation as a relation between soul and body without sacrificing classical theology.[27] The model's primary disadvantage probably consists in the fact that to most people it is only a curious antiquity. On the other hand, even if the 'Platonic' picture of the soul–body relation is inadequate, it may still provide an appropriate analogue of the God–world relationship.

According to Hartshorne, the relation between divine occasions and non-divine occasions is importantly similar to that which obtains between those occasions which constitute our soul and those occasions which constitute our body.[28] There is, therefore, real point in speaking of the world as God's body. At the same time, we must remember that Hartshorne's position involves the acceptance of a Whiteheadian analysis of the soul–body relationship and a rejection of much classical theology. Those who find this too high a price to pay must either adopt the 'Platonic' (or some similar) model, or reject the view that the world is God's body.

[27] The Neo-Platonic theory of the soul and body includes elements which are not compatible with classical Christian theology, e.g., the claim that body is not produced by choice but necessarily. Whether this claim is essential to what can reasonably be called a 'Platonic' view of the soul–body relation is a moot point, but in my opinion it is not essential.

[28] Perhaps most significantly, God and non-divine events prehend each other with the immediacy with which soul occasions and brain occasions prehend each other.

III

DIVINE GOODNESS

5

MUST GOD CREATE THE BEST?

ROBERT MERRIHEW ADAMS

I

MANY philosophers and theologians have accepted the following propositions:

(*P*) If a perfectly good moral agent created any world at all, it would have to be the very best world that he could create.

The best world that an omnipotent God could create is the best of all logically possible worlds. Accordingly, it has been supposed that if the actual world was created by an omnipotent, perfectly good God, it must be the best of all logically possible worlds.

In this paper I shall argue that ethical views typical of the Judaeo-Christian religious tradition do not require the Judaeo-Christian theist to accept (*P*). He must hold that the actual world is a good world. But he need not maintain that it is the best of all possible worlds, or the best world that God could have made.[1]

The position which I am claiming that he can consistently hold is that *even if* there is a best among possible worlds, God could create another instead of it, and still be perfectly good. I do not in fact see any good reason to believe that there is a best among possible worlds. Why can't it be that for every possible world there is another that is better? And if there is no maximum degree of perfection among possible worlds, it would be unreasonable to blame God, or to think less highly of his goodness, because he created a world less excellent than he could have created.[2] But I do

Reprinted from, *Philosophical Review*, Vol. 81, No. 3, July 1972, 317–332, by permission of the Managing Editor and the author.

[1] What I am saying in this paper is obviously relevant to the problem of evil. But I make no claim to be offering a complete theodicy here.

[2] Leibniz held (in his *Theodicy*, pt. i, s. 8) that if there were no best among possible worlds, a perfectly good God would have created nothing at all. But

not claim to be able to prove that there is no best among possible worlds, and in this essay I shall assume for the sake of argument that there is one.

Whether we accept proposition (*P*) will depend on what we believe are the requirements for perfect goodness. If we apply an act-utilitarian standard of moral goodness, we will have to accept (*P*). For by act-utilitarian standards it is a moral obligation to bring about the best state of affairs that one can. It is interesting to note that the ethics of Leibniz, the best-known advocate of (*P*), is basically utilitarian.[3] In his *Theodicy* (part 1, s. 25) he maintains, in effect, that men, because of their ignorance of many of the consequences of their actions, ought to follow a rule-utilitarian code, but that God, being omniscient, must be a perfect act utilitarian in order to be perfectly good.

I believe that utilitarian views are not typical of the Judaeo-Christian ethical tradition, although Leibniz is by no means the only Christian utilitarian. In this essay I shall assume that we are working with standards of moral goodness which are not utilitarian. But I shall not try either to show that utilitarianism is wrong or to justify the standards that I take to be more typical of Judaeo-Christian religious ethics. To attempt either of these tasks would unmanageably enlarge the scope of the paper. What I can hope to establish here is therefore limited to the claim that the rejection of (*P*) is consistent with Judaeo-Christian religious ethics.

Assuming that we are not using utilitarian standards of moral goodness, I see only two types of reason that could be given for (*P*). (1) It might be claimed that a creator would necessarily wrong someone (violate someone's rights), or be less kind to someone than a perfectly good moral agent must be, if he knowingly created a less excellent world instead of the best that he could. Or (2) it might be claimed that, even if no one would be wronged or treated

Leibniz is mistaken if he supposes that in this way God could avoid choosing an alternative less excellent than others He could have chosen. For the existence of no created world at all would surely be a less excellent state of affairs than the existence of some of the worlds that God could have created.

[3] See Gaston Grua, *Jurisprudence universelle et théodicée selon Leibniz* (Paris, 1953), pp. 210–18.

unkindly by the creation of an inferior world, the creator's choice of an inferior world must manifest a defect of character. I will argue against the first of these claims in section II. Then I will suggest, in section III, that God's choice of a less excellent world could be accounted for in terms of his grace, which is considered a virtue rather than a defect of character in Judaeo-Christian ethics. A counter-example, which is the basis for the most persuasive objections to my position that I have encountered, will be considered in sections IV and V.

II

Is there someone *to* whom a creator would have an obligation to create the best world he could? Is there someone whose rights would be violated, or who would be treated unkindly, if the creator created a less excellent world? Let us suppose that our creator is God, and that there does not exist any being, other than himself, which he has not created. It follows that if God has wronged anyone, or been unkind to anyone, in creating whatever world he has created, this must be one of his own creatures. To which of his creatures, then, might God have an obligation to create the best of all possible worlds? (For that is the best world he could create.)

Might he have an obligation to the creatures in the best possible world, to create them? Have they been wronged, or even treated unkindly, if God has created a less excellent world, in which they do not exist, instead of creating them? I think not. The difference between actual beings and merely possible beings is of fundamental moral importance here. The moral community consists of actual beings. It is they who have actual rights, and it is to them that there are actual obligations. A merely possible being cannot be (actually) wronged or treated unkindly. A being who never exists is not wronged by not being created, and there is no obligation to any possible being to bring it into existence.

Perhaps it will be objected that we believe we have obligations to future generations, who are not yet actual and may never be actual. We do say such things, but I think what we mean is something like the following. There is not merely a logical possibility, but a probability greater than zero, that future generations will really exist; and *if* they will in fact exist, we will have wronged them if we act or fail to act in certain ways. On this analysis we cannot have an obligation to future generations to bring them into existence.

I argue, then, that God does not have an obligation to the creatures in the best of all possible worlds to create them. If God has chosen to create a world less excellent than the best possible, he has not thereby wronged any creatures whom he has chosen not to create. He has not even been unkind to them. If any creatures are wronged, or treated unkindly, by such a choice of the creator, they can only be creatures that exist in the world he has created.

I think it is fairly plausible to suppose that God could create a world which would have the following characteristics:

(1) None of the individual creatures in it would exist in the best of all possible worlds.
(2) None of the creatures in it has a life which is so miserable on the whole that it would be better for that creature if it had never existed.
(3) Every individual creature in the world is at least as happy on the whole as it would have been in any other possible world in which it could have existed.

It seems obvious that, if God creates such a world, he does not thereby wrong any of the creatures in it, and does not thereby treat any of them with less than perfect kindness. For none of them would have been benefited by his creating any other world instead.[4]

If there are doubts about the possibility of God's creating such a world, they will probably have to do with the third characteristic. It may be worth while to consider two questions, on the supposition (which I am not endorsing) that no possible world less excellent than the best would have characteristic (3), and that God has created a world which has characteristics (1) and (2) but not

[4] Perhaps I can have a right to something which would not benefit me (e.g., if it has been promised to me). But if there are such non-beneficial rights, I do not see any plausible reason for supposing that a right not to be created could be among them.

(3). In such a case, must God have wronged one of his creatures? Must He have been less than perfectly kind to one of His creatures?

I do not think it can reasonably be argued that in such a case God must have wronged one of his creatures. Suppose a creature in such a case were to complain that God had violated its rights by creating it in a world in which it was less happy on the whole than it would have been in some other world in which God could have created it. The complaint might express a claim to special treatment: 'God ought to have created *me* in more favourable circumstances (even though that would involve his creating some *other* creature in less favourable circumstances than he could have created it in).' Such a complaint would not be reasonable, and would not establish that there had been any violation of the complaining creature's rights.

Alternatively, the creature might make the more principled complaint, 'God has wronged me by not following the principle of refraining from creating any world in which there is a creature that would have been happier in another world he could have made.' This also is an unreasonable complaint. For if God followed the stated principle, he would not create any world that lacked characteristic (3). And we are assuming that no world less excellent than the best possible would have characteristic (3). It follows that, if God acted on the stated principle, he would not create any world less excellent than the best possible. But the complaining creature would not exist in the best of all possible worlds; for we are assuming that this creature exists in a world which has characteristic (1). The complaining creature, therefore, would never have existed if God had followed the principle that is urged in the complaint. There could not possibly be any advantage to this creature from God's having followed that principle; and the creature has not been wronged by God's not following the principle. (It would not be better for the creature if it had never existed; for we are assuming that the world God created has characteristic (2).)

The question of whether in the assumed case God must have been unkind to one of his creatures is more complicated than the question of whether he must have wronged one of them. In fact it is too complicated to be discussed adequately here. I will just make three observations about it. The first is that it is no clearer that the best of all possible worlds would possess characteristic (3) than that some less excellent world would possess it. In fact, it has often been supposed that the best possible world might not possess it. The problem we are now discussing can therefore arise also for those who believe that God has created the best of all possible worlds.

My second observation is that, if kindness to a person is the same as a tendency to promote his happiness, God has been less than perfectly (completely, unqualifiedly) kind to any creature whom he could have made somewhat happier than he has made it. (I shall not discuss here whether kindness to a person is indeed the same as a tendency to promote his happiness; they are at least closely related.)

But in the third place I would observe that such qualified kindness (if that is what it is) toward some creatures is consistent with God's being perfectly good, and with his being very kind to all his creatures. It is consistent with his being very kind to all his creatures because he may have prepared for all of them a very satisfying existence even though some of them might have been slightly happier in some other possible world. It is consistent with his being perfectly good because even a perfectly good moral agent may be led, by other considerations of sufficient weight, to qualify his kindness or beneficence toward some person. It has sometimes been held that a perfectly good God might cause or permit a person to have less happiness than he might otherwise have had, in order to punish him, or to avoid interfering with the freedom of another person, or in order to create the best of all possible worlds. I would suggest that the desire to create and love all of a certain group of possible creatures (assuming that all of them would have satisfying lives on the whole) might be an adequate ground for a perfectly good God to create them, even if his creating *all* of them must have the result that some of them are less happy than they might otherwise have been. And they need not be the best of all possible creatures, or included in the best of all possible worlds, in order for this qualification of his kindness to be consistent with his perfect goodness. The desire to create *those* creatures is as legitimate a ground for him to qualify his kindness toward some, as is the desire to create the best of all possible worlds. This suggestion seems to me to be in keeping with the aspect of the Judaeo-Christian moral ideal which will be discussed in section III.

These matters would doubtless have to be discussed more fully if we were considering whether the *actual* world can have been created by a perfectly good God. For our present purposes, however, enough may have been said—especially since, as I have noted, it seems a plausible assumption that God could make a world having characteristics (1), (2) and (3). In that case he could certainly make a less excellent world than the best of all possible worlds without wronging any of his creatures or failing in kindness to any of them. (I have, of course, *not* been arguing that there is *no* way in which God could wrong anyone or be less kind to anyone than a perfectly good moral agent must be.)

III

Plato is one of those who held that a perfectly good creator would make the very best world he could. He thought that if the creator chose to make a world less good than he could have made, that could be understood only in terms of some defect in the creator's character. Envy is the defect that Plato suggests.[5] It may be thought that the creation of a world inferior to the best that he could make would manifest a defect in the creator's character even if no one were thereby wronged or treated unkindly. For the perfectly good moral agent must not only be kind and refrain from violating the rights of others, but must also have other virtues. For instance, he must be noble, generous, high-minded, and free from envy. He must satisfy the moral ideal.

There are differences of opinion, however, about what is to be included in the moral ideal. One important element in the Judaeo-Christian moral ideal is *grace*. For present purposes, grace may be defined as a disposition to love which is not dependent on the

[5] *Timaeus*, 29E–30A.

merit of the person loved. The gracious person loves without worrying about whether the person he loves is worthy of his love. Or perhaps it would be better to say that the gracious person sees what is valuable in the person he loves, and does not worry about whether it is more or less valuable than what could be found in someone else he might have loved. In the Judaeo-Christian tradition, it is typically believed that grace is a virtue which God does have and men ought to have.

A God who is gracious with respect to creating might well choose to create and love less excellent creatures than he could have chosen. This is not to suggest that grace in creation consists in a preference for imperfection as such. God could have chosen to create the best of all possible creatures, and still have been gracious in choosing them. God's graciousness in creation does not imply that the creatures he has chosen to create must be less excellent than the best possible. It implies, rather, that even if they are the best possible creatures, that is not the ground for his choosing them. And it implies that there is nothing in God's nature or character which would require him to act on the principle of choosing the best possible creatures to be the object of his creative powers.

Grace, as I have described it, is not part of everyone's moral ideal. For instance, it was not part of Plato's moral ideal. The thought that it may be the expression of a virtue, rather than a defect of character, in a creator, *not* to act on the principle of creating the best creatures he possibly could, is quite foreign to Plato's ethical viewpoint. But I believe that thought is not at all foreign to a Judaeo-Christian ethical viewpoint.

This interpretation of the Judaeo-Christian tradition is confirmed by the religious and devotional attitudes toward God's creation which prevail in the tradition. The man who worships God does not normally praise him for his moral rectitude and good judgement in creating *us*. He thanks God for his existence as for an undeserved personal favour. Religious writings frequently deprecate the intrinsic worth of human beings, considered apart from God's love for them, and express surprise that God should concern himself with them at all.

When I look at thy heavens, the work of thy fingers, the moon and the stars which thou hast established;
What is man that thou art mindful of him, and the son of man that thou dost care for him?
Yet thou hast made him little less than God, and dost crown him with glory and honour.
Thou hast given him dominion over the works of thy hands; thou hast put all things under his feet [Psalm 8: 3–6].

Such utterances seem quite incongruous with the idea that God created us because if he had not he would have failed to bring about the best possible state of affairs. They suggest that God has created human beings and made them dominant on this planet although he could have created intrinsically better states of affairs instead.

I believe that in the Judaeo-Christian tradition the typical religious attitude (or at any rate the attitude typically encouraged) toward the fact of our existence is something like the following. 'I am glad that I exist, and I thank God for the life he has given me. I am also glad that other people exist, and I thank God for them. Doubtless there could be more excellent creatures than we. But I believe that God, in his grace, created us and loves us; and I accept that gladly and gratefully.' (Such an attitude need not be complacent; for the task of struggling against certain evils may be seen as precisely a part of the life that the religious person is to accept and be glad in.) When people who have or endorse such an attitude say that God is perfectly good, we will not take them as committing themselves to the view that God is the kind of being who would not create any other world than the best possible. For they regard grace as an important part of perfect goodness.

IV

On more than one occasion, when I have argued for the positions I have taken in sections II and III above, a counter-example of the following sort has been proposed. It is the case of a person who, knowing that she intends to conceive a child and that a certain drug invariably causes severe mental retardation in children conceived by those who have taken it, takes the drug and conceives a severely retarded child. We all, I imagine, have a strong inclination to say that such a person has done something wrong. It is objected to me that our moral intuitions in this case (presumably including the moral intuitions of religious Jews and Christians) are inconsistent with the views I have advanced above. It is claimed that consistency requires me to abandon those views unless I am prepared to make moral judgements that none of us are in fact willing to make.

I will try to meet these objections. I will begin by stating the case in some detail, in the most relevant form I can think of. Then I will discuss objections based on it. In this section I will discuss an objection against what I have said in section II, and a more general objection against the rejection of proposition (*P*) will be discussed in section V.

Let us call this case (*A*). A certain couple become so interested in retarded children that they develop a strong desire to have a retarded child of their own—to love it, to help it realize its potentialities (such as they are) to the full, to see that it is as happy as it can be. (For some reason it is impossible for them to *adopt* such a child.) They act on their desire. They take a drug which is known to cause damaged genes and abnormal chromosome structure in reproductive cells, resulting in severe mental retardation of children conceived by those who have taken it. A severely retarded child is conceived and born. They lavish affection on the child. They have ample means, so that they are able to provide for special needs, and to ensure that others will never be called on to pay for the child's support. They give themselves unstintedly, and do develop the child's capacities as much as possible. The child is, on the whole, happy, though incapable of many of the higher intellectual, aesthetic, and social joys. It suffers some pains and frustrations, of course, but does not feel miserable on the whole.

The first objection founded on this case is based, not just on the claim that the parents have done something wrong (which I certainly grant), but on the more specific claim that they have *wronged the child*. I maintained, in effect, in section II that a creature has not been wronged by its creator's creating it if both of the following conditions are satisfied.[6] (4) The creature is not, on the whole, so miserable that it would be better for him if he had never existed. (5) No being who came into existence in better or happier circumstances would have been the same individual as the creature in question. If we apply an analogous principle to the parent–child relationship in case (*A*), it would seem to follow that the retarded child has not been wronged by its parents. Condition (4) is satisfied: the child is happy rather than miserable on the whole. And condition (5) also seems to be satisfied. For the retardation in case (*A*), as described, is not due to pre-natal injury but to the genetic constitution of the child. Any normal child the parents might have conceived (indeed any normal child at all) would have had a different genetic constitution, and would therefore have been a different person, from the retarded child they actually did conceive. But—it is objected to me—we do regard the parents in case (*A*) as having wronged the child, and therefore we cannot consistently accept the principle that I maintained in section II.

My reply is that if conditions (4) and (5) are really satisfied the child cannot have been wronged by its parents' taking the drug and conceiving it. If we think otherwise we are being led, perhaps by our emotions, into a confusion. If the child is not worse off than if it had never existed, and if *its* never existing would have been a sure consequence of its not having been brought into existence as retarded, I do not see how *its* interests can have been injured, or *its* rights violated, by the parents' bringing it into existence as retarded.

It is easy to understand how the parents might come to feel that they had wronged the child. They might come to feel guilty (and rightly so), and the child would provide a focus for the guilt. Moreover, it would be easy, psychologically, to assimilate case (*A*) to cases of culpability for pre-natal injury, in which it is more

[6] I am not holding that these are necessary conditions, but only that they are jointly sufficient conditions, for a creature's not being wronged by its creator's creating it. I have numbered these conditions in such a way as to avoid confusion with the numbered characteristics of worlds in section II.

reasonable to think of the child as having been wronged.[7] And we often think very carelessly about counter-factual personal identity, asking ourselves questions of doubtful intelligibility, such as, 'What if I had been born in the Middle Ages?' It is very easy to fail to consider the objection, 'But that would not have been the same person.'

It is also possible that an inclination to say that the child has been wronged may be based, at least in part, on a doubt that conditions (4) and (5) are really satisfied in case (*A*). Perhaps one is not convinced that in real life the parents could ever have a reasonable confidence that the child would be happy rather than miserable. Maybe it will be doubted that a few changes in chromosome structure, and the difference between damaged and undamaged genes, are enough to establish that the retarded child is a different person from any normal child that the couple could have had. Of course, if conditions (4) and (5) are not satisfied, the case does not constitute a counter-example to my claims in section II. But I would not rest any of the weight of my argument on doubts about the satisfaction of the conditions in case (*A*), because I think it is plausible to suppose that they would be satisfied in case (*A*) or in some very similar case.

V

Even if the parents in case (*A*) have not wronged the child, I assume that they have done something wrong. It may be asked *what* they have done wrong, or *why* their action is regarded as wrong. And these questions may give rise to an objection, not specifically to what I said in section II, but more generally to my rejection of proposition (*P*). For it may be suggested that what is wrong about the action of the parents in case (*A*) is that they have violated the following principle:

[7] It may be questioned whether even the pre-natally injured child is the same person as any unimpaired child that might have been born. I am inclined to think it is the same person. At any rate there is *more* basis for regarding it as the same person as a possible normal child than there is for so regarding a child with abnormal genetic constitution.

(*Q*) It is wrong to bring into existence, knowingly, a being less excellent than one could have brought into existence.[8]

If we accept this principle we must surely agree that it would be wrong for a creator to make a world that was less excellent than the best he could make, and therefore that a perfectly good creator would not do such a thing. In other words, (*Q*) implies (*P*).

I do not think (*Q*) is a very plausible principle. It is not difficult to think of counter-examples to it.

Case (*B*): A man breeds goldfish, thereby bringing about their existence. We do not normally think it is wrong, or even *prima facie* wrong, for a man to do this, even though he could equally well have brought about the existence of more excellent beings, more intelligent and capable of higher satisfactions. (He could have bred dogs or pigs, for example.) The deliberate breeding of human beings of subnormal intelligence is morally offensive; the deliberate breeding of species far less intelligent than retarded human children is not morally offensive.

Case (*C*): Suppose it has been discovered that if intending parents take a certain drug before conceiving a child, they will have a child whose abnormal genetic constitution will give it vastly superhuman intelligence and superior prospects of happiness. Other things being equal, would it be wrong for intending parents to have normal children instead of taking the drug? There may be considerable disagreement of moral judgement about this. I do not think that the parents who chose to have normal children rather than take the drug would be doing anything wrong, nor that they would necessarily be manifesting any weakness or defect of moral character. Parents' choosing to have a normal rather than a superhuman child would not, at any rate, elicit the strong and universal or almost universal disapproval that would be elicited by the action of the parents in case (*A*). Even with respect to the offspring of human beings, the principle we all confidently endorse is not that it is wrong to bring about, knowingly and voluntarily,

[8] Anyone who was applying this principle to human actions would doubtless insert an 'other things being equal' clause. But let us ignore that, since such a clause would presumably provide no excuse for an agent who was deciding an issue so important as what world to create.

the procreation of offspring less excellent than could have been procreated, but that it is wrong to bring about, knowingly and voluntarily, the procreation of a human offspring which is deficient by comparison with normal human beings.

Such counter-examples as these suggest that our disapproval of the action of the parents in case (*A*) is not based on principle (*Q*), but on a less general and more plausible principle such as the following:

(*R*) It is wrong for human beings to cause, knowingly and voluntarily, the procreation of an offspring of human parents which is notably deficient, by comparison with normal human beings, in mental or physical capacity.

One who rejects (*Q*) while maintaining (*R*) might be held to face a problem of explanation. It may seem arbitrary to maintain such a specific moral principle as (*R*), unless one can explain it as based on a more general principle, such as (*Q*). I believe, however, that principle (*R*) might well be explained in something like the following way in a theological ethics in the Judaeo-Christian tradition, consistently with the rejection of (*Q*) and (*P*).[9]

God, in his grace, has chosen to have human beings among his creatures. In creating us he has certain intentions about the qualities and goals of human life. He has these intentions for us, not just as individuals, but as members of a community which in principle includes the whole human race. And his intentions for human beings as such extend to the offspring (if any) of human beings. Some of these intentions are to be realized by human voluntary action, and it is our duty to act in accordance with them.

It seems increasingly possible for human voluntary action to influence the genetic constitution of human offspring. The religious believer in the Judaeo-Christian tradition will want to be extremely cautious about this. For he is to be thankful that we exist as the beings we are, and will be concerned lest he bring about the procreation of human offspring who would be deficient in their capacity to enter fully into the purposes that God has for human beings as such. We are not God. We are his creatures, and

[9] I am able to give here, of course, only a very incomplete sketch of a theological position on the issue of 'biological engineering'.

we belong to him. Any offspring we have will belong to him in a much more fundamental way than they can belong to their human parents. We have not the right to try to have as our offspring just any kind of being whose existence might on the whole be pleasant and of some value (for instance, a being of very low intelligence but highly specialized for the enjoyment of aesthetic pleasures of smell and taste). If we do intervene to affect the genetic constitution of human offspring, it must be in ways which seem likely to make them *more* able to enter fully into what we believe to be the purposes of God for human beings as such. The deliberate procreation of children deficient in mental or physical capacity would be an intervention which could hardly be expected to result in offspring more able to enter fully into God's purposes for human life. It would therefore be sinful, and inconsistent with a proper respect for the human life which God has given us.

On this view of the matter, our obligation to refrain from bringing about the procreation of deficient human offspring is rooted in our obligation to God, as his creatures, to respect his purposes for human life. In adopting this theological rationale for the acceptance of principle (*R*), one in no way commits oneself to proposition (*P*). For one does not base (*R*) on any principle to the effect that one must always try to bring into existence the most excellent things that one can. And the claim that, because of his intentions for human life, we have an obligation to God not to try to have as our offspring beings of certain sorts does not imply that it would be wrong for God to create such beings in other ways. Much less does it imply that it would be wrong for God to create a world less excellent than the best possible.

In this essay I have argued that a creator would not necessarily wrong anyone, or be less kind to anyone than a perfectly good moral agent must be, if he created a world of creatures who would not exist in the best world he could make. I have also argued that from the standpoint of Judaeo-Christian religious ethics, a creator's choice of a less excellent world need not be regarded as manifesting a defect of character. It could be understood in terms of his *grace*, which (in that ethics) is considered an important part of perfect goodness. In this way I think the rejection of proposition (*P*) can be seen to be congruous with the attitude of gratitude and respect for human life as God's gracious gift which is encouraged in the Judaeo-Christian religious tradition. And that attitude (rather than any belief that one ought to bring into existence only the best beings one can) can be seen as a basis for the disapproval of the deliberate procreation of deficient human offspring.[10]

[10] Among the many to whom I am indebted for help in working out the thoughts contained in this paper, and for criticisms of earlier drafts of it, I must mention Marilyn McCord Adams, Richard Brandt, Eric Lerner, the members of my graduate class on theism and ethics in the Fall term of 1970 at the University of Michigan, and the editors of the *Philosophical Review*.

6

DUTY AND DIVINE GOODNESS

THOMAS V. MORRIS

THROUGHOUT the history of Western theology, divine goodness has been explicated in a number of different ways. Central among these is the important religious claim that God is morally good. This form of divine goodness usually is thought to consist in God's acting always in accordance with universal moral principles, satisfying without fail moral duties and engaging in acts of gracious supererogation. Divine moral goodness is understood basically on the model of human moral goodness. Let us refer to the part of this conception having to do with duty as 'the duty model' of divine goodness. According to the common employment of this model, God like us has moral duties, but unlike us satisfies those duties perfectly.

Now of course God is not thought on any reasonable construal of the duty model to have all and only those moral duties also had by human beings. We, for example, have a duty to worship God and be thankful for his benefits. Presumably, he has no such duty. Conversely, in virtue of his exalted role *vis-à-vis* the entire universe, God may well have duties shared by no one else, and even duties of which we have no conception. So divine and human duties presumably diverge. But it is a widespread and fundamental religious belief that they must also overlap. If God deigns to communicate with us, he will speak the truth, in accordance with a universal duty. Likewise, if he makes a promise, he will keep it, consistent with another general duty. This area of overlap between human and divine obligation is vital to religious faith. In our ability to know moral principles which bind human conduct we have the ability to anticipate features of divine activity. The belief that such

Reprinted with permission from, *American Philosophical Quarterly*, Vol. 21, No. 3, July 1984, 261–268.

duties as truth-telling and promise-keeping govern divine conduct grounds the trust the religious believer has in God.

Yet two other common, and also quite important, traditional theistic commitments create a serious logical problem for the duty model of divine goodness. I shall indicate what this problem is, comment on some unsatisfactory attempts to avoid it, and then propose an adequate solution which involves a new account of the way in which the notion of a moral duty can be used to characterize divine action.

I

A great many theists favour a libertarian (agent-causation) analysis of free action. Nearly all are committed to a libertarian account of divine action. At the same time, it is a standard theistic belief that God is necessarily good, that goodness is an essential property of the individual who in fact, and of necessity, is God. If God is necessarily good, and part of what that goodness involves is given by the duty model, then it follows that God necessarily acts in accordance with moral principles. But if this is so, a quite modest libertarian principle will entail that God does not exemplify the kind of freedom requisite for being a moral agent with any duties at all. On this principle it will be logically impossible for any individual to have moral duties he necessarily satisfies. In short, there can be no necessarily good moral agent. It is this entailment which will generate our problem. The logical problem, then, is one of compatibility among three common theistic commitments: (1) the duty model of divine goodness, (2) a libertarian account of moral freedom, and (3) the claim that God is necessarily good.

Most accounts of free action include a condition to the effect that an act is performed freely only if its agent in some sense *could have done otherwise*. The libertarian characteristically insists on a strong, categorical construal of this condition. It is exceedingly difficult to state an unproblematic formulation of this requirement, but it is clear that it must contain *at least* the relatively modest principle that an agent *S* performs an act *A* at a time *t* freely only if no conditions exist prior to *t* which render it necessary, or unavoidable, in a broadly logical sense, and by doing so in fact bring it about, that S performs A.[1] Let us refer to this condition as the Principle of Avoidance (PA). The libertarian will insist on conditions a good deal more stringent than PA as well, but at least all forms of the libertarian account of freedom will incorporate this requirement, and it is all that is needed to produce our problem. According to the libertarian, it is only acts satisfying this minimal condition which are free acts. And only free acts are morally characterizable as the satisfaction or violation of duties.

PA is to be understood as specifying that whenever there are *any* conditions prior to the time of an act (other than any immediately efficacious decision or intention of the agent to perform that act) which render it in a broadly logical sense unavoidable, it is not a morally characterizable act. Such an act will be judged not to exemplify the sort of freedom necessary for its being morally assessable. Likewise, any *feature* of an act which is such that it can not be avoided by the agent is not such that the agent is morally responsible for it. And this in particular is relevant to the case of God.

Suppose God promises to bless Abraham. If God necessarily acts in accordance with moral principles, it seems that once the promise is made he is logically bound, bound in such a way as to deprive him of the freedom the libertarian analysis requires of a morally characterizable act. Suppose the promise is made at t to bless Abraham at $t + n$. At that later time, is God free to bless and free to refrain from blessing Abraham, all relevant prior conditions remaining the same? If he is free to refrain, he is free to break a promise. But God can be free to break a promise only if there is a possible world in which he does so. And if he is necessarily good, there is no such world. Jonathan Edwards once put this point strongly by saying:

> God's absolute promise of any things makes the things promised necessary and their failing to take place impossible.[2]

[1] The principle stated here circumvents well known counter-examples to the stronger Principle of Alternate Possibilities. See for example Harry Frankfurt's 'Alternate Possibilities and Moral Responsibility', *Journal of Philosophy* 66 (1969).

[2] *Freedom of the Will*, ed. Paul Ramsey (New Haven, 1957), p. 283.

There is no possible world containing both a promise of God's and the everlasting lack of that promise's fulfilment. So when God blesses Abraham, his act of blessing fails to satisfy PA. Conditions prior to the time of his act render it necessary, or unavoidable, in a broadly logical sense that he perform that act. Thus, on the libertarian analysis, it is not morally characterizable, and so cannot count as the fulfilment of a duty. And surely this result of PA will be entirely general. From the necessity of God's acting in accordance with moral principles, it will follow, for example, that no divine act can possibly constitute in a moral sense the keeping of a promise, and so it will follow that God cannot make any promises at all. Likewise, analogous reasoning will show that God cannot act in such a way as *morally* to satisfy *any* duty, and thus cannot be such as to have any moral duties at all.[3]

It should be pointed out at this stage that libertarian principles do not entail that God is not in any sense free. Nor do they entail that, by making a promise, he would deprive himself of all freedom with respect to the act promised. God always has a range of free choice, but the argument is that it is not such as to ground moral characterization with respect to duty. For example, if God were to promise to give Abraham a son, he could not then do otherwise. But suppose that in keeping his promise he gives Abraham Isaac. The exact way in which he keeps the promise is such that he could have done otherwise. He could have given Abraham another son. It was in no sense necessary or unavoidable that he give Abraham Isaac. There is always this sort of 'open texture' to promises and promise-keeping. This sort of freedom God does have. And of course God is presumably free with regard to whether he will ever make such a promise in the first place. So God is free both to promise and not to promise. Likewise, he is free in exactly how he keeps the promise. He lacks freedom only with respect to whatever feature of a state of affairs or event will render his actualization of it the keeping of his promise. He is not free to refrain from bringing it about that something have that

[3] The argument here treats God as a temporal agent lacking power to change the past, but this is strictly unnecessary for the generation of our problem. Note also that the inference bears a superficial resemblance to, but on reflection can be seen not to commit, a famous modal fallacy.

particular feature. Given prior conditions it is necessary or unavoidable in the broadly logical sense that he bring that about. So on the libertarian analysis he is not free in his bringing it about that that feature obtain.

The case of truth-telling may serve to highlight these distinctions. Suppose God chooses to reveal some proposition *P* at time *t*. If he is necessarily good, then anything he asserts must be true. He cannot lie. Now, according to PA, why cannot we count God's telling the truth in uttering *P* at *t* as the satisfaction of a moral duty not to lie? Is God free to assert *P* at *t* and free to refrain from asserting *P* at *t*? Surely circumstances are easily conceivable in which this is so, in which God's revealing *P* satisfies PA. He could have revealed some other true proposition *Q* instead, or just have chosen not to communicate anything at *t*. His act of revelation is thus in this sense a free act. But the libertarian principle generates the following argument. At *t* God freely tells a truth. But there is a sense in which he could not have done otherwise. He could not have asserted intentionally a falsehood at *t*. This is the morally significant alternative from which he is debarred by his character. And his having such a character is a condition which obtains, and obtains of necessity, prior to *t*. If he chooses to communicate, God cannot refrain from bringing about that feature of an assertion which alone would render its utterance the satisfaction of a duty not to lie. If he decides to speak, his goodness logically necessitates his telling the truth. So, on the libertarian analysis, since he is not free to utter a falsehood knowingly, he does not have the sort of freedom requisite for his uttering a true statement to count as morally characterizable, and thus as the satisfaction of any duty.

This can be put in another way. Those states of affairs which God can actualize fall into two categories—those in which he communicates and those in which he refrains from communicating. It is a simple necessary truth that if he does not communicate, he does not lie. And if he essentially acts in accordance with moral principles, it follows that, necessarily, if he does communicate, he does not lie. Thus it is impossible that God actualize a state of affairs in which he refrains from not lying. Being such that in it God does not lie is the feature of any state of affairs which would render God's actualization of it the satisfaction of a moral duty not to lie. But it is not a feature which God is, in the sense of PA, both free to actualize and free to refrain from actualizing. Thus, at no time does God's not lying satisfy PA.

Again, the libertarian PA does not impugn the divine freedom in any wholesale way. It just precludes God's having the sort of freedom which is a necessary condition of his having moral duties. It seems therefore that a libertarian theist must deny that a necessarily good moral agent is possible, and thus deny that God is necessarily good—where his goodness is at least partially explicated by the duty model—or else reject the duty model of divine goodness.

II

Faced with such a choice, the theist committed both to the position that God is necessarily good and to the duty model of divine goodness might consider rethinking his account of freedom and moral responsibility. He might consider adopting a general account of moral freedom which will not give rise to this dilemma. However, this way out of our problem is unattractive initially for at least three reasons. First, it is not altogether obvious that even the most lenient compatabilism of any merit will allow an act to count as free and morally significant if at its performance it is *logically impossible* (in the broadly logical sense) that its agent refrain from doing it. And this is what we have in the case of God's acting in accordance with moral principles. Secondly, even if such an account of freedom is available, it may not be consistent with other standard doctrines of traditional theism concerning human sin, divine punishment, and the compatibility of God's goodness with the evil in the world. And finally, with all the data of common sense and theological backing which can be marshalled in favour of a libertarian position, the traditional theist will probably find this resolution of the problem no more attractive than either horn of the dilemma which otherwise faces him.

In light of this, it can be tempting for the theist to jettison the duty model altogether. For there are other traditional explications of divine goodness available. There is, for example, in patristic and medieval theology what we might call 'the plenitude of being model' of divine goodness. According to this tradition, to attribute goodness to God is to hold that he is in some sense the fullness of being and the ground of all value. He is said to have necessarily the maximally perfect set of compossible, ontological great-making properties, construed along Anselmian lines. Such affirmations clearly constitute a metaphysical rather than a moral explication of God's goodness.

Another understanding of divine goodness may be referred to as 'the benevolence model'. On this model, to say that God is good is to say that he freely actualizes moral value he is not obligated to bring about. The goodness of God is thought of as consisting in divine grace, kindness, mercy, and other dispositions to supererogation. Some philosophers may find this explication alone quite satisfying. It can seem to circumvent altogether the difficult issue of whether God has moral duties, and it avoids the sort of metaphysical assumptions involved in talk about plenitude of being which nowadays are so dubious to many philosophers and theologians. So it might appear easy for the libertarian theist to give up the duty model in order to attain consistency within his overall position. Either, or both, of these other models may seem to give him all he needs for a satisfactory explication of divine goodness.

However, I am afraid that to substitute either or both of these other models for the duty model would be religiously unacceptable within any remotely orthodox variant of the Judaeo-Christian tradition. For in the Biblical tradition, God has been experienced as one who makes and keeps promises, who enters into covenant relations, and who does not lie. Repeatedly, the Biblical authors affirm not only that God is concerned with moral behaviour on the part of his people, but also that he himself will surely do justice for them as well. He is presented as engaging in just the sort of behaviour to be expected of a perfectly good moral agent. The duty model thus captures an important element in the Biblical experience and portrayal of God. As such it seems indispensable to any orthodox account of his character and activity.

If the theist wishes to retain both a libertarian account of moral freedom and the duty model of divine goodness, it can look as if the only way to avoid our logical problem is to abandon the claim that God is good of logical necessity. This can even seem at first to be a relatively attractive way out, since the thesis that God is necessarily good can appear to be in some sense the most remotely theoretical of our three conflicting commitments, the one least supported by the data of experience and reflective common sense. In a recent book,[4] Bruce Reichenbach has argued that the sort of problem I have articulated forces us to conclude that being morally perfect is not one of God's essential properties. Recognizing a distinction between the moral and the metaphysical goodness of God, he holds that the proposition that God is good is necessary *de dicto* with respect to both forms of goodness but necessary *de re* only in the case of metaphysical goodness. It is a necessary condition of deity that an individual be both morally and metaphysically good. It may even be required that he have metaphysical goodness as one of his necessary, or essential, properties. But because of logical incompatibility with PA and the duty model, it cannot be a requisite of deity that an individual be morally good of necessity, or essentially. And, of course, on the same ground Reichenbach holds that the individual who in fact is God just cannot himself be necessarily good in a moral sense. The conclusion Reichenbach draws then is that the libertarian who holds God to be a moral agent must allow that he is in fact morally good only contingently.

Of course, Reichenbach is not the first philosopher to think that the theist is forced by some logical problem to hold that God's moral goodness is only contingent. In a well-known article,[5] Nelson Pike has drawn the same conclusion from a different problem, one allegedly arising between omnipotence and necessary goodness. I have suggested elsewhere that Pike's argument in no way forces the theist to give up the traditional claim that God's moral goodness has the modal status of *de re* necessity.[6] And I think it is even easier to see that the abandonment of necessary goodness is not called for to solve our problem here—primarily

[4] *Evil and a Good God* (New York, 1982), ch. 7.

[5] 'Omnipotence and God's Ability to Sin', *American Philosophical Quarterly* 6 (1969), pp. 208–16.

[6] I argue this in 'Impeccability', *Analysis* 43 (1983), pp. 106–12.

because this move will not itself circumvent the problem at all unless other quite radical and unacceptable alterations are made to the traditional concept of God as well.

Reichenbach assumes that if the individual who is God, say, Yahweh, is morally good only contingently, it follows that it is at least possible, in a broadly logical sense, for him to cease being good at any time, by contravening at that time some moral duty. It is only if this entailment holds that Yahweh's being good only contingently would guarantee that his acting in accordance with moral principles could satisfy PA and thus qualify as his moral fulfilment of duties. But, unfortunately, the entailment does not hold. From the fact that a property is contingent for an individual, such that the individual could have existed without ever having it at all, it does not follow that the individual can ever possibly cease to have it. God, for example, has now the property of having once spoken to Abraham. He has this property contingently. But even though it is among God's contingent properties, it is not the sort of property he could ever *cease* to exemplify. This should be clear. And the same will be true for a number of different kinds of contingent properties.[7] It is perfectly compatible with a property's being exemplified contingently that its full mode of exemplification be such that the individual having it cannot cease to have it. So even if God were morally good only contingently, it would not follow straightforwardly that he could ever act in such a way as to cease being perfectly good.

In fact, in the case of God, it can be strictly demonstrated from other divine attributes that if he is ever morally good at any time, even contingently, he can never thereafter cease to be good. As I have advanced proofs of this elsewhere at some length, I shall not rehearse the arguments here.[8] However, I should at least indicate their direction. If God is necessarily omnipotent, and essentially omniscient, it will follow that he cannot possibly cease to be good in a moral sense. The goodness of his character will have a strong stability. So, to circumvent our logical problem in Reichenbach's manner, the theist will have to abandon a good deal more than

[7] I have argued this in a manner relevant to the present discussion in 'Properties, Modalities, and God', *Philosophical Review* 93 (1984), pp. 35–55.

[8] The arguments appear in 'Properties, Modalities, and God', s. 4.

merely the necessity *de re* of God's moral goodness. He will have to relinquish the *de re* necessity of his power and knowledge as well. But even this will not be enough. For even if God's omniscience and omnipotence are among his contingent properties, it is implied by even a modest form of the doctrine of divine immutability that they are not such that the individual who is God could ever cease to have them. And if this is the mode of their contingent exemplification, it also follows that God can never cease to be good. So, in order to take Reichenbach's way out, the theist would have to alter the traditional concept of God a great deal more than he might initially expect. He would have to deny the stability of divine power and knowledge in order to arrive at a conception of deity according to which God's acting in concurrence with moral principles could satisfy the libertarian principle PA, and thus count as morally good. Any theist of remotely orthodox inclinations will find this prospect quite unsatisfactory. So this way out of our problem has little to recommend it, as little as either of the other obvious avenues of escape.

III

I would like to suggest that there is a way of applying the duty model to God which avoids completely the logical problem which otherwise arises between the libertarian account of freedom, the claim that God is necessarily good, and the use of that model as at least a partial explication of what religious people mean to convey when they ascribe goodness to God. Should it be judged successful, there will be no need to give up any of the three commitments which have seemed to form an inconsistent triad. If what I have to suggest is right, employing the duty model as at least a partial explication of divine goodness need not commit one to holding that God actually has any duties at all. A fairly simple distinction will render intelligible this admittedly paradoxical claim.

For a number of years, philosophers have drawn a distinction between following a rule and merely acting in accordance with a rule. Behaviour which results from obeying a rule can be distinguished logically from behaviour which otherwise accords with that rule, even though the two may be empirically indistinguishable to an observer. Although we cannot appropriate this precise distinction to solve our problem, the application of this *sort* of distinction to our employment of the duty model of divine goodness is relatively simple, and will give us exactly what we need. We can hold that those moral principles which function as either deontically prescriptive or proscriptive for human conduct stand in some other relation to divine conduct. We could even go so far as to claim that they are merely descriptive of the shape of divine activity. But the important difference is as follows. We human beings exist in a state of being *bound* by moral duty. In this state we act under obligation, either satisfying or contravening our duties. Because of his distinctive nature, God does not share our ontological status. Specifically, he does not share our relation to moral principles—that of being bound by some of these principles as duties. Nevertheless, God acts *in accordance with* those principles which would express duties for a moral agent in his relevant circumstances. And he does so necessarily. So although God does not literally have any duties on this construal of the duty model, we still can have well-grounded expectations concerning divine conduct by knowing those moral principles which would govern the conduct of a perfect, duty-bound moral agent who acted as God in fact does. We understand and anticipate God's activity by analogy with the behaviour of a completely good moral agent. And this is an application of analogy in our understanding of God which in no way impedes that understanding. On this application of the duty model, just as much as on its literal employment, we know that if God says that he will do *A*, then he will do *A*. We can depend on it. Likewise, if he communicates any proposition, we can be assured that it will be a true one. When we use the duty model in this way, we retain all that is religiously important about it while avoiding the problems a literal application would generate.

A couple of objections to this application of the duty model easily come to mind. First, it might be pointed out that, on this interpretation, God can never actually make any promises, since promising generates literal duties. And this surely seems counter-intuitive. Don't traditional theists often talk of 'the promises of God'?

There is no substance to this objection. R. L. Franklin has characterized the purpose of promising as 'that of committing a man reliably to future acts'.[9] God can certainly declare his intention to bless Abraham, thereby committing himself reliably to do so (where 'committing himself' amounts to intentionally generating justified expectations in his hearers). The libertarian can hold that, in making this sort of declaration, God is doing something for his creatures with an effect analogous to that of promising, or even that in an analogical sense he is making a promise. In holding that God cannot literally make promises, the libertarian would only be acknowledging in a particular type of case that the relation holding between God and moral principles is different from that holding between us and those moral principles. And so long as God necessarily acts in the way a perfectly good moral agent would act, nothing of religious importance is lost in this difference.

A more substantial objection would go as follows. If God does not actually have any moral duties he satisfies, we have no basis on which to praise him. Praise, according to this line of thought, is appropriate only for acts which satisfy moral duties, and only for agents in so far as they perform such acts. On this understanding of praise, a theology which claims that God can have no duties thereby debars God from ever being praiseworthy.

This objection is based on a very common mistaken assumption about moral praise. It is the position that fulfilment of duty, and that alone, merits praise. I would argue, on the contrary, that praise is never strictly appropriate for duty satisfactions. The proper response of one moral agent to another when the latter has done his duty, and when none other than moral considerations obtain, is something weaker than, and distinct from, praise. One who does his duty ought to be morally acknowledged, accepted, or commended by his follows, not praised. Admittedly, in this world of ours, where duty fulfilment under difficult conditions is somewhat rare, there can be significant social utility in praising such accomplishment. But strictly speaking, praise is morally proper only for acts of supererogation.

[9] *Free Will and Determinism* (New York, 1968), p. 41.

God's lacking duties, then, will not amount to his being unworthy of praise. In so far as he actualizes great value he is not bound to bring about, he is worthy of praise. For example, when God 'makes a promise', do we praise him for being so good as to keep it? I think not. When he speaks to his people, is he praised for restraining himself from lying? Clearly not. What we praise him for is for condescending to make us promises or communicate with us at all, for deigning to involve himself at all in our small lives. And these are acts of supererogation, not fulfilments of duty.

Are there any costs incurred by employing the duty model in this new analogical manner? It might seem that at least we lose any answer for such questions as 'Why does God keep his promises?' or 'Why does God do what is morally right?' We can no longer say 'Because he ought to'. But actually nothing is lost. It can be maintained that as a maximally perfect being, God necessarily acts in accordance with those principles which lesser beings sought to comply with. This is his nature. And as his activity and nature is, in a less than Cartesian sense, the ground of all possibility, it is impossible that he should not act thus. We would have a troubling unanswered question about his activity only if it were a contingent fact that his conduct accords perfectly with moral principles. But of course, the traditional theist denies that this is a contingent matter.

IV

One final question remains. In applying the duty model in an analogical manner, are we any longer giving an account of God's *goodness*? Can divine goodness even partially consist in God's acting in accordance with moral principles if none of those principles provides him with moral duties? The most obvious answer to this may seem to be—no. Human action in accord with moral principles can count as the moral satisfaction of duties, because of the nature of the human condition. Our ontological status and our freedom is such that we have duties we can morally fulfil and thereby count as good agents. With the analogical deployment of the duty model, the theist could say that it is not strictly true that God's goodness partly consists in his acting in accordance with moral principles. With this model, we are just explicating part of what religious people usually *mean to convey* when they say that God is good. Strictly speaking, God's non-metaphysical goodness consists only in his disposition to, and effectuation of, supererogatory activity.

But this answer is not forced on the theist. It seems at least possible to argue without absurdity that some conditions for goodness vary with the ontological status of the agent concerned. I have referred to both moral and metaphysical goodness in the case of God. It is possible to treat both these sorts of goodness as species of a broader category of what we might call 'axiological goodness'. To be an agent, such as a human being, who gladly engages in deeds of supererogation and freely acts in accordance with moral principles, satisfying moral duties, is to be in a state of axiological goodness. To be an agent such as God who freely engages in acts of grace, or supererogation, but necessarily acts in accordance with moral principles, is to be in the greatest possible state of axiological goodness. It may be held that for human beings, axiological goodness and moral goodness coincide. For God, however, one form of moral goodness (supererogation) is a component of his axiological goodness; whereas another aspect of his axiological goodness is his necessarily acting in accordance with moral principles—not literally a form of moral goodness at all on the libertarian analysis, but on this view a contributing element or aspect of divine axiological goodness.

On this possible view, God's intentionally acting in accordance with what for us are moral principles specifying duties would be sufficient, given his nature and ontological status, for that conduct counting as good, not morally but axiologically. Axiological agency need not be thought of as logically incompatible, on every ontological level, with all forms of necessitation. Brand Blanshard once argued that being determined by the moral law is, unlike being causally determined by prior states of the physical universe, a condition of the highest (i.e. most valuable) sort of freedom.[10] Of course, because of PA the libertarian cannot hold this to be true of moral freedom. But it could be reasonable for the libertarian theist

[10] See 'The Case For Determinism', in *Determinism and Freedom in The Age of Modern Science*, ed. Sidney Hook (New York, 1958).

to hold that a form of moral necessitation is compatible with, indeed a condition of, God's being a perfectly good axiological agent, a greater than which is not possible.

With these distinctions in hand, the theist could say that an analogical employment of the duty model is indeed a partial explication of divine goodness. Part of God's goodness does consist in his acting in perfect accord with those principles which would provide duties for a lesser being. This use of the model would be an explication, not of God's moral goodness, but of his axiological goodness. When religious people claim that God is morally good, meaning that he acts in accord with moral principles, they are merely using that axiological conception with which they are most familiar, moral goodness, to describe or model an aspect of divinity functionally isomorphic with, though ontologically different from, human goodness. The point of importance here is that either answer to our question could be defended, whichever is preferred. And neither is obviously inimical to traditional theology.

It seems then that a traditional theist can hold to (1) a libertarian analysis of free action, (2) the position that God is necessarily good, and (3) the duty model of divine goodness without incurring any logical inconsistency among these commitments just by employing the duty model in a carefully controlled analogical manner. The resolution of the problem we have examined seems to be attended by no peculiar difficulties of its own, and seems to be perfectly consistent with any broadly orthodox theology in the Judaeo-Christian tradition. And as the same problem of logical consistency may arise on any plausible analysis of free action, this new understanding of the duty model of divine goodness may be of importance to any traditional theist, whatever reasonable position he adopts concerning the conditions of moral freedom.

IV

OMNIPOTENCE

7

THE DEFINITION OF OMNIPOTENCE

ANTHONY KENNY

It is by no means easy to state concisely and coherently what is meant by 'omnipotence'. Omniscience appears to be analogous to omnipotence: just as omniscience is knowing everything, so omnipotence is being able to do everything. But whereas it is easy to define what it is to be omniscient, it is not so easy to define omnipotence. A being X is omniscient if, for all *p*, if *p*, then X knows that *p*. We cannot offer a simply parallel definition of omnipotence: X is omnipotent if, for all *p*, if *p*, then X can bring it about that *p*. For this, though it would attribute considerable power to X, would not attribute to him power to do anything which has not already been done, or will not sometime be done. On the other hand, if we drop the if-clause, and say that X is omnipotent iff for all *p*, X can bring it about that *p*, then we attribute to X a power far beyond what has traditionally been ascribed to God. For, with the possible exception of Descartes, no theologian or philosopher has seriously maintained that God can bring it about that contradictories are true together. But if, for all *p*, God can bring it about that *p*, then, by substitution we can conclude that he can bring it about that both *p* and not *p*; that mice are both larger and smaller than elephants, or what you will. Nor can one say that, for all $\emptyset$, God can $\emptyset$; for it seems clear that there will be some substitutions for '$\emptyset$' which will not give truths when applied to God, such as 'cough', 'sin', or 'die'.

Aquinas rehearses some of the difficulties about omnipotence in the seventh article of the first question of the *De Potentia*. He concludes that God cannot be said to be omnipotent in the sense of being simply able to do everything (*quia omnia possit absolute*). He considers a number of other suggestions. One, attributed to St

Augustine, is that God is omnipotent in the sense that he can do whatever he wants to do. But to this there are serious objections. The blessed in heaven, St Thomas says, and perhaps even the happy on earth, can do whatever they want; otherwise there would be something lacking in their happiness. But they are not called omnipotent. So it is not enough for the omnipotence which is a divine attribute that God should be able to do whatever he wants. Indeed, a wise man restricts his wants to what is within his power. If he succeeds in this degree of self-control, it will be true of him that he can do whatever he wants. But it is not true that every wise man is an omnipotent man.

Aquinas turns to the formulation: God can do whatever is possible. He raises the question: what does 'possible' mean here? Does it mean: whatever is naturally possible, or whatever is supernaturally possible, i.e. possible to God? If the former, then divine omnipotence does not exceed the power of nature and is no great thing. If the latter, then to say that God is omnipotent is a tautology and the analysis a circumlocution: to say that God is omnipotent is merely to say that God can do all that God can do. And once again, in this sense one can claim that everyone is as omnipotent as God: for everyone can do what he can do.

Aquinas's own account is tantamount to the proposal that the omnipotence of God is the ability to do whatever is logically possible. 'We are left with the alternative', he wrote in the *Summa Theologiae*, 'that he is omnipotent because he can do everything that is absolutely possible.' This possibility is absolute possibility in contrast to the relative possibility just discussed, which was possibility relative to a particular agent's powers. 'Something is judged to be possible or impossible from the relationship between its terms: possible when the predicate is compatible with the subject, as, for Socrates to sit; impossible when it is not compatible, as for a man to be a donkey.'

St Thomas offers a rather dubious reason for this, saying that as God is pure being, not being of any particular kind, anything which qualifies as being (*habet rationem entis*) is a fit object of God's action. He goes on:

Whatever implies being and not being simultaneously is incompatible with the absolute possibility which falls under the divine omnipotence. Such a contradiction is not subject to it, not from any impotence in God, but because it simply does not have the nature of being feasible or possible. Whatever, then, does not involve a contradiction is in that realm of the possible with respect to which God is called omnipotent. Whatever involves a contradiction is not within the scope of omnipotence because it cannot qualify for possibility. Better, however, to say that it cannot be done, rather than that God cannot do it.[1]

Aquinas's solution, however, does not solve the difficulties. We cannot define omnipotence by saying 'For all *p*, if it is logically possible that *p*, then God can bring it about that *p*.' For there are many counter-examples to this which St Thomas would himself have admitted as counter-examples. For instance, it is no doubt logically possible that Troy did not fall, but according to the common view God cannot (now at any rate) bring it about that Troy did not fall. Moreover, by itself Aquinas's formula does not show us how to deal with a number of familiar puzzles about the idea of omnipotence. It does not show us, for instance, how to answer such questions as 'Can God make an object too heavy for him to lift?' 'Has God the power to make an immovable lamp-post and the power to make an irresistible cannon-ball?'

St Thomas does indeed mention some difficulties of this kind; but before considering them it is worth noting that he seems to prefer the formulation 'God's power is infinite' to the formulation 'God is omnipotent'. I shall later argue that this is a sound instinct. However, St Thomas's argument to this effect is unconvincing. God's active power, he says, is in proportion to his actual being; his actual being is infinite; therefore his active power is infinite. Or, in slightly different terms: the more perfect an agent's form, the more powerful it is (e.g. the hotter something is, the better it can heat); therefore, since God's form or essence is infinite, so is his power.

The sense in which God's being is infinite is, however, obscure. From time to time St Thomas explains it along the following lines: while I am a man and this is a table, there are all kinds of things which I am not and which this table is not; for example, I am not a

[1] *Summa Theologiae* Ia, 25, 3.

horse and this table is not a chair. In the case of God, however, he just *is*, and his being is not limited by having any cramping predicates stuck on after the copula. Or, as he puts it in the present article, 'God's being is infinite in so far as it is not limited by any container (*recipiens*).' *Esse* appears to be pictured as a sort of fluid which is boundless in itself, and is given form and boundaries by being poured into a particular object as into a bucket. In reading Aquinas on Being, one is constantly torn between considering *esse* in terms of vivid but inapplicable metaphors, and abstract but ill-formed formulas.[2]

Among the difficulties which Aquinas raises for his account of omnipotence, however, there is one which deserves to be pondered: 'Every power is manifested by its effects; otherwise it would be a vain power. So if God's power were infinite he could produce an infinite effect.' In the *Summa* the answer is given that God is not a univocal agent (i.e., not an agent whose effect is something of the same kind as itself). A human begetter, being an univocal agent, cannot do anything more than breed men, so that the whole of its power is manifested in its effect. The case is different with analogous agents like God and (in Aristotelian cosmology) the sun. The *De Potentia* gives an alternative answer; the very notion of *being made* or *being an effect* is incompatible with infinity, because whatever is made from nothing has some defect. Hence the notion of an infinite effect is incoherent. But might one not go on to conclude that the notion of an infinite power is no less incoherent than the notion of an infinite effect?

Aquinas's objection is an ancestor of a number of modern difficulties. We may consider an instructive question posed by John Mackie in his article 'Evil and Omnipotence':

> Can an omnipotent being make things which he cannot control? It is clear that this is a paradox; the question cannot be answered satisfactorily either in the affirmative or in the negative. If we answer 'Yes' it follows that if God actually makes things which he cannot control, he is not omnipotent once he has made them: there are then things which he cannot do. But if we answer 'No' we are immediately asserting that there are

[2] See my *Aquinas: A Collection of Critical Essays* (London, 1969), pp. 70 ff.

things which he cannot do, that is to say that he is already not omnipotent.[3]

It is, I think, clear that the answer to Mackie's question is 'No, he cannot': the problem is to show how this answer is not incompatible with omnipotence.

This cannot be done simply by appeal to the notion of logical impossibility: for whether 'There exists a being whom an omnipotent God cannot control' is a logically possible state of affairs or not depends on what definition we give of omnipotence, and whether the concept is a coherent one.

On the other hand, it seems that we can reverse Mackie's dilemma and ask: Does it make sense to say 'X is a being which even an omnipotent being cannot control'? If it does, then God can make such a being without any loss to his omnipotence, since the ascribing of sense to the formula, however it is done, will have shown that failure to control X is not incompatible with omnipotence. If it does not, then it is no limitation on God's omnipotence to say that God cannot bring it about that such a being exists.

Of course 'X makes a being which X cannot control' is not an impossible sentence frame; but that does not mean that it will give a possibility with every substitution for 'X', especially if we allow as substitutions phrases like 'a being which can control everything'. Similarly, the fact that both 'X shaves Y' and 'X shaves X' are possible sentence frames does not mean that there can be a barber who shaves all and only those who do not shave themselves.

In discussing Mackie's paradox, Plantinga[4] considers a suggested definition of omnipotence different from those we have been criticizing:

> X is omnipotent iff X is capable of performing any logically possible action.

This will not do, Plantinga says, because making a table that God did not make is a logically possible action, but God cannot make a table which God did not make. Nor can we say:

[3] 'Evil and Omnipotence', *Mind* 64 (1955).
[4] Alvin Plantinga, *God and Other Minds* (Ithaca, 1967), p. 168.

> X is omnipotent iff X is capable of performing any action A such that the proposition 'X performs A' is logically possible.

For the unfortunate man who is capable only of scratching his ear is capable of performing any action A such that the proposition 'the man who is capable only of scratching his ear performs A' is logically possible, for the only such action A is the action of scratching his ear:

> We might consider the suggestion that God is omnipotent iff God can do any A such that 'God does A' is logically possible.

This, of course, would not be a definition of omnipotence but only an explication of divine omnipotence. But even so, Plantinga remarks, it would be an unsuccessful explication. For let A be the action of 'doing what I am thinking of'. Then 'God does A' will be logically possible: it is logically possible for God to do what I am thinking of; but if what I am thinking of is creating a square circle, then God cannot do what I am thinking of.

Plantinga in the end abandons the search for a totally satisfactory account of omnipotence, believing rightly that such an account is not necessary in order to counter Mackie's argument. More recently Geach[5] has concluded, from difficulties such as the ones we have considered, that the notion of omnipotence is incapable of coherent formulation, and suggests that it be abandoned in favour of the notion of being *almighty*, i.e., as having power over all things. And Swinburne[6] thinks that in answer to puzzles like Mackie's we must say that an omnipotent being can indeed create a being which he cannot control, but that he can exercise this power only at the cost of thereby ceasing to be omnipotent.

I agree with Plantinga that it is difficult to formulate a coherent and elegant definition of omnipotence; and I agree with Geach that the notion of God as almighty is a more essential element in Western theism than the comparatively philosophical notion of omnipotence. But I think that an account of divine omnipotence simpler than Swinburne's can be devised to avoid the difficulties we have been discussing.

[5] Peter Geach, 'Omnipotence', *Philosophy* 48 (1973).
[6] R. G. Swinburne, *The Coherence of Theism* (Oxford, 1977), p. 156.

Let us consider the following definition of omnipotence: A being is omnipotent if it has every power which it is logically possible to possess.[7]

The definition must first of all be supplemented with an account of when it is logically possible to possess a power. It is logically possible to possess a power, I suggest, if the exercise of the power does not as such involve any logical impossibility. When I say that the exercise of the power does not *as such* involve any logical possibility, I mean that there is no logical incoherence in the description of what it is to exercise the power. For a power to be a logically possible power, it is not necessary that every exercise of it should be coherently conceivable, but only that some exercise of it should be.

I shall try to explain the definition, and bring out its merits, by applying it to some of the difficult cases current in the literature.

An omnipotent being can make an irresistible cannon-ball, and he can make an immovable lamp-post; there is nothing incoherent in the supposition that these powers are exercised. Of course there would be an incoherence in the idea of them both being exercised simultaneously; but our definition of the logical possibility of possessing a power did not imply that every formulatable exercise of that power should be logically possible, but only that some should.

The man who is capable only of scratching his ear is not omnipotent by our definition; for there are many logically possible powers which he does not possess (the ability to create a world, for example).

An omnipotent being has the power to do what I am thinking of. It is true that if I am thinking of something which it is impossible to do, then an omnipotent God cannot, on that occasion, exercise the power he has of doing what I am thinking about. But powers are not tied to particular occasions, and it is not necessary, for a power to be genuinely possessed, that it can be coherently exercised on

[7] The reader may be disappointed that this definition is not given quasi-logical form like the definitions rejected above. This is no accident. I have argued, in my paper 'Human Abilities and Logical Modalities' in R. Tuomela (ed.) *Essays on Explanation and Understanding* (Dordrecht, 1974), that the current resources of logic are inadequate to analyse the relevant notion of power.

all occasions and in all circumstances. Though God has the power to do what I am thinking of, he cannot exercise this power if I am thinking a nonsensical thought; just as, though he possesses the power to make an immovable lamp-post, he cannot exercise that power if he has just then exercised his power to make an irresistible cannon-ball.

It will be seen that the definition of omnipotence by generalizing over powers is an attempt to preserve the merits, without the disadvantages, of St Thomas's formulation of omnipotence as infinite power. St Thomas was, I think, right in saying that powers are manifested by their effects or, as he elsewhere puts it, specified by their exercises. That is to say, the power to $\emptyset$ can only be defined and understood by someone who knows what $\emptyset$-ing is. But it is not true that powers are specified by their effects in such a way that an infinite power must have an infinite effect. No power, whether finite or infinite, is logically exhausted by its effect: even the human power to beget, with which Aquinas contrasts divine power, is not a limited power in the sense that the power to beget children is a power to beget some specified number of children.

There are advantages, then, in defining omnipotence as the totality of logically possible powers rather than as the power to perform all logically possible actions or to bring about all logically possible states of affairs. But even so defined as the totality of logically possible powers, omnipotence cannot be ascribed to God. For there are many powers which it is logically possible to have which God cannot have, such as the power to make a table which God has not made. The power to change, to sin, and to die are instances of powers which it is logically possible to have—since we human beings have them—and yet which traditional theism denies to God.

Divine omnipotence, therefore, if it is to be a coherent notion, must be something less than the complete omnipotence which is the possession of all logically possible powers. It must be a narrower omnipotence, consisting in the possession of all logically possible powers which it is logically possible for a being with the attributes of God to possess. (If the definition is not to be empty, 'attributes' must here be taken to mean those properties of Godhead which are not themselves powers: properties such as immutability and goodness.) This conception of divine omnipotence is close to traditional accounts of the doctrine while avoiding some of the incoherences we have found in them.

On this account, an omnipotent God will not have the power to make a table that God did not make. The power to make a table that one has not made is not a power that anyone can have; and the power to make a table that God did not make is not a power it is logically possible for someone to have who is identical with God. Any being with all the attributes of God will of course have, *inter alia*, the attribute of being identical with God.

What are we to say, on this account, in answer to the question whether an omnipotent God can make a being whom he cannot control? The power to create, while remaining omnipotent, a being that one cannot control is not a logically possible power, since the description of the power contains a hidden contradiction. The power to create a being that one cannot control and thereby give up one's omnipotence is not a power that could logically be possessed by a being who had the attributes of God including immutability. Consequently, the answer to the conundrum is in the negative: but this does not clash with the notion of divine omnipotence as we have now described it.

Powers such as the power to weaken, sicken, and die will not be parts of divine omnipotence since they clash with other divine attributes. What of the power to do evil? Clearly, the actual performance of an evil deed would be incompatible with divine goodness: but some theologians have thought that the mere power to do evil, voluntarily unexercised, is not only compatible with, but actually enhances the splendour of divine beneficence. If so, then the power to do evil, since it is clearly in itself a logically possible power, would be part of divine omnipotence.

8

MAXIMAL POWER

THOMAS P. FLINT AND ALFRED J. FREDDOSO

CHRISTIANS profess that God is almighty. He has created the world and conserves it in being. Whatever can or does occur is within his control. His great power guarantees the fulfilment of his providential designs.

Theologians and philosophers have typically commenced their explications of divine power with the assertion that God is omnipotent, i.e., that in some sense or other God can do everything. But Peter Geach has recently charged that this assertion is wrong-headed:

> When people have tried to read into 'God can do everything' a signification not of Pious Intention but of Philosophical Truth, they have only landed themselves in intractable problems and hopeless confusions; no graspable sense has ever been given to this sentence that did not lead to self-contradiction or at least to conclusions manifestly untenable from the Christian point of view.[1]

Geach goes on to argue that in all probability any philosophically adequate analysis of omnipotence will have the consequence that, in order to be omnipotent, an agent has to be able to act in morally reprehensible ways. For instance, it seems reasonable to think that any omnipotent being must have the power, whether or not it is in fact exercised, to perform actions which constitute the breaking of his previously made promises. Yet Christians have traditionally believed that God is impeccable, i.e., absolutely incapable of such behaviour. Once God has promised to send his Son, for example, it appears that he no longer even has the power not to send him.

[1] Peter Geach, *Providence and Evil* (Cambridge, 1977), p. 4. The chapter entitled 'Omnipotence' first appeared as an article by the same name in *Philosophy* 48 (1973), pp. 7–20.

But this could not be true if God were omnipotent. In short, omnipotence on any plausible construal turns out to be incompatible with impeccability.

Nelson Pike had earlier reached the same conclusion by a somewhat different route.[2] Accepting the common view that an omnipotent being is one who can bring about any consistently describable state of affairs, Pike argues that some consistently describable states of affairs are necessarily such that anyone who brings them about is morally blameworthy for so doing. So any agent capable of bringing about such a state of affairs is also capable of acting in a morally reprehensible way, and hence is not impeccable in the sense specified above.

Pike responds to this dilemma by urging us to abandon the belief that the person who is God lacks the ability to act in a morally blameworthy fashion. But Geach testily (though correctly, we believe) dismisses this suggestion as patently unorthodox. He counsels us instead to jettison the belief that God is omnipotent. We must simply be careful to distinguish the suspect proposition that God is omnipotent from the theologically central proposition that God is almighty. The latter entails, for instance, that God has power over all things, that he is the source of all power, and that his intentions cannot be thwarted; but it is compatible with the evident truth that there are many things that an agent with all of God's attributes—including, most notably, impeccability—cannot do.

[2] Nelson Pike, 'Omnipotence and God's Ability to Sin', *American Philosophical Quarterly* 6 (1969), pp. 208–16. In fairness to Pike, we should point out that he distinguishes three senses of the claim that God cannot sin: viz. (*a*) that it is logically impossible that someone both is God and sins; (*b*) that the person who is God is incapable of sinning; and (*c*) that the person who is God 'cannot bring himself' to sin even though he is capable of sinning. Pike accepts (*a*) and (*c*), but rejects (*b*) as incompatible with the claim that the person who is God is omnipotent. Our response is that (*b*) expresses the correct understanding of the claim in question—and it is (*b*) which we hope to show, *pace* Pike, to be compatible with the claim that the person who is God is omnipotent. Later we will endorse the stronger, Anselmian thesis that the person who is God is *essentially* incapable of sinning, which again, given our analysis of omnipotence, is compatible with that person's being omnipotent. Hence, we admit Pike's contention that God is not morally praiseworthy for not sinning. But we hasten to add that God is still morally praiseworthy, since he performs many supererogatory acts, such as sending us his only begotten son.

At first Geach's 'way out' seems little more than a verbal ploy. After all, it is hardly self-evident that being almighty differs from being omnipotent, or that having power *over* all things differs from having the power *to do* all things (or, as we prefer to say, having maximal power). Nonetheless, further reflection reveals that Geach's position does not essentially depend on the dubious claim that the terms 'almighty' and 'omnipotent' are normally used to express two distinct concepts. Rather, it depends only on the more plausible claim that there are two distinct concepts to be expressed. And here, we believe, Geach is correct.

The term 'almighty', as he uses it, expresses a properly religious concept, i.e., a concept whose explication is subject to overtly theological constraints. To say that God is almighty is to attribute to God all the power that a being with his nature can have.[3] This way of characterizing God's power is not very informative, since it gives one no more insight into the nature of God or the extent of his power than is had antecedently from the sources of revelation. However, there is no danger that the belief that God is almighty will engender any pernicious theological consequences. Most importantly, we can know *a priori* that it is possible for an agent to be both almighty and impeccable, since this possibility is already explicitly packed into the notion of being almighty.

The term 'omnipotent', on the other hand, is used by Geach to express what we might call a properly secular concept, i.e., one whose explication is subject only to those non-theological constraints which emerge from a careful consideration of the ordinary notion of power, and of the relation of power to other properties. It is clear, for instance, that an analysis of omnipotence

[3] Jerome Gellman contends that *omnipotence* should be explicated in this way, so that an omnipotent agent is one who has all the power that an essentially perfect being can have. See Jerome Gellman, 'Omnipotence and Impeccability', *New Scholasticism* 51 (1977), pp. 21–37. In support of this analysis, Gellman argues for the dubious thesis that omnipotence is conceptually inextricable from the other properties (e.g., impeccability) a perfect being must have. In effect, then, he assimilates omnipotence to almightiness. By contrast, in *The Coherence of Theism* (Oxford, 1977), pp. 158–61, Richard Swinburne admits that God cannot be omnipotent in the strongest sense, but he goes on to claim, *pace* Geach, that it is perfectly appropriate to use the term 'omnipotent' in a weaker sense in which omnipotence is compatible with impeccability. We believe that these moves made by Gellman and Swinburne are undesirable and, as we will argue, unnecessary.

should not be constructed so as to ensure that there cannot be a morally imperfect omnipotent agent, or a non-omniscient omnipotent agent, or an agent who is only contingently or perhaps even only temporarily omnipotent. But God cannot be an agent of any of these types. So even if God has all the power that a being with his nature can have, there is no *a priori* guarantee that he has maximal power, absolutely speaking. If Geach is right, then all our evidence points to just the opposite conclusion, viz. that God does not have, indeed cannot have, maximal power.

We concur with Geach that almightiness and omnipotence are distinct properties. However, we will argue in what follows that an orthodox believer need not for this reason give up the hallowed belief that God is omnipotent. For, *pace* Geach, an adequate analysis of maximal power will show that God can be both almighty and omnipotent; and, *pace* both Geach and Pike, such an analysis will show that it is possible for an agent—even a divine agent—to be both omnipotent and impeccable. We will begin by proposing five conditions of philosophical adequacy for an account of maximal power, indicating in the footnotes which of these conditions are not satisfied by one or another of the numerous recent attempts to explicate omnipotence. Then we will present an analysis which meets all five conditions, and argue that it is both philosophically adequate and theologically benign.

I

1. Our first condition of adequacy is that an analysis of maximal power should be stated in terms of an agent's power to actualize or bring about states of affairs. (Since we are assuming that there is an exact isomorphism between states of affairs and propositions, we can also speak equivalently of an agent's power to make propositions true.) Though this condition is now widely accepted, some writers have employed the alternative strategy of casting their accounts of omnipotence in terms of an agent's ability to perform tasks, where a task is expressed linguistically by the nominalization of a verb phrase rather than, like a state of affairs, by the nominalization of a complete declarative sentence. The problems with this alternative strategy are well known. Suppose

we claim that an agent *S* is omnipotent just in case *S* can perform any logically possible task, i.e., any task which is possibly such that someone performs it. This proposal rules out Smith as omnipotent simply on the ground that Smith cannot perform the logically possible task of saying something which is (at the same time) being said only by Jones. Yet it is clear intuitively that this fact about Smith in no way points to a lack of power on his part. Moreover, when we attempt to amend our analysis by claiming that *S* is omnipotent just in case *S* has the power to perform any task that it is logically possible *for S* to perform, we find that we are forced to count as omnipotent the notorious weakling Mr McEar, who is capable of scratching his left ear but essentially incapable of performing any other task.[4]

Such difficulties are obviated by our first condition. For the state of affairs of Smith's saying something which is being said only by Jones is logically impossible and thus unproblematically not within anyone's power to actualize, whereas the state of affairs of Jones's (or: someone's) saying something which is being said only by Jones may well be one which agents other than Jones can actualize, and which we should expect an omnipotent being to have the power to actualize.

Nevertheless, even though our first condition is commonplace today, few writers on omnipotence have explicitly entertained the following question: Is it possible for one agent to actualize (and hence to have the power to actualize) a state of affairs consisting in, or at least involving in some way, the free actions of other agents? If we assume a compatibilist account of freedom, the answer to this question is uncontroversially affirmative. For it is obviously possible for a suitably powerful and aptly situated agent

[4] To the best of our knowledge, McEar makes his first contemporary appearance in Alvin Plantinga's *God and Other Minds* (Ithaca, 1967), pp. 168–73. But a similar difficulty was recognized at least as early as the later Middle Ages. For instance, the following note was added by an anonymous writer to one of the manuscripts of Ockham's *Ordinatio* I, distinction 42: 'Nor is a being said to be omnipotent because he can do all things which are possible for him to do . . . since it would follow that a minimally powerful being is omnipotent. For suppose that Socrates performs one action and is not capable of performing any others. Then one argues as follows: "He is performing every action which it is possible for him to perform, therefore he is omnipotent." See Gerald Etzkorn and Francis Kelly (eds.) *Ockham: Opera Theologica*, vol. iv (St Bonaventure, NY, 1979), p. 611.

to bring it about that another agent has desires or needs and also opportunities that are together causally sufficient for his behaving freely (in this compatibilist sense) in a specified way. So on this view of freedom, bringing about the free actions of others is not relevantly different from actualizing states of affairs that in no way involve the free actions of others. In both sorts of cases the agent in question simply does something which, in conjunction with other operative causal factors, is sufficient for the obtaining of the state of affairs in question.

However, we believe along with many others that there are good reasons for rejecting this account of freedom in favour of the position that every free action must involve the occurrence of an event for which there is no antecedent sufficient causal condition—an event, that is, which has only an agent and no other event as its cause. Given this libertarian conception of freedom, there is a clear and familiar sense of 'actualize' in which it is logically impossible for one agent to actualize another agent's free actions. Following Alvin Plantinga, we call this sense of actualization *strong actualization*.[5] Roughly, an agent *S* strongly actualizes a state of affairs *p* just when *S* causally determines *p*'s obtaining, i.e., just when *S* does something which in conjunction with other operative causal factors constitutes a sufficient causal condition for *p*'s obtaining. Since an agent's freely performing (or, perhaps better, freely endeavouring to perform) a given action cannot have a sufficient causal condition, it follows straightforwardly that no such state of affairs can be strongly actualized by anyone other than the agent in question.

But even granted the libertarian conception of freedom, there is a weaker sense of actualization—discussed in rather different contexts by both Plantinga and Roderick Chisholm[6]—in which one agent can actualize (and hence can have the power to actualize)

[5] See Alvin Plantinga, *The Nature of Necessity* (Oxford, 1974), pp. 172–3.

[6] Plantinga's discussion of weak actualization is in the place cited in note 5. Chisholm's discussion occurs in *Person and Object* (LaSalle, 1976), pp. 67–9. (Chisholm takes as basic the concept of causally contributing to a state of affairs rather than the notion of actualizing a state of affairs.) It is no mean feat to formulate an exact analysis of weak actualization, but an intuitive grasp of this notion will suffice for our purposes in this paper.

the free actions of another. In such cases the agent in question, by his actions or omissions, strongly brings it about that another agent *S* is in a situation *C*, where it is true that if *S* were in *C*, then *S* would freely act in a specified way. For instance, a mother might actualize her child's freely choosing to have Rice Krispies for breakfast by limiting his choices to Rice Krispies and the hated Raisin Bran. Or she might bring it about that the child freely donates his allowance to a relief agency by telling him poignantly of the plight of those who do not have enough to eat. In short, it is a familiar truth that one agent may contribute causally to the free actions of another in any number of ways which stop short of being incompatible with the other's acting freely. In such cases it seems perfectly legitimate to say that the one has actualized the other's acting freely in the way in question. Again adopting Plantinga's terminology, we will call this sense of actualization *weak actualization*. Further, it is not only the free actions of another which a given agent may weakly actualize. In addition, an agent *S* may weakly actualize a state of affairs *p through the mediation of* the free actions of another agent *S**. This occurs when *S* weakly actualizes *S**'s freely acting in such a way as to bring about *p*. Thus, in the second of the above examples, the mother weakly actualizes not only her son's freely donating his allowance to a relief agency but also—among others—the state of affairs of someone's hunger being alleviated.

We want to insist that in an analysis of omnipotence the term 'actualize' (or 'bring about') should be construed broadly to include both strong and weak actualization. For it is intuitively evident that a person's power is normally judged in large measure by his ability to influence the free actions of others in one or another of the ways intimated above, for example, by restricting their options, or by providing them with information or opportunities, or by commanding them, or by persuading or dissuading them, etc. So an omnipotent being should be expected to have the maximal amount of this sort of power. This underscores nicely the impressive nature of maximal power, extending as it does even to the free actions of others. On the other hand, even though the use of this liberal sense of actualization helps us to capture the pervasiveness of an omnipotent agent's power, it also points to an almost universally ignored limitation on that power. We will discuss this limitation below.[7]

2. Our second condition is that an omnipotent being should be expected to have the power to actualize a state of affairs *p* only if it is logically possible that someone actualize *p*, i.e., only if there is a possible world *W* such that in *W* someone actualizes *p*. We take this claim to be self-evident.

One generally acknowledged consequence of this condition of adequacy is that the scope of an omnipotent agent's power is limited to logically contingent states of affairs, where a logically contingent state of affairs is one that possibly obtains and also possibly fails to obtain. However, it should be obvious that an analysis of maximal power will not by itself determine just which states of affairs are logically contingent and which are not. Indeed, one could trivialize the consequence in question by espousing the extreme view, sometimes attributed to Descartes, that every state of affairs is logically contingent. Or one might weaken it considerably by embracing the slightly more modest position—and perhaps this is what Descartes actually had in mind—that many allegedly paradigmatic necessary truths, for example, logical laws or simple mathematical truths, are in fact logically contingent. We do not endorse such views, but nothing we say about maximal power itself will rule them out. Their truth or falsity must be decided independently.

Also, we will explicitly assume below that all states of affairs (and propositions) are tensed. If this assumption is correct, then it is reasonable to think that at least some logically contingent past-tense states of affairs are not possibly such that someone actualizes them.[8] For instance, one might hold that, even though it is

[7] For some analyses of omnipotence *not* stated in terms of actualizing states of affairs, see Richard Francks, 'Omniscience, Omnipotence and Pantheism', *Philosophy* 54 (1979), pp. 395–9; Jerome Gellman, 'The Paradox of Omnipotence, and Perfection', *Sophia* 14 (1975), pp. 31–9; and (though less explicitly) J. L. Mackie, 'Evil and Omnipotence', *Mind*, 64 (1955), pp. 200–12.

[8] We say 'at least some', since those who espouse an Ockhamistic response to the problem of future contingents might want to insist that we can have the power to actualize certain 'future-infected' past-tense states of affairs. See Alfred J. Freddoso, 'Accidental Necessity and Power over the Past', *Pacific Philosophical Quarterly* 63 (1982), pp. 54–68.

logically possible for someone to bring it about that Jones will some day be in Chicago, it is logically impossible that anyone ever bring it about that Jones has already been in Chicago. Again, however, an account of maximal power will not by itself decide whether such a claim is true.[9]

3. Many contemporary philosophers not only have accepted our first two conditions of adequacy but also have taken them to be sufficient by themselves. This is evident from the widespread acceptance, until fairly recently, of analyses equivalent to the following:

(A) *S* is omnipotent if and only if for any state of affairs *p*, if there is a world *W* such that in *W* someone actualizes *p*, then *S* has the power to actualize *p*.

However, philosophers at least as far back as Aristotle have realized that, if the past is in some sense necessary, then there are further, purely temporal restrictions on the power of any agent. The medievals, in fact, had a moderately well articulated theory of temporal (*per accidens*) modality, from which it follows that at any given time there are states of affairs which meet the condition specified in (A) and yet are such that they cannot be within the power of any agent to actualize. Interestingly, even those like Aquinas, who held that God is not 'in time', recognized this sort of restriction on God's power.

So, for instance, suppose that Jones played basketball two days ago. Then, the claim goes, not only is it *true* now that Jones once played basketball, but it is also *necessary* now that Jones once played basketball. That is, in any possible world just like ours prior to the present moment *t*, it is true at *t* and at every moment after *t* that Jones once played basketball. And from this it follows that no one can *now* have the power to actualize the following state of affairs:

[9] Despite what we have said, it may be the case that Descartes is an offender rather than just a trivializer of our second condition. See Harry Frankfurt, 'Descartes on the Creation of the Eternal Truths', *Philosophical Review*, 86 (1977), pp. 36–57.

(1) Its being the case that it will be true at some time that Jones has never played basketball.

For it is a minimal and non-controversial constraint on any agent's having the power at a time *t* to actualize a state of affairs *p* that there be a possible world *W* just like ours prior to *t* such that at *t* in *W* someone actualizes *p*.[10] But, the argument continues, there is no such world in the case of (1). Nevertheless, (1) satisfies the condition laid down in (A), since it is easy enough to conceive of a possible world in which someone actualizes it. Such an agent might, for example, prevent Jones's coming into existence, or arrange for him not to play basketball for a long time after his birth. So it is logically possible for some one to have the power to actualize (1), even though it is logically impossible that both (*a*) the world should have the history it has had until now and (*b*) someone should now have the power to actualize (1). Furthermore, there are any number of states of affairs which are like (1) in these respects. So any adequate account of omnipotence must be relativized to a time. In addition, these purely temporal restrictions on power may vary not only from moment to moment but also from possible world to possible world. And so an account of omnipotence should also be relativized to a possible world. Hence, our analysandum should be '*S* is omnipotent at *t* in *W*', and we should incorporate into our analysis the purely temporal restrictions on any agent's power.

This argument rests on two metaphysical presuppositions. The first is that states of affairs (and propositions) are tensed. We find this claim both natural and defensible, and so we accept it. (However, it may be possible for the friends of 'tenseless' propositions to recast the argument in their own idiom.) One important consequence is that some logically contingent states of affairs may obtain at some times and not at others within the same possible world. For instance, the state of affairs of Jones's having played basketball does not obtain before Jones plays basketball for the first time but always obtains afterwards. Again, the state of

[10] This condition on power, despite first appearances, is consistent even with compatibilism. The compatibilist would, however, deny the libertarian claim that we can add the further condition that *W* and our world continue to share the same laws of nature (with no violations) at *t* itself.

affairs of its being the case that Jones will play basketball may obtain now, but it will not obtain after Jones plays basketball for the last time. Further, some states of affairs may first obtain, and then not obtain, and still later obtain again. An example is the present-tense state of affairs of Jones's (now) playing basketball.

The second metaphysical presupposition is that it is logically impossible that someone travel into the past. This claim, though eminently reasonable, has been challenged of late by several writers, who have asserted in effect that there are no purely temporal restrictions on any agent's power.[11] These philosophers would say that, in the case alluded to above, it is at least conceivable that someone now should travel backwards two days into the past and find himself in a position to prevent Jones from playing basketball. Assuming that Jones has played basketball just this one time, our time traveller would have it within his power to actualize (1). If such a scenario is coherent, it may not be incompatible with our analysis of maximal power, since our third condition of adequacy is simply that an account of omnipotence should accommodate the (epistemic) possibility that there are purely temporal restrictions on the power of an omnipotent agent. We will satisfy this condition by claiming that an omnipotent agent should be expected to have the power at t in W to actualize p only if there is a world W^* such that (i) W^* shares the same history with W at t and (ii) at t in W^* someone actualizes p. Perhaps a proponent of the conceivability of time travel can find a plausible interpretation of the notion of two worlds sharing the same history that allows him to accept this third condition while maintaining that it adds no restrictions on power beyond those already embodied in our second condition of adequacy. (We will return shortly to the notion of sharing the same history.) On the other hand, it may be that any theory of time travel is incompatible with our suggestion for satisfying the third condition. If this is the case, then so much the worse for time travel.

Two points of clarification should be made here. First, we

[11] See, for instance, Jack W. Meiland, 'A Two-Dimensional Passage Model of Time for Time Travel', *Philosophical Studies* 26 (1974), pp. 153–73; and David Lewis, 'The Paradoxes of Time Travel', *American Philosophical Quarterly* 13 (1976), pp. 145–52.

assume that it is logically possible for agents to actualize future-tense states of affairs. For instance, an agent may bring it about at *t* that Jones will be in Chicago within two hours or that Jones will be in Chicago two hours after *t*. (Below, we will claim that an agent brings about a future-tense state of affairs by bringing it about that a given present-tense state of affairs will obtain at the appropriate future time. So someone brings it about at *t* that Jones will be in Chicago within two hours by bringing it about that the present-tense state of affairs of Jones's being in Chicago will obtain within two hours after *t*.) Some may even go so far as to say that, where *p* is a present-tense state of affairs, it is not possible for any agent *S* to bring it about at *t* that *p* obtains at *t*. That is, *S*'s actualizing *p* cannot be simultaneous with *p*'s obtaining but must rather precede *p*'s obtaining. If this is so, then every instance of actualization involves the actualization of a future-tense state of affairs. In any case, it is reasonable to expect that an agent who is omnipotent at *t* will have extensive control over what can happen at any time after *t*—subject to the restriction which will be set down by our fourth condition of adequacy discussed below.

Second, it should be noted that our third condition of adequacy does not by itself rule out the possibility that someone have the power to bring about (as opposed to alter) the past. This is a separate issue which, as noted above, falls under our second condition of adequacy. So, for example, if it is logically possible that someone now, given the history of our world, brings it about that Carter was elected president in 1976, then an omnipotent agent now has the power to actualize this past-tense state of affairs. Given that Carter was in fact elected in 1976, the argument presented at the beginning of this section does not by itself rule out such backward causation. Again, this is an issue that must be decided independently.

We claimed above that an omnipotent being should be expected to have the power at *t* in *W* to actualize *p* only if there is a world *W** such that (i) *W** shares the same history with *W* and *t* and (ii) at *t* in *W** someone actualizes *p*. But so far we have said nothing about what it is for two worlds to share the same history at a given time. Perhaps it is not fair to demand that one who gives an analysis should provide an exact characterization of each concept used in that analysis, especially when those concepts are tolerably clear on their own. Nevertheless, in this case we feel obliged to say something more, since the concept in question is open to seemingly acceptable construals which would undermine the adequacy of our account of maximal power.

Consider, for instance, the following 'natural' explication of sharing the same history:

(2) *W* shares the same history with *W** at *t* if and only if for any state of affairs *p* and time *t** earlier than *t*, *p* obtains at *t** in *W* if and only if *p* obtains at *t** in *W**.

Since we are assuming that states of affairs are tensed, if we take (2) together with the analogue of the law of bivalence for states of affairs, the net effect is that *W* can share the same history with *W** at *t* only if *W* also shares the same present and future with *W** at *t*, i.e., only if *W* is identical with *W**. For among the states of affairs that obtain at any time prior to *t* in *W* are future-tense states of affairs which specify exactly what will be true in *W* at and after *t*. Moreover, even if we deny that the law of bivalence holds for so-called 'future contingent' states of affairs, so that no such state of affairs ever obtains, (2) will still be unacceptable. For on the most popular construal of the notion of a future contingent, a state of affairs is a future contingent at a given time only if it is future-tense and not causally necessary at that time. So even when we make an exception for future contingents, it still follows from (2) that *W* and *W** share the same history at *t* only if they share at *t* what we might call their causally necessitated futures. Such a result is particularly unwelcome when one is trying to explicate maximal power, since it is generally conceded that an agent who is omnipotent at *t* has the power at *t* to bring about events whose occurrence is in some sense contrary to nature.[12]

[12] For a dissenting view cf. Dennis M. Ahern, 'Miracles and Physical Impossibility', *Canadian Journal of Philosophy* 7 (1977), pp. 71–9. Our own inclination, on the other hand, is to believe that laws of nature specify the causal powers or dispositions of natural substances. Hence, such a law, e.g., that potassium has by nature a disposition to ignite when exposed to oxygen, might remain true even when the manifestation of the disposition in question is prevented solely by the action of a supernatural agent.

Our own account of two worlds sharing the same history at a given time, which is Ockhamistic in inspiration, has been set out in detail elsewhere.[13] So we will simply outline it rather broadly here. The basic insight involved is that what is temporally independent —or, to use Chisholm's phrase, rooted in the present—at any given time can be specified in terms of the present-tense (or, as we prefer to say, immediate) states of affairs which obtain at that time. All non-immediate, or temporally dependent, states of affairs that obtain at a time *t* obtain at *t* only in virtue of the fact that the appropriate immediate states of affairs did or will obtain at moments other than *t*. So, for instance, the non-immediate state of affairs of Jones's having played basketball obtains now in virtue of the fact that the immediate state of affairs of Jones's playing basketball obtained at some past time. Likewise, the non-immediate state of affairs of its being the case that Jones will play basketball obtains now in virtue of the fact that Jones's playing basketball will obtain at some future time. This is why it is reasonable to believe that an agent brings it about that Jones will play basketball only *by* bringing it about that Jones's playing basketball will obtain.

Our claim is that for any moment *t* in a world *W* there is a set *k* of immediate states of affairs which determines what obtains at *t* in a temporally independent way, i.e., what obtains at *t* but does not obtain at *t* in virtue of what occurs at moments other than *t*. We call *k* the *sub-moment* of *t* in *W*, and say that *k* obtains in *W* when and only when each of its members obtains in *W*. Then *W* and *W** share the same history at *t* if and only if they share all and only the same sub-moments, obtaining in exactly the same order, prior to *t*. Since no future-tense state of affairs is immediate or, consequently, a member of any sub-moment, it follows that *W* and *W** may share the same history at *t* even if their futures are radically diverse at *t*—and this diversity may extend even to their laws of nature at and after *t* or to events contrary to the laws of nature that they share at or after *t*.

[13] See Alfred J. Freddoso, 'Accidental Necessity and Logical Determinism', *Journal of Philosophy* 80 (1983), pp. 257–78. This paper argues for our account of sharing the same history on purely philosophical grounds rather than on the theological grounds suggested below.

Given this general picture, the most pressing task is to provide a plausible characterization of the distinction between immediate and non-immediate states of affairs. However, our account of this distinction is much too complicated to be presented in passing here. Since it has been worked out in sufficient detail elsewhere, we will simply note one result which will become relevant below. As far as we can tell, this is the only consequence of what we say about the purely temporal restrictions on power that may prove troublesome for our claim that even a divine being may have maximal power.

According to our explication of immediacy, states of affairs involving present-tense propositional attitudes directed at future-tense propositions, for example,

(3) Jones's believing that Smith will arrive at 2 p.m.

and

(4) Jones's promising that Smith will receive a gift,

are immediate unless they entail the future-tense propositions which they involve.[14] On the other hand, if these entailments do hold, then such states of affairs are non-immediate and hence not members of any sub-moment. But now consider the following states of affairs:

(5) God's believing that Smith will be saved

and

(6) God's promising that Smith will be saved.

Since (5) and (6) both entail that Smith will be saved, each is on our account non-immediate, and hence not eligible for membership in a sub-moment. This is a welcome result in the case of (5), since it enables us to reconcile divine foreknowledge with human freedom. In short, even if (5) has already obtained, there may still be a world *W* such that (i) *W* shares the same history with our world at the present moment and yet (ii) Smith is never saved in

[14] A state of affairs *p* may be said to entail a proposition *q* just in case it is logically impossible that *p* obtains and *q* does not. And *p* may be said to involve *q* just in case *p* is necessarily such that whoever conceives it conceives *q*.

W. So even if it has already been true that God believes that Smith will be saved, Smith may still have it within his power to bring it about that he will never be saved. However, this same result is somewhat more troublesome in the case of (6)—for reasons that we will discuss in some detail at the end of this essay.[15]

4. Some might suspect that what we have already said is sufficient for explicating maximal power. For at this point we have the resources to formulate the following analysis:

(B) *S* is omnipotent at *t* in *W* if and only if for any state of affairs *p*, if there is a world *W** such that (i) *W** shares the same history with *W* at *t*, and (ii) at *t* in *W** someone actualizes *p*, then *S* has the power at *t* in *W* to actualize *p*.

Though this analysis is surely appealing, we believe that it is nonetheless inaccurate. Its insufficiency can be traced to one primary deficiency: such an analysis fails to take account of the way in which the free actions (and dispositions to free action) of other beings would necessarily limit the power of any omnipotent being. Let us now show how this limitation arises.

As noted above in our discussion of actualization, there seems to be good reason to think that the libertarian analysis of freedom is correct. If so, it follows that not even an omnipotent being can causally determine the free actions of another agent. This fact, of course, was what accounted for the distinction between strong and weak actualization, a distinction which allows that a being can bring about a state of affairs in two distinct ways.

However, if libertarianism is true, it has a second and equally significant impact on the analysis of omnipotence. To see this, let us imagine the following situation. Suppose that at a time *t* a non-omnipotent being named Jones is free with respect to writing a letter to his wife. In that case Jones has the power at *t* to actualize

(7) Jones's freely deciding at *t* to write a letter to his wife,

[15] Many recent philosophers have failed to recognize explicitly that any being's power is necessarily limited to states of affairs which are 'temporally contingent'. In addition to Francks, Gellman, and Mackie, see George Mavrodes, 'Defining Omnipotence', *Philosophical Studies* 32 (1977), pp. 191–202; Pike, 'Omnipotence and God's Ability to Sin'; and Richard Purtill, *Thinking about Religion* (Englewood Cliffs, NJ, 1978), p. 31.

and he also has the power at *t* to actualize

(8) Jones's freely deciding at *t* to refrain from writing a letter to his wife.

From this it follows that there is a world *W*, sharing the same history with our world at *t*, such that at *t* in *W* someone (viz., Jones) actualizes (7); and it also follows that there is a world *W**, sharing the same history with our world at *t*, such that at *t* in *W** someone (viz., Jones) actualizes (8). So given (B), any agent who is omnipotent at *t* in our world must have at *t* both the power to actualize (7) and the power to actualize (8).

However, on the assumption that libertarianism is true it is fairly easy to show that no one distinct from Jones—not even an omnipotent agent—*can* have at *t* both the power to actualize (7) and the power to actualize (8). Let *C* stand for the circumstances in which Jones finds himself at *t*. If libertarianism is true, then *C* includes the fact that there is a temporal interval beginning before *t* and including *t*, in which there is no causally sufficient condition either for Jones's deciding at *t* to write the letter or for his deciding at *t* not to write the letter. But now consider the following counter-factual:[16]

(9) If Jones were in *C* at *t*, he would freely decide at *t* to refrain from writing a letter to his wife.

Like any proposition, (9) is either true or false. Furthermore, since (9) tells us what Jones would do if left free in a certain situation, no one other than Jones can simply decide to make (9) true or false, for no one other than Jones can determine how Jones would *freely* act. Therefore, not even an omnipotent being can decide by himself to make (9) true or false; its truth value is something he is powerless to affect.

The consequence of this inescapable powerlessness is that, regardless of whether (9) is true or false, there will be a state of affairs which, despite meeting the conditions set down in (B),

[16] Throughout this essay we shall follow David Lewis's practice of not presupposing that the term 'counter-factual' is to be applied only to conditionals with false antecedents. See David Lewis, *Counterfactuals* (Cambridge, Mass., 1973), p. 3.

cannot be actualized at *t* by any being other than Jones—even if that being is omnipotent at *t*. For suppose (9) is true. In that case, even an agent who is omnipotent at *t* does not have the power at *t* to actualize (7). He cannot, of course, strongly actualize (7), for he cannot causally determine Jones's acting freely in a certain way. But neither can he weakly actualize (7). He can, perhaps, arrange things so that Jones is in *C* at *t*. But if he does so arrange things, then (9) tells us that Jones will freely refrain from writing the letter and thereby actualize (8) rather than (7). On the other hand, if (9) is false, then our omnipotent agent cannot at *t* weakly actualize (8). The most he can do in an attempt to bring about (8) is to bring it about that Jones is in *C* at *t*. But if (9) is false, then it is *not* the case that if Jones were in *C* at *t*, he would strongly actualize (8). And no one weakly actualizes (8) unless Jones strongly actualizes it. So if (9) is in fact false, then not even an omnipotent agent has the power at *t* to actualize (8).[17]

Therefore, whether or not (9) is true, there will be some state of affairs satisfying the conditions specified in (B) which even an omnipotent agent is incapable of actualizing. And since this inability results solely from the *logically necessary* truth that one being cannot causally determine how another will freely act, it should not be viewed (as (B) does view it) as a kind of inability which disqualifies an agent from ranking as omnipotent.

It follows, then, that an adequate analysis of omnipotence must acknowledge the logically inescapable limitations which counter-factuals such as (9) would place on an omnipotent agent. Now it should be obvious that there are many counter-factuals which, like (9), tell us how beings would freely act. In fact, since there are presumably an infinite number of circumstances in which a being can find himself, there will be an infinite number of such counter-factuals for any free agent. Nor can we limit our consideration exclusively to *actual* free beings. For though an omnipotent agent might well have the power to create free beings who are not now actual, he would nonetheless be limited by the counter-factuals relating to the free actions of these beings as well. Hence, our

[17] The argument here is little more than a variant of Alvin Plantinga's argument against the thesis that God must have the ability to actualize any possible world. See Plantinga, *The Nature of Necessity*, pp. 180–84.

analysis of omnipotence must recognize the importance of counter-factuals of freedom regarding not only *actual* beings but *possible* beings as well. If we believe that, strictly speaking, there are no possible but non-actual beings, we can make this last point by saying that the relevant counterfactuals relate not to individuals but to *individual essences*, where *P* is an individual essence if and only if *P* is a property which is such that (i) in some possible world there is an individual *x* who has *P* essentially and (ii) there is no possible world in which there exists an individual distinct from *x* who has *P*.[18] An individual *x* will thus be said to be an *instantiation* of individual essence *P* just in case *x* has *P*.

Now suppose we call a complete set of such counter-factuals of freedom a *world type*. If the law of conditional excluded middle were true—i.e., if it were the case that for any propositions *p* and *q*, either *p* counter-factually implies *q* or *p* counter-factually implies the negation of *q*—then a world type could be defined as a set of counter-factuals indicating, for every individual essence and every possible set of circumstances and times in which it could be instantiated and left free, how an instantiation of that essence would freely act if placed in those circumstances.

However, many philosophers reject the law of conditional excluded middle, for they feel there are at least some cases in which *p* counter-factually implies neither *q* not its negation.[19] Hence, it would probably be wiser for us to provide a more general

[18] The definition of an individual essence is taken from Plantinga, *The Nature of Necessity*, p. 72.

[19] For a discussion of conditional excluded middle, see Lewis, *Counterfactuals*, pp. 79–82. We wish to note in passing, however, that even if the law of conditional excluded middle is false, there may be a weaker analogue of that law which is true, and which would be sufficient for our present purposes if we chose to invoke it. For the antecedents of the counter-factual conditionals which concern us here are all of the form 'Individual essence *P* is instantiated in circumstances *C* at time *t*, and *P*'s instantiation is left free with respect to action *A*.' Now suppose we stipulate that the substituend for '*C*' must be a complete description of the past at *t* along with a clause specifying that the same laws of nature continue to hold at *t*. In that case there seems to be good reason to believe that where *p* is a proposition expressed by a sentence of *this* form, then for any proposition *q*, either *p* counter-factually implies *q* or *p* counter-factually implies the negation of *q*. However, a complete defence of this position is impossible here, and so we will proceed on the assumption that there is no acceptable version of the law of conditional excluded middle.

definition of a world type which does not presuppose the truth of this law. Let us say, then, that a world type is a set which is such that for any *counter-factual of freedom*—i.e., any proposition which can be expressed by a sentence of the form 'If individual essence *P* were instantiated in circumstances *C* at time *t* and its instantiation were left free with respect to action *A*, the instantiation of *P* would freely do *A*'—either that counter-factual or its negation is a member of the set. (To obviate certain esoteric technical problems, we might also stipulate that for any two members of the set, the conjunction of those two members is a member of the set as well.) Let us also say that a world type is *true* just in case every proposition which is a member of it is true. (Since we are assuming an exact isomorphism between propositions and states of affairs, we may take a world type to be, alternatively, a set of counter-factual states of affairs.)

Now any free being will have some say in determining which world type is true. For example, since Jones is free to decide whether or not to write that letter to his wife, it is up to him whether the true world type includes (9) or its negation. However, the vast majority of the counter-factuals which go to make up a world type relate to beings other than Jones, and Jones, of course, is powerless to make such counter-factuals true or false. So for any free agent *x* there will be a set of all and only those true counter-factuals of freedom (or true negations of such counterfactuals) over whose truth value *x* has no control. Since such a set will clearly be a subset of the true world type and will be characteristic only of *x*, let us refer to it as the *world-type-for-x*.[20]

So it is a necessary truth that every being is in a sense simply presented with a set of counter-factuals whose truth values he is

[20] The relationship between the world-type-for-God and divine freedom is discussed at length in Thomas P. Flint, 'The Problem of Divine Freedom', *American Philosophical Quarterly* 20 (1983), pp. 255–64. One terminological point suggested there might also be noted in passing here: God's knowledge of the world-type-for-God is identical with what is generally referred to as God's *middle knowledge*. The Molinist thesis that God has middle knowledge of contingent propositions whose truth values he cannot control is hotly contested in traditional theological discussions of grace, providence, and predestination. We cannot pursue the matter here, but simply wish to note our belief that it is only by adopting some version of Molinism that one can preserve a suitably strong understanding of both (*a*) the doctrine of divine providence and (*b*) the thesis that human beings are free.

powerless to control. That is, for any agent *x* the world-type-for-*x* will remain true regardless of what *x* does. So it is logically impossible for *x* to bring about any state of affairs which is inconsistent with the truth of the world-type-for-*x* with which he happens to be confronted. That is, it is logically impossible for him to bring about any state of affairs which does not obtain in any world in which that world-type-for-*x* is true. And since it is also logically impossible for any agent to escape this type of limitation, we cannot allow such a limitation of power to disqualify a being from ranking as omnipotent. Hence, if we allow '*Lx*' to stand for the true world-type-for-*x*, then *x* should not be required, in order to rank as omnipotent, to possess the power to actualize any state of affairs that does not obtain in any world in which *Lx* is true. We can consider this as our fourth condition for an adequate analysis of omnipotence.

So the power of any being *x* will necessarily be limited by the set of counter-factuals of freedom which constitute the true world-type-for-*x*. Moreover, since these counter-factuals do relate to the *free* actions of agents, none of them will be a logically necessary truth. Even if (9) is true in the actual world, it could not be a necessary truth, for Jones could not be free regarding letter-writing if there were no world in which he does decide to write in the circumstances in question. So though the true world-type-for-*x* (where *x* is distinct from Jones) in our world may include (9), there are other worlds in which the true world-type-for-*x* includes the negation of (9). Hence, different world-types-for-*x* may be true in different worlds. And this gives further support to the claim, made above, that an analysis of omnipotence must be relativized to a possible world.[21]

5. If our first four conditions of adequacy were pedantically specific, our fifth and final condition is refreshingly vague. Simply stated, it is that no being should be considered omnipotent if he

[21] Among authors discussed previously, Francks, Gellman, Mackie, Pike, and Purtill all fail to satisfy this fourth condition. In addition, see Gary Rosenkrantz and Joshua Hoffman, 'What an Omnipotent Agent Can Do', *International Journal for Philosophy of Religion* 11 (1980), pp. 1–19; James Ross, *Philosophical Theology* (Indianapolis, 1969), p. 221; and Douglas Walton, 'Some Theorems of Fitch on Omnipotence', *Sophia* 15 (1976), pp. 20–7.

lacks the kind of power which it is clear an omnipotent agent ought to possess. Such a requirement might appear redundant at this point. However, it is actually needed to rule out an analysis like the following, which satisfies our first four conditions:

(C) *S* is omnipotent at *t* in *W* if and only if for any state of affairs *p* and world-type-for-*S Ls* such that *p* is not a member of *Ls*, if there is a world *W** such that
(i) *Ls* is true in both *W* and *W**, and
(ii) *W** shares the same history with *W* at *t*, and
(iii) at *t* in *W* S* actualizes *p*,
then *S* has the power at *t* in *W* to actualize *p*.[22]

Instead of furnishing us with an analysis of absolute maximal power, the right-hand side of (C) merely provides an analysis of the maximal amount of power that can be had at *t* in *W* by *any being with S's nature*. As such, it may be satisfied by a being obviously lacking omnipotence, for example, the infamous Mr McEar. To avoid this result we will satisfy our fifth condition by insisting that, to count as omnipotent, a being should have the maximal amount of power consistent with our first four conditions.[23]

II

Though we are aware of no previously offered analysis which satisfies each of these five conditions, it seems to us that an

[22] The stipulation that *p* not be a member of *Ls* is required if we assume that by their free actions agents actualize the corresponding counter-factuals of freedom. In the example used above, this assumption would amount to the claim that by actualizing (8) Jones also actualizes (9). If, on the other hand, we deny that a counter-factual of freedom can properly be said to be actualized by anyone, then the stipulation in question is, though superfluous, completely harmless. So we have added it just to be safe.

[23] Despite Richard Swinburne's protestations to the contrary, the conceivability of McEar disqualifies his analysis. See Richard Swinburne, 'Omnipotence', *American Philosophical Quarterly* vol. 10 (1973), pp. 231–7. For much the same reason, an analysis offered tentatively by Plantinga must also be deemed unacceptable. On this analysis, a being *S* is viewed as omnipotent at time *t* in world *W* if and only if (1) there are states of affairs *S* can strongly actualize at *t*, and (2) for any state of affairs *p* such that there is a possible world which shares the initial world segment prior to *t* with *W* and in which *S* at *t* strongly actualizes *p*, *S* can at *t* strongly actualize *p*.

acceptable analysis of omnipotence can be formulated. For consider:

(D) *S* is omnipotent at *t* in *W* if and only if for any state of affairs *p* and world-type-for-*S* *Ls* such that *p* is not a member of *Ls*, if there is a world *W** such that
(i) *Ls* is true in both *W* and *W**, and
(ii) *W** shares the same history with *W* at *t*, and
(iii) at *t* in *W** someone actualizes *p*,
then *S* has the power at *t* in *W* to actualize *p*.

(D) appears to satisfy each of our desiderata. It is stated in terms of actualizing states of affairs, and does not presuppose that an omnipotent being would have strongly to actualize every state of affairs he brings about; in other words, it leaves a place for weak actualization. The inability of even an omnipotent being to actualize necessarily unactualizable states of affairs is acknowledged by (iii), while his inability to change the past is recognized by (ii) and (iii) together. Furthermore, by employing the notion of a world-type-for-*S*, (D) satisfies our fourth condition. And, finally, (D) requires that an agent who is omnipotent at *t* in *W* should have the power to actualize *any* state of affairs (other than a member of *Ls*) which *any* agent actualizes at *t* in *any* world satisfying conditions (i) and (ii). Consequently, it seems to us that (D) does provide a philosophically adequate analysis of maximal power.

(D) also appears to be immune to the so-called paradoxes of omnipotence. Suppose that Sam is omnipotent at *t* in our world. Does (D) require that Sam have the power at *t* to actualize the state of affairs

(10) Its being the case that there will be a stone which Sam, though he exists, cannot move?

The answer depends upon what further properties Sam has. If Sam is essentially omnipotent, then he cannot at *t* actualize (10). But (D) does not require that he have this power, since in that case (10) is a logically impossible state of affairs and thus not possibly such that anyone actualizes it. On the other hand, if Sam is only contingently omnipotent, then (D) might well require that he have the power at t to actualize (10). But there is no paradox here. By actualizing (10) Sam would merely bring it about that at some future time he will be non-omnipotent.[24]

Again, take the following state of affairs:

(11) Its being the case that a completely uncaused event will occur.

Does (D) require that Sam have the power at t to actualize (11)? If one can actualize (11) only by causing the event in question, then (D) does not require that Sam be able to actualize (11). For in that case it is logically impossible for anyone to actualize (11), even if (11) is a logically contingent state of affairs. On the other hand, if (11) is possibly actualized by someone, then Sam must have the power at t to actualize it. In neither case is there a paradoxical result.

But what of this state of affairs:

(12) Someone is actualizing p, and Sam, though omnipotent, is not actualizing p,

where p is a state of affairs which even non-omnipotent agents can normally actualize? Must Sam have the power at t to bring it about that (12) will obtain? One might have doubts about whether it is logically possible for any agent to actualize (12). However, anyone who holds a fairly liberal position with respect to the diffusiveness of power might plausibly contend that it is logically possible. For instance, a non-omnipotent being could bring it about at t that (12) will obtain at t^* by bringing it about that he will be actualizing p at t^*, when in fact it is true that Sam will not be actualizing p at t^*. But then, by the same token, it appears that Sam too may have the power at t to bring it about that (12) will obtain at t^*. Sam would do this by bringing it about that he will not be actualizing p at t^*, when in fact it is true that someone else will be actualizing p at t^*.

Of course, it is plausible to think that, if Sam is an essentially divine (i.e., eternally omnipotent, omniscient, and provident) being, then he weakly or strongly actualizes at any time t every

[24] This response to the stone paradox conforms to that given by Rosenkrantz and Hoffman in 'What an Omnipotent Agent Can Do'.

state of affairs (other than a member of the true world-type-for-Sam) which *anyone* actualizes at *t*. In that case Sam would never have the power to bring it about that (12) will obtain. But neither would any other agent ever have this power in any world containing an essentially divine being. So (D) would not in this case require that Sam have the power at *t* to bring it about that (12) will obtain. In short, (12) seems to present no serious problem for our analysis of omnipotence. Perhaps there are other states of affairs which would present a problem, but we have not been able to think of any.

Furthermore, our analysis has not been 'corrupted' by theological considerations. Indeed, (D) appears to be quite neutral with regard to what additional properties an omnipotent being might conceivably have. Given (D), there is no obvious conceptual requirement that an omnipotent agent be eternal, necessary, essentially omnipotent, uniquely omnipotent, omniscient, or morally impeccable—a being could conceivably lack any or all of these attributes at a time *t* in a world *W* and yet still be omnipotent at *t* in *W*. Of course, for all that (D) tells us, an omnipotent being could equally well possess any or all of these attributes (leaving open for now the question of moral impeccability, which will be discussed below). In short, it appears that (D) neither requires nor forbids an omnipotent being to possess the theologically significant properties mentioned above, and thus does exhibit the kind of independence from religious matters which we would presumably prefer our analysis to exhibit.

III

So it appears that (D) meets our conditions for philosophical adequacy. But what of its theological adequacy? Does (D) allow the traditional religious believer to consider God both omnipotent and incapable of acting reprehensibly? That is, does it permit one to evade the Geachian abandonment of divine omnipotence without endorsing the Pikean rejection of divine impeccability?

In attempting to answer these questions, we would perhaps be well advised to begin by noting that, given our analysis of omnipotence, there is no conceptual problem with an omnipotent agent's being impeccable. For though our analysis does apparently require that an omnipotent being have the power at a given time *t* to actualize many evil states of affairs, for example,

(13) An innocent child's being maliciously tortured,

it does not require that our omnipotent being also possess omniscience at *t*. Indeed, it does not require that he be very knowledgeable at all. He could conceivably be utterly ignorant of the consequences of his actions and hence bring about evil states of affairs such as (13) unintentionally. Provided that his own ignorance is not a state for which he is himself culpable, it would seem to follow that he could not be held morally blameworthy for those evil states of affairs which he might unintentionally actualize at *t*. Hence, the ability to actualize such states of affairs at *t* does not entail the ability to act in a morally reprehensible fashion at *t*. The possibility of an omnipotent but impeccable being is thus left open by our analysis.

Of course, this demonstration of the compatibility of omnipotence and impeccability lends little assistance to the traditional theist who professes belief in a God who, in addition to possessing both of these attributes, is omniscient as well. How, one might ask, could an impeccable God who knew with certainty the ramifications of any action he might take have the power to actualize evil states of affairs such as (13)?

Troubling though such a question might appear, it would seem that our analysis provides the theist with a rather obvious response, a response which should sound familiar to those conversant with theistic replies to the atheological argument from evil. The analysis of omnipotence which we have proposed does not require an omnipotent being to have the power *strongly* to actualize states of affairs like (13); the ability *weakly* to actualize them is sufficient to satisfy the conditions laid down by (D). Once this is recognized, it no longer appears strange to contend that God, while remaining impeccable, might well have the power to actualize a state of affairs such as (13). For (13) could be part of some world *W* which is itself such that God's actualizing it might be morally justifiable. Perhaps the actuality of (13) in *W* leads to greater good than would have occurred had (13) not obtained; perhaps it leads to less evil. In any event, it is surely conceivable that God should recognize that his allowing one of his creatures freely to torture an innocent child would as a matter of fact result in a world so good that this allowance was morally acceptable—and this despite the fact that the actual torturing would remain an evil state of affairs and the torturer would remain blameworthy. Hence, since even an impeccable God could have the power weakly to actualize worlds such as *W* which contain moral evil, and since in actualizing such worlds he must weakly actualize the evil states of affairs such as (13) which they contain, it follows that God can indeed remain impeccable even though he has the power to actualize evil states of affairs.

Now it might be thought that this response is still inadequate. It might be thought that there are some states of affairs which are *so* evil that *no* possible world containing them is a world that anyone could be morally justified in actualizing. Hence, since no divine being could ever have the power even weakly to actualize these states of affairs, no such being could rank as omnipotent. (We are willing to accept the assumption, made by this objection, that a being who is divine at *t* at least weakly actualizes any state of affairs (other than a member of the true world-type-for-him) that is actualized by anyone at *t*.)

Though this objection might well be potent against the theist who views Yahweh, the person who is in fact God, as a contingently divine being, it lacks efficacy against one who holds the more traditional belief that Yahweh is an essentially divine—and so essentially impeccable—being. For, on this view, no state of affairs of the sort just described obtains (or, consequently is actualized by anyone) in any possible world in which Yahweh exists. Hence, (D) does not require that, in order to be omnipotent, Yahweh must ever have the power tō actualize any state of affairs which is necessarily such that anyone who even weakly actualizes it is morally reprehensible for so doing. In fact, if we go one step further, and adopt the Anselmian claim that Yahweh is a necessary being as well as an essentially divine being, it follows that no such state of affairs obtains (or, as a result, is actualized by anyone) in *any* possible world. Some such states of affairs might be *conceivable*, but they are not, according to the Anselmian, *logically possible*.[25]

However, even for the Anselmian, Geach's challenge to the notion of an omnipotent God remains to be met. If God is essentially impeccable, there is no world in which he fails to fulfil a promise he has made. But if this is so, does it not follow that, by making a promise, God limits his ability to act in the future and thus renders himself less than omnipotent?

It appears at first that we have a straightforward answer to this question, viz., that by making a promise to his creatures God indeed limits his power, but not in a way which compromises his omnipotence. For suppose, to use one of Geach's examples, that God has already promised that Israel will be saved.[26] And assume that from this it follows that God does not now (at *t*) have the power to actualize

(14) Its being the case that Israel will never be saved.

Can we conclude, given (D), that God is not now omnipotent? A close look at (D) reveals that the answer to this question is negative. For in any possible world which shares the same past with our world at *t*, an essentially divine being who is essentially incapable of breaking his promises has promised prior to *t* that Israel will be saved. So in every such world Israel is saved. Hence, no one actualizes (14) at *t* in any such world. So (D) does not

[25] The Anselmian response to Pike was first formulated by Joshua Hoffman in 'Can God Do Evil?' *Southern Journal of Philosophy*, vol. 17 (1979), pp. 213–20.

[26] In his comments on this essay, William Wainwright argued that, if our account of freedom is correct, then God cannot make promises like the alleged promise to save Israel. For a 'promise' of this sort would be such that God could not fulfil it on his own, as it were, since he does not have the power to determine causally the free actions of his creatures. At best, Wainwright contends, God could (in virtue of his foreknowledge) 'assure' some creatures that they would be saved. But he could not 'promise' this. We are not completely convinced by this argument, since it may be that God, in virtue of his knowledge of the future free acts of his creatures, can make promises where non-omniscient beings can only give assurances. But even if Wainwright is correct, it seems that an orthodox believer could comfortably construe talk of God's promises as talk about God's assurances, at least in those cases where free human actions are involved. Indeed, as Wainwright himself notes, we often give assurances by using the expression 'I promise you that . . .'. One who is sympathetic to Wainwright's argument should simply construe our talk below of 'conditioned promises' as talk about assurances.

require that, in order to be omnipotent now, God must now have the power to actualize (14).

This solution to Geach's problem is extremely attractive, and if all else should fail, we will resort to using it. However, we can adopt it only if we abandon the account sketched above of what it is for two worlds to share the same history at a given time. For on that account the state of affairs

(15) God's promising that Israel will be saved

is non-immediate, since it entails the future-tense proposition that Israel will be saved. Hence, (15) is not a member of any sub-moment, i.e., it does not count as part of what is temporally independent at the time at which it obtains. And from this it follows that a world *W* might share the same history (in our sense) with our world now at *t* even if (15) has already obtained in our world but never obtains prior to *t* in *W*. So, given our official interpretation of condition (ii) in (D), it may very well be the case that, in order to be omnipotent, God must now have the power to actualize (14). But this seems to entail the theologically odious conclusion that God now has the power to break a promise and so is not impeccable.

Still, we are reluctant to scrap our explication of what it is for two worlds to share the same history at a given time, and this reluctance itself is in part motivated by theological concerns. For our explication of this notion allows us to avoid the deterministic claim that if

(16) God's believing (the future-contingent proposition) that Israel will be saved

now obtains, then it is now no longer within the power of the children of Israel to lead, without exception, lives heavily laden with moral turpitude. Rather, we can say that God's present belief that Israel will be saved is temporally dependent on the fact that the children of Israel will freely accept his grace and live accordingly.[27] So it is conceivable that (16) never obtains in a

[27] We acknowledge that this way of speaking is infected with (some might say 'infested' with) Molinist assumptions about the relation between grace and freedom. See note 20 above.

world which shares the same history with our world at the present moment *t*, since in that world God believes at *t* that the children of Israel will freely reject his grace and choose to separate themselves from him.

Of course, philosophers have devised other, non-Ockhamistic, strategies for dealing with the problem of foreknowledge and freedom. Some argue in effect that (16) is a logically impossible state of affairs, either because a future-contingent proposition can be neither true nor false, or because—as Prior would have it—a future-contingent proposition expressible by a sentence of the form 'It will be the case that *p*' cannot be true.[28] However, if one accepts this way out of the deterministic problem, then it seems to follow that (15) is logically impossible as well. For it obtains at a time *t* only if it is *true* at *t* that Israel will be saved. So on this view one cannot make sense of the central religious claim that God makes promises (or gives assurances) which in some way or other guarantee the truth of contingent propositions about the future.

Geach himself employs the alternative tactic of claiming that statements ostensibly about the future are really about present intentions, dispositions, tendencies, or trends.[29] So (16) obtains just in case God believes that things are presently tending toward Israel's salvation. But this is compatible with the freedom of the children of Israel, since they may by their free actions reverse this trend, in which case at some future date (before the Judgement) it would turn out to be true that Israel will not be saved. Their freedom is preserved, however, only at the expense of the traditional belief that God now knows exactly what will happen at every future moment. It is sufficient, Geach contends, that God, like a grand chess master, knows all the possible moves we might freely make and also knows exactly how he would counter each of those moves in order to accomplish his purposes.[30] Nevertheless, it

[28] See A. N. Prior, 'The Formalities of Omniscience', in *Papers on Time and Tense* (Oxford, 1968), pp. 26–44.

[29] Geach, *Providence and Evil*, ch. 2, esp. pp. 44–54.

[30] The image of God as a grand chess master, first popularized by William James in his essay 'The Dilemma of Determinism', is in many ways reminiscent of Jacques Maritain's image of God as an almighty stage manager who incorporates our improvisations into his providential play. See Maritain's *God and the Permission of Evil* (Milwaukee, 1966), p. 79. 'The Dilemma of Determinism' is found in William

is difficult to see how an orthodox Christian can accept this emasculation of the notion of divine providence. Like the promise to save Israel, many of God's promises seem to presuppose foreknowledge of exactly how his creatures will freely act. Once we deny such foreknowledge, as Geach does, then we open up the possibility that God makes promises which he will not and cannot fulfil. For even Geach insists that God cannot cause his creatures to act freely in the way he desires them to act. And suppose that they all freely reject his grace. Will he than save them? Will his kingdom then come? The answer, it is clear, is no. But if God does not have foreknowledge, then he cannot discount this possibility when deciding what to promise. The grand chess master cannot accomplish his purpose if, unbeknown to him, his opponent will refuse to move according to the rules or will simply decline his invitation to play. So, given Geach's view, either God cannot in good conscience, as it were, promise that Israel will be saved—which is false according to faith—or it is logically possible that God's promise to save Israel go unfulfilled—which is also false according to faith.

So our disinclination to abandon a broadly Ockhamistic account of divine foreknowledge stems in large part from a consideration of the theological consequences of the alternative accounts. Now it may be, of course, that even within an Ockhamistic framework one could find some acceptable reason to count (15) as immediate while counting (16) as non-immediate. For perhaps it is plausible to think that, while God's beliefs about the future depend on what will happen, his promises with respect to the future are by contrast efficacious. However, we can see at present no way to formulate a general account of immediacy which preserves this asymmetry between God's promising and God's believing without producing other unacceptable consequences—especially in cases like (15), where God promises to actualize future-tense states of affairs whose actualization depends in part on the free actions of his creatures. Moreover, there are theological reasons for thinking that God's beliefs about the future are in some sense or other causally efficacious.

James, *The Will to Believe and Other Essays in Popular Philosophy* (New York, 1897, reprinted 1956), pp. 145–83.

Instead of pursuing this line of enquiry, we will close with a very tentative sketch of an alternative strategy for reconciling, within the parameters of our Ockhamistic account of sharing the same history, God's omnipotence with his impeccability. But we wish to reiterate that, if this strategy turns out to be irremediably defective, then we will jettison our account of what it is for two worlds to share the same history at a given moment. In that case, the previously noted 'straightforward' response to the promising problem would, at the cost of some vagueness in our analysis of omnipotence, become available to us.

Now it is not unreasonable to think that some of God's promises to us reflect necessary truths about how God treats his creatures. For example, perhaps it is a necessary truth that any sinful free creature whom God creates is offered divine forgiveness. Suppose that this is so, and suppose further that God has promised that Jones, a sinful free creature of God's who now exists, will be offered divine forgiveness. Given this scenario, even though the state of affairs

(17) God's promising that Jones will be offered divine forgiveness

is non-immediate, it is still the case that there is no possible world *W* sharing the same history with our world at the present moment *t* such that at *t* in *W* someone brings it about that Jones will never be offered divine forgiveness. For in any such world Jones is a sinful free agent created by God, and so he is offered divine forgiveness. Let us call promises of this sort God's *standing* promises. It should be obvious that (D) does not require that God ever have, in order to be omnipotent, the power to break a standing promise.

It is also reasonable to believe that many of God's promises to us reflect at least in part his beliefs about how he and his free creatures will freely choose to act in the future. For instance, his promise that Israel will be saved presumably depends in part on his belief that the children of Israel will, under the influence of grace, freely act in the ways appropriate for their salvation. And perhaps his promise never again to destroy the world by flood reflects his knowledge of his own present, but constant, intentions and hence his foreknowledge of his own future free actions. Let us call promises of this sort God's *conditioned* promises.

Now suppose that God's promise to save Israel is indeed a conditioned promise, and suppose that he has already made this promise. Since (15) is non-immediate, it may follow from our account of omnipotence (given the Ockhamistic construal of condition (ii) in (D)) that God now has the power to bring it about that Israel will never be saved. Suppose that this does in fact follow. Does it follow further that God has the power to break a promise or to act in a morally reprehensible way? The answer, it should be clear, is no. For take a world *W* which shares the same history (in our sense) with our world now at *t* and in which Israel is never saved. Since in *W* God knows that the children of Israel will reject his grace, he never promises in *W* that Israel will be saved. So it is compatible with all the assumptions made above that there is no possible world in which God breaks a previously made conditioned promise. That is, even if God now has the power to bring it about that Israel will never be saved, it does not follow that God now has the power to act in a way which is such that if he were to act in that way, he would have broken a promise. For if he were to bring it about now that Israel will never be saved, then in those possible worlds most similar to ours in which Israel is never saved, God never promises to save Israel—where the relevant notion of two worlds being similar at *t* is at least partially defined in terms of the notion of two worlds sharing the same history at *t*. (We are, for present purposes, assuming a standard possible-worlds account of the truth conditions for counter-factuals.)

While this line of thought admittedly requires further elaboration and defence, we believe that even this brief sketch shows it to have some merit. If some such account of God's promises is indeed correct, then to complete our argument we have only to add the claim that necessarily, any promise made by God is either a standing promise or a conditioned promise. Since neither of these types of promise undermines the claim that God is both omnipotent and impeccable—or even the stronger claim that God is both essentially omnipotent and essentially impeccable—our analysis of omnipotence does not succumb to Geach's objection even if (D) is construed Ockhamistically.

Hence, we conclude that (D) does provide the type of analysis of the concept of omnipotence which Geach and Pike held to be impossible. The theist does not *need* to choose between divine omnipotence and divine impeccability. And neither, fortunately, does God.[31]

[31] We wish to thank William Wainwright, our commentator at the conference at Notre Dame at which this paper was first presented, along with Nelson Pike and Philip Quinn, for their helpful comments on an earlier version of this essay.

V

OMNISCIENCE

9

ON OCKHAM'S WAY OUT

ALVIN PLANTINGA

Two essential teachings of Western theistic religions—Christianity, Judaism, and Islam—are that God is omniscient and that human beings are morally responsible for at least some of their actions. The first apparently implies that God has knowledge of the future and thus has foreknowledge of human actions; the second, that some human actions are *free*. But divine foreknowledge and human freedom, as every twelve-year-old Sunday school student knows, can seem to be incompatible; and at least since the fifth century AD philosophers and theologians have pondered the question whether these two doctrines really do conflict. There are, I think, substantially two lines of argument for the *incompatibility thesis*—the claim that these doctrines are indeed in conflict; one of these arguments is pretty clearly fallacious, but the other is much more impressive. In section I I state these two arguments; in section II I explain (and endorse) Ockham's reply to them; in section III I point out some startling implications of Ockham's way out; and finally, in section IV I offer an account of accidental necessity.

I. FOREKNOWLEDGE AND THE NECESSITY OF THE PAST

In *De Libero Arbitrio* Augustine puts the first line of argument in the mouth of Evodius:

That being so, I have a deep desire to know how it can be that God knows all things beforehand and that, nevertheless, we do not sin by necessity. Whoever says that anything can happen otherwise than as God has foreknown it, is attempting to destroy the divine foreknowledge with the most insensate impiety. . . . But this I say. Since God foreknew that man

Reprinted from *Faith and Philosophy*, Vol. III, No. 3 (July, 1986), pp. 235–269, by permission of the editors.

would sin, that which God foreknew must necessarily come to pass. How then is the will free when there is apparently this unavoidable necessity?[1]

(Replies Augustine: 'You have knocked vigorously.') Evodius's statement of the argument illustrates one parameter of the problem: the conception of freedom in question is such that a person *S* is free with respect to an action *A* only if (1) it is within *S*'s power to perform *A* and within his power to refrain from performing *A*, and (2) no collection of necessary truths and causal laws—causal laws outside *S*'s control—together with antecedent conditions outside *S*'s control entails that *S* performs *A*, and none entails that he refrains from doing so. (I believe that the first of these conditions entails the second, but shall not argue that point here.) Of course, if these conditions are rejected, then the alleged problem dissolves.

The essential portion of Evodius's argument may perhaps be put as follows:

(1) If God knows in advance that *S* will do *A*, then it must be the case that *S* will do *A*.
(2) If it *must* be the case that *S* will do *A*, then it is not within the power of *S* to refrain from doing *A*.
(3) If it is not within the power of *S* to refrain from doing *A*, then *S* is not free with respect to *A*.

Hence

(4) If God knows in advance that *S* will do *A*, then *S* is not free with respect to *A*.

Augustine apparently found this argument perplexing. In some passages he seems to see its proper resolution; but elsewhere he reluctantly accepts it and half-heartedly endorses a compatibilist account of freedom according to which it is possible both that all of a person's actions be determined and that some of them be free.

Thomas Aquinas, however, saw the argument for the snare and delusion that it is:

If each thing is known by God as seen by Him in the present, what is

[1] St Augustine, *On Free Will*, in *Augustine: Earlier Writings*, tr. J. H. S. Burleigh, vol. 6 (Philadelphia, 1953), bk. 3, ii, 4.

known by God will then have to be. Thus, it is necessary that Socrates be seated from the fact that he is seen seated. But this is not absolutely necessary or, as some say, with the *necessity of the consequent*; it is necessary conditionally, or with the *necessity of the consequence*. For this is a necessary conditional proposition: *if he is seen sitting, he is sitting.*[2]

Aquinas's point may perhaps be put more perspicuously as follows. (1) is ambiguous as between

(1)(*a*) Necessarily, if God knows in advance that *S* will do *A*, then *S* will do *A*.

and

(1)(*b*) If God knows in advance that *S* will do *A*, then it is necessary that *S* will do *A*.

Now consider

(1)(c) If God knows in advance that *S* will do *A*, then *S* will do *A*.

(1)(*a*), says Aquinas, is a true proposition expressing 'the necessity of the consequence'; what it says, sensibly enough, is just that the consequent of (1)(*c*) follows with necessity from its antecedent. (1)(*b*), on the other hand, is an expression of the necessity of the *consequent*; what *it* says, implausibly, is that the necessity of the consequent of (1)(*c*) follows from its antecedent. Aquinas means to point out that (1)(*a*) is clearly true but of no use to the argument. (1)(*b*), on the other hand, is what the argument requires; but it seems flatly false—or, more modestly, there seems not the slightest reason to endorse it.

If the above argument is unconvincing, there is another, much more powerful, that is also considered by Aquinas.[3] The argument in question has been discussed by a host of philosophers both before and after Aquinas; it received a particularly perspicuous formulation at the hands of Jonathan Edwards:

1. I observed before, in explaining the nature of necessity, that in things

[2] St Thomas Aquinas, *Summa Contra Gentiles*, bk. i, ch. 67, p. 10.

[3] See *Summa Contra Gentiles*, bk. i, ch. 67, and *Summa Theologiae*, pt. i, q. 14, art. 13.

which are past, their past existence is now necessary: having already made sure of existence, 'tis now impossible, that it should be otherwise than true, that that thing has existed.

2. If there be any such thing as a divine foreknowledge of the volitions of free agents, that foreknowledge, by the supposition, is a thing which already has, and long ago had existence; and so, now its existence is necessary; it is now utterly impossible to be otherwise, than that this foreknowledge should be, or should have been.

3. 'Tis also very manifest, that those things which are indissolubly connected with other things that are necessary, are themselves necessary. As that proposition whose truth is necessarily connected with another proposition, which is necessarily true, is itself necessarily true. To say otherwise, would be a contradiction; it would be in effect to say, that the connection was indissoluble, and yet was *not so*, but might be broken. If that, whose existence is indissolubly connected with something whose existence is now necessary, is itself not necessary, then it may possibly not exist, notwithstanding that indissoluble connection of its existence.—Whether the absurdity ben't glaring, let the reader judge.

4. 'Tis no less evident, that if there be a full, certain and infallible foreknowledge of the future existence of the volitions of moral agents, then there is a certain infallible and indissoluble connection between those events and that foreknowledge; and that therefore, by the preceding observations, those events are necessary events; being infallibly and indissolubly connected with that whose existence already is, and so is now necessary, and can't but have been.[4]

Edwards concludes that since 'God has a certain and infallible prescience of the acts and wills of moral agents', it follows that 'these events are necessary' with the same sort of necessity enjoyed by what is now past.

The argument essentially appeals to two intuitions. First, although the past is not necessary in the broadly logical sense (it is possible, in that sense, that Abraham should never have existed), it *is* necessary in *some* sense: it is fixed, unalterable, outside anyone's control. And second, whatever is 'necessarily connected' with what is necessary in some sense, is itself necessary in that sense; if a proposition *A*, necessary in the way in which the past is necessary, entails a proposition *B*, then *B* is necessary in that same way. If Edwards's argument is a good one, what it shows is that if

[4] Jonathon Edwards, *Freedom of the Will* (Boston, 1745), s. 12.

at some time in the past God knew that I will do *A*, then it is necessary that I will do *A*—necessary in just the way in which the past is necessary. But then it is not within my power to refrain from doing *A*, so that I will not do *A* freely. So, says Edwards, suppose God knew, eighty years ago, that I would mow my lawn this afternoon. This foreknowledge is, as he says, a 'thing that is past'. Such things, however, are now necessary; ''tis now impossible, that it should be otherwise than true, that that thing has existed.' So it is now necessary that God had that knowledge eighty years ago; but it is also *logically* necessary that, if God knew that I would mow my lawn today, then I will mow my lawn today. It is therefore now necessary that I will mow; it is thus not within my power to refrain from mowing; hence, though I will indeed mow, I will not mow freely.

Edwards's argument is for what we might call 'theological determinism'; the premiss is that God has foreknowledge of the 'acts and wills of moral agents' and the conclusion is that these acts are necessary in just the way the past is. Clearly enough the argument can be transformed into an argument for *logical* determinism, which would run as follows. It was true, eighty years ago, that I would mow my lawn this afternoon. Since what is past is now necessary, it is now necessary that it was true eighty years ago that I would mow my lawn today. But it is logically necessary that, if it was true eighty years ago that I would mow my lawn today, then I will mow my lawn today. It is therefore necessary that I will mow my lawn—necessary in just the sense in which the past is necessary. But then it is not within my power not to mow; hence I will not mow freely.

Here a Boethian bystander might object as follows. Edwards's argument involves divine *fore*knowledge—God's having known at some time in the past, for example, that Paul will mow his lawn in 1995. Many theists, however, hold that God is *eternal*,[5] and that his eternity involves at least the following two properties. First, his being eternal means, as Boethius suggested, that everything is *present* for him; for him there is no past or future. But then God does not know any such propositions as 'Paul *will* mow in 1995';

[5] See E. Stump and N. Kretzmann, 'Eternity', *Journal of Philosophy* 78 (8) (Aug. 1981), pp. 429–58; reprinted in this volume.

what he knows, since everything is present for him, is just that Paul mows in 1995. And secondly, God's being eternal means that God is atemporal, 'outside of time'—outside of time in such a way that it is an error to say of him that he knew some proposition or other *at a time*. We thus cannot properly say that God *now* knows that Paul mows in 1995, or that at some time in the past God knew this; the truth, instead, is that he knows this proposition *eternally*. But then Edwards's argument presupposes the falsehood of a widely accepted thesis about the nature of God and time.

I am inclined to believe that this thesis—the thesis that God is both atemporal and such that everything is present for him—is incoherent. If it *is* coherent, however, Edwards's argument can be restated in such a way as not to presuppose its falsehood. For suppose in fact Paul will mow his lawn in 1995. Then the proposition 'God (eternally) knows that Paul mows in 1995' is now true. That proposition, furthermore, was true eighty years ago; the proposition 'God knows (eternally) that Paul mows in 1995' not only *is* true *now*, but *was* true *then*. Since what is past is necessary, it is now necessary that this proposition was true eighty years ago. But it is logically necessary that, if this proposition was true eighty years ago, then Paul mows in 1995. Hence his mowing then is necessary in just the way the past is. But, then it neither now is nor in the future will be within Paul's power to refrain from mowing.

Of course this argument depends upon the claim that a proposition can be true *at a time*—eighty years ago, for example. Some philosophers argue that it does not so much as make sense to suggest that a proposition *A* is or was or will be true at a time; a proposition is true or false *simpliciter* and no more true at a time than, for example, true in a mail-box or a refrigerator.[6] (Even if there is no beer in the refrigerator, the proposition 'there is no beer' is not true in the refrigerator.) We need not share their scruples in order to accommodate them; the argument can be suitably modified. Concede for the moment that it makes no sense to say of a *proposition* that it was true at a time; it nonetheless

[6] See, for example, Peter van Inwagen, *An Essay on Free Will*, (Oxford, 1983), pp. 35 ff.; and Nelson Pike, *God and Timelessness*, (New York, 1970), pp. 67 ff. (More exactly, Pike's objection is not to temporally indexed propositions as such, but to alleged propositions of the sort 'It is true at T_1 that S does A at T_2'.)

makes good sense, obviously, to say of a sentence that it expressed a certain proposition at a time. But it also makes good sense to say of a sentence that it expressed a truth at a time. Now eighty years ago the sentence

(5) God knows (eternally) that Paul mows in 1995

expressed the proposition that God knows eternally that Paul mows in 1995 (and for simplicity let us suppose that proposition was the only proposition it expressed then). But if in fact Paul will mow in 1995, then (5) also expressed a truth eighty years ago. So eighty years ago (5) expressed the proposition that Paul will mow in 1995 and expressed a truth; since what is past is now necessary, it is now necessary that eighty years ago (5) expressed that proposition and expressed a truth. But it is necessary in the broadly logical sense that if (5) then expressed that proposition (and only that proposition) and expressed a truth, then Paul will mow in 1995. It is therefore necessary that Paul will mow then; hence his mowing then is necessary in just the way the past is.

Accordingly, the claim that God is outside of time is essentially irrelevant to Edwardsian arguments. In what follows I shall therefore assume, for the sake of expository simplicity, that God does indeed have foreknowledge, and that it is quite proper to speak of him both as holding a belief at a time and as having held beliefs in the past. What I shall say, however, can be restated so as to accommodate those who reject this assumption.

II OCKHAM'S WAY OUT

As Edwards sees things, then, 'in things which are past, their existence is now necessary . . . , 'Tis too late for any possibility of alteration in that respect: 'tis now impossible that it should be otherwise than true, that that thing has existed.' Nor is Edwards idiosyncratic in this intuitiion; we are all inclined to believe that the past, as opposed to the future, is fixed, stable, unalterable, closed. It is outside our control and outside the control even of an omnipotent being. Consider, for example, Peter Damian, often (but mistakenly) cited as holding that the power of God is limited by nothing at all, not even the laws of logic. In *De Divina*

Omnipotentia, a letter to Desiderio of Cassino, Damian recalls and discusses a dinner conversation with the latter, a conversation that touched off a centuries-long discussion of the question whether it was within the power of God to restore to virginity someone who was no longer a virgin. The topic is God's power over the past:

> I feel obliged to respond to an objection that many put forward. They say: 'If God', as you affirm, 'is omnipotent in all things, can he so act that things that are made, are not made? He can certainly destroy all things that have been made, so that they exist no more: but it is impossible to see how he can bring it about that those things which were made should never have been made at all. He can bring it about that from now and henceforth Rome should no longer exist, but how can the opinion be maintained that he can bring it about that it should never have been built of old?'[7]

Damian's response is not entirely clear. In chapter 15, which is substantially his concluding chapter, he suggests that 'it is much the same thing to ask "How can God bring it about that what once happened did not happen?" or "Can God act in such a way that what he made, he did not make?" as to assert that what God has made, God did not make.'[8] (Damian takes a relatively strong line with respect to this last; anyone who asserts it, he says, is contemptible, not worthy of a reply, and should instead be branded.) Here it isn't clear whether he is holding that the proposition 'What has happened is such that God can bring it about that it has not happened' is equivalent to the proposition 'God can bring it about that what has happened hasn't happened' and is thus false, or whether he simply fails to distinguish these propositions. He goes on to make heavy weather over the relation of God's eternity to the question under discussion, apparently holding that 'relative to God and his unchangeable eternity', it is correct to say that God *can* bring it about that Rome was never founded; 'relative to *us*', on the other hand, the right thing to say is

[7] Peter Damian, *De Divina Omnipotentia*, ch. 4, in J. Migne's *Patrologia Latina*, vol. 145 (Paris, n.d.), p. 599. The translation of the last two sentences is from Anthony Kenny's *The God of the Philosophers* (Oxford, 1979), p. 101.

[8] Ibid., p. 618. The translation is by Owen J. Blum, and is taken from John Wippel and Alan Wolter, *Medieval Philosophy* (New York, 1969), p. 147.

that God *could have* brought it about that Rome was never founded.[9]

Damian's views on the matter are not altogether clear; what *is* clear is that he, like the rest of us, saw an important asymmetry between past and future. This asymmetry consists in part in the fact that the past is outside our control in a way in which the future is not. Although I now have the power to raise my arm, I do not have the power to bring it about that I raised my arm five minutes ago. Although it is now within my power to think about Vienna, it is not now within my power to bring it about that five minutes ago I was thinking about Vienna. The past is fixed in a way in which the future is open. It is within my power to help determine how the future shall be; it is too late to do the same with respect to the past.

Edwards, indeed, speaks in this connection of the *unalterability* of the past; and it is surely natural to do so. Strictly speaking, however, it is not alterability that is here relevant; for the future is no more alterable than the past. What after all, would it be to alter the past? To bring it about, obviously, that a temporally indexed proposition which is true and about the past before I act, is false thereafter. On 1 January 1982, I was not visiting New Guinea. For me to change the past with respect to that fact would be for me to perform an action *A* such that prior to my performing the action, it is true that on 1 January 1982 I was not in New Guinea, but after I perform the action, false that I was not in New Guinea then. But of course I can't do anything like that, and neither can God, despite his omnipotence.

But neither can we alter the future. We can imagine someone saying, 'Paul will in fact walk out the door at 9.21 AM; hence "Paul will walk out at 9.21 AM" is true; but Paul has the power to refrain from walking out then; so Paul has the power to alter the future.' But the conclusion displays confusion; Paul's not walking out then, were it to occur, would effect no alteration at all in the future. To alter the future, Paul must do something like this: he must perform some action *A* at a time *t* before 9.21 such that prior to *t* it is true that Paul will walk out at 9.21, but after *t* (after he performs *A*) false that he will. Neither Paul nor anyone—not even God—can

[9] Ibid., p. 619.

do something like that. So the future is no more alterable than the past.

The interesting asymmetry between past and future, therefore, does not consist in the fact that the past is unalterable in a way in which the future is not; nonetheless, this asymmetry remains. Now, before 9.21, it is within Paul's power to make it false that he walks out at 9.21; after he walks out at 9.21 he will no longer have that power. In the same way, in 1995 BC God could have brought it about that Abraham did not exist in 1995 BC; now that is no longer within his power. As Edwards says, it's too late for that.

Recognizing this asymmetry, Ockham, like several other medieval philosophers, held that the past is indeed in some sense necessary: it is *necessary per accidens*:

> I claim that every necessary proposition is *per se* in either the first mode or the second mode. This is obvious, since I am talking about all propositions that are necessary *simpliciter*. I add this because of propositions that are necessary *per accidens*, as is the case with many past tense propositions. They are necessary *per accidens*, because it was contingent that they be necessary, and because they were not always necessary.[10]

Here Ockham directs our attention to propositions about the past: past-tense propositions together with temporally indexed propositions, such as:

(8) *Columbus sails the ocean blue* is true in 1492[11]

whose index is prior to the present time. Such propositions, he says, are accidentally necessary if true; they are *accidentally* necessary because they *become* necessary. Past-tense propositions become necessary when they become true; temporally indexed propositions such as (8), on the other hand, do not become true—(8) was always true—but they become necessary, being necessary after but not before the date of their index. And once a proposition acquires this status, says Ockham, not even God has the power to make it false.

[10] William of Ockham, *Ordinatio*, vol. i, prologue, q. 6.

[11] I take it that (8) is equivalent to

(8*) 'Columbus sails the ocean blue' is, was or will be true in 1492

I am here ignoring allegedly tenseless propositions, if indeed there are any such things.

In *Predestination, God's Foreknowledge and Future Contingents*, Ockham goes on to make an interesting distinction:

Some propositions are about the present as regards both their wording and their subject matter (*secundum vocem et secundum rem*). Where such propositions are concerned, it is universally true that every true proposition about the present has (corresponding to it) a necessary one about the past:—e.g., 'Socrates is seated', 'Socrates is walking', 'Socrates is just', and the like.

Other propositions are about the present as regards their wording only and are equivalently about the future, since their truth depends on the truth of propositions about the future. Where such (propositions) are concerned, the rule that every true proposition about the present has corresponding to it a necessary proposition about the past is not true.[12]

Ockham means to draw the following contrast. Some propositions about the present 'are about the present as regards both their wording and their subject matter'; for example,

(9) Socrates is seated.

Such propositions, we may say, are *strictly* about the present; and if such a proposition is now true, then a corresponding proposition about the past—

(10) Socrates was seated—

will be accidentally necessary from now on. Other propositions about the present, however, 'are about the present as regards their wording only and are equivalently about the future'; for example,

(11) Paul correctly believes that the sun will rise on 1 January 2000.

Such a proposition is 'equivalently about the future', and it is not the case that if it is true, then the corresponding proposition about the past—

(12) Paul correctly believed that the sun will rise on 1 January 2000

[12] William Ockham, *Predestination, God's Foreknowledge, and Future Contingents*, tr. with Introduction, Notes, and Appendices by Marilyn Adams and Norman Kretzmann (Ithaca, 1969), pp. 46–7.

in this case—will be accidentally necessary from now on. (Of course we hope that (12) will be accidentally necessary after 1 January 2000.)

What Ockham says about the present, he would also say about the past. Just as some propositions about the present are 'about the present as regards their wording only and are equivalently about the future', so some propositions about the past are about the past as regards their wording only and are equivalently about the future; (12) for example, or

(13) Eighty years ago, the proposition 'Paul will mow his lawn' in 1999 was true

or (to appease those who object to the idea that a proposition can be true at a time):

(14) Eighty years ago, the sentence 'Paul will mow his lawn in 1999' expressed the próposition 'Paul will mow his lawn in 1999' and expressed a truth.

These propositions are about the past, but they are also equivalently about the future. Furthermore, they are not necessary *per accidens*—not yet, at any rate. We might say that a true proposition like (12)–(14) is a *soft* fact about the past, whereas one like:

(15) Paul mowed in 1981

—one strictly about the past—is a *hard* fact about the past.[13]

Now of course the notion of aboutness, as Nelson Goodman has reminded us[14] is at best a frail reed; *a fortiori*, then, the same goes for the notion of being *strictly* about. But we do have something of a grasp of this notion, hesitant and infirm though perhaps it is. It may be difficult or even impossible to give a useful criterion for the distinction between hard and soft facts about the past, but we do have *some* grasp of it, and can apply it in many cases. The idea of a

[13] See Nelson Pike, 'Of God and Freedom: A Rejoinder', *Philosophical Review* 75 (1966), p. 370; and Marilyn Adams, 'Is the Existence of God a "Hard" Fact?', *Philosophical Review* 76 (1966), pp. 493–94.

[14] Nelson Goodman, 'About', *Mind* 70 (1962), pp. 1–24.

hard fact about the past contains two important elements: *genuineness* and *strictness*. In the first place, a hard fact about the past is a genuine fact about the past. This cannot be said, perhaps, for (13). It is at least arguable that if (13) is a fact about the past at all, it is an ersatz fact about the past; it tells us nothing about the past except in a Pickwickian, Cantabridgian sort of way. What it really tells us is something about the future: that Paul will mow in 1999. (12) and (14), on the other hand, do genuinely tell us something about the past: (12) tells us that Paul believed something and (14) that a certain sentence expressed a certain proposition. But (12) and (14) aren't *strictly* about the past; they also tell us something about what will happen in 1999. It may be difficult to give criteria, or (informative) necessary and sufficient conditions for either genuineness or strictness; nevertheless, we do have at least a partial grasp of these notions.

Accordingly, let us provisionally join Ockham in holding that there is a viable distinction between hard and soft facts about the past. The importance of this distinction, for Ockham, is that it provides him with a way of disarming the arguments for logical and theological determinism from the necessity of the past. Each of those arguments, when made explicit, has as a premise

(16) If *p* is about the past, then *p* is necessary

or something similar. Ockham's response is to deny (16): *hard* facts about the past are indeed accidentally necessary, but the same cannot be said for soft facts. Such propositions as (13) and (14) are not hard facts about the past; each entails that Paul will mow his lawn in 1999, and is therefore, as Ockham says, 'equivalently about the future'. Not all facts about the past, then, are hard facts about the past; and only the hard facts are plausibly thought to be accidentally necessary. (16), therefore, the general claim that all facts about the past are accidentally necessary, is seen to be false—or, at any rate, there seems to be no reason at all to believe it. And thus dissolves any argument for theological determinism which, like Edwards's, accepts (16) in its full generality.

I believe Ockham is correct here; furthermore, there is no easy way to refurbish Edwards's argument. Given Ockham's distinction between hard and soft facts, what Edwards's argument needs is the premise that such propositions as

(17) God knew eighty years ago that Paul will mow in 1999

are hard facts about the past. Clearly, however, (17) is not a hard fact about the past; for (like (13) and (14)), it entails

(18) Paul will mow his lawn in 1999;

and no proposition that entails (18) is a hard fact about the past.

Let me be entirely clear here; I say that none of (13), (14), and (17) is a hard fact about the past, because each entails (18). In so saying, however, I am not endorsing a *criterion* for hard fact-hood; in particular I am not adopting an 'entailment' criterion, according to which a fact about the past is a hard fact about the past if and only if it entails no proposition about the future. No doubt *every* proposition about the past, hard fact or not, entails *some* proposition about the future; 'Socrates was wise', for example, entails 'It will be true from now on that Socrates was wise', and 'Paul played tennis yesterday' entails 'Paul will not play tennis for the first time tomorrow'. What I *am* saying is this: no proposition that entails (18) is a hard fact about the past, because no such proposition is *strictly* about the past. We may not be able to give a criterion for being strictly about the past; but we do have at least a rough and intuitive grasp of this notion. Given our intuitive grasp of this notion, I think we can see two things. First, no conjunctive proposition that contains (18) as a conjunct is (now, in 1986) strictly about the past. Thus 'Paul will mow his lawn in 1999 and Socrates was wise', while indeed a proposition about the past, is not *strictly* about the past. And second, hard fact-hood is closed under logical equivalence: any proposition equivalent (in the broadly logical sense) to a proposition strictly about the past is itself strictly about the past.[15] But any proposition that entails (18) is equivalent, in the broadly logical sense, to a conjunctive

[15] I think it is clear that hard fact-hood *is* closed under broadly logical equivalence; this argument, however, does not require the full generality of that premise. All it requires is that no proposition strictly about the past is equivalent in the broadly logical sense to a conjunction one conjunct of which, like (18), is a contingent proposition paradigmatically about the future.

proposition one conjunct of which is (18); hence each such proposition is equivalent to a proposition that is not a hard fact about the past, and is therefore itself not a hard fact about the past. Thus the Edwardsian argument fails.

III ON OCKHAM'S WAY OUT

As we have seen, Ockham responds to the arguments for theological determinism by distinguishing hard facts about the past—facts that are genuinely and strictly about the past—from soft facts about the past; only the former, he says, are necessary *per accidens*. This response is intuitively plausible. It is extremely difficult, however, to say precisely what it is for a proposition to be strictly about the past, and equally difficult to say what it is for a proposition to be accidentally necessary. According to Ockham, a proposition is not strictly about the past if its 'truth depends on the truth of propositions about the future'. This suggests that if a proposition about the past *entails* one about the future, then it isn't strictly about the past; we might therefore think that a proposition is strictly about the past if and only if it does not entail a proposition about the future. We might then concur with Ockham in holding that a proposition about the past is accidentally necessary if it is true and *strictly* about the past. But as John Fischer points out, difficulties immediately rear their ugly heads.[16] I shall mention only two. In the first place, suppose we take 'about the future' in a way that mirrors the way we took 'about the past'; a proposition is then about the future if and only if it is either a future-tense proposition or a temporally indexed proposition whose index is a date later than the present. Then obviously any proposition about the past will entail one about the future;

(24) Abraham existed a long time ago

and

(25) Abraham exists in 1995 BC

entail, respectively,

[16] John Fischer, 'Freedom and Foreknowledge', *Philosophical Review* 92 (1983), pp. 73–5.

(26) It will be the case from now on that Abraham existed a long time ago

and

(27) It will always be true that Abraham exists in 1995 BC.

But then the distinction between propositions strictly about the past and propositions about the past *simpliciter* becomes nugatory.

Perhaps you will reply that propositions like (26) and (27) are at best ersatz propositions about the future, despite their future tense or future index; on a less wooden characterization of 'about the future', they wouldn't turn out to be about the future. Perhaps so; I won't here dispute the point. But other and less tractable difficulties remain. First, (24) and (25) both entail that Abraham will not begin to exist (i.e., exist for the first time) in 1999;[17] and that isn't, or isn't obviously, an ersatz fact about the future. Second, on that more adequate characterization, whatever exactly it might be, it will no doubt be true that

(28) It was true eighty years ago either that God knew that Friesland will rule the world in 2000 AD or that Paul believed that Friesland will rule the world in 2000 AD[18]

entails no non-ersatz future propositions and is thus strictly about the past. Now suppose, *per impossibile*, that Friesland will indeed rule the world in 2000 AD. Then (28) (given divine omniscience) will be true by virtue of the truth of the first disjunct; the second disjunct, however, is false (by virtue of Paul's youth). And then on the above account (28) is accidentally necessary; but is it really? Isn't it still within someone's power—God's, let's say—to act in such a way that (28) would have been false (Fischer, p. 74)?[19]

Necessity *per accidens* and *being strictly about the past* thus present difficulties when taken in tandem in the way Ockham takes them. The former, furthermore, is baffling and perplexing in its own right; and this is really the fundamental problem here. If, as its proponents claim, accidental necessity isn't any sort of logical

[17] Ibid., p. 75.

[18] I leave it to the reader to restate (28) in such a way as to accommodate those who hold that propositions are not true at times.

[19] Fischer, 'Freedom and Foreknowledge', p. 74.

or metaphysical or causal necessity, what sort of necessity is it? How shall we understand it? Ockham, Edwards, and their colleagues don't tell us. Furthermore, even if they (or we) had a plausible account of *being strictly about the past*, we couldn't sensibly *define* accidental necessity in terms of being strictly about the past; for the whole point of the argument for theological determinism is just that propositions about the future that are entailed by accidentally necessary propositions about the past will themselves be accidentally necessary. So how shall we understand accidental necessity?

Perhaps we can make some progress as follows. In explaining accidental necessity, one adverts to facts about the power of agents—such facts, for example, as that not even God can now bring it about that Abraham did not exist; it's too late for that. Furthermore, in the arguments for logical and theological determinism, accidental necessity functions as a sort of middle term. It is alleged that a proposition of some sort or other is about or strictly about the past; but then, so the claim goes, that proposition is accidentally necessary—in which case, according to the argument, it is not now within the power of any agent, not even God, to bring it about that it is false. Why not eliminate the middleman and *define* accidental necessity in terms of the powers of agents? If a proposition *p* is accidentally necessary, then it is not possible—possible in the broadly logical sense—that there be an agent who has it within his power to bring it about that *p* is false; why not then define accidental necessity as follows?

(29) *p* is accidentally necessary at *t* if and only if *p* is true at *t* and it is not possible both that *p* is true at *t* and that there is a being that at *t* or later has the power to bring it about that *p* is false?[20]

But how shall we understand this 'has the power to bring it about

[20] The appropriate atemporalist counterpart of (29) is

(29*) *p* is accidentally necessary if and only if *p* is true and it is not possible both that *p* is true and that there is or will be a being that has or will have the power to bring it about that *p* is false

of which (29) is a generalization. (31), (39), (42), and (44) below have similar counterparts.

that *p* is false'? Pike speaks in this connection of 'its being within Jones' power to do something that would have brought it about that' *p*, and Fisher of 'being able so to act that *p* would have been false'. This suggests

(30) *S* has the power to bring it about that *p* is false if and only if there is an action it is within *S*'s power to perform such that if he were to perform it, *p* would have been false.

(30) is perhaps inadequate as a *general* account of what it is to have the power to bring it about that a proposition is false. For one thing, it seems to imply that I have the power with respect to necessarily false propositions (as well as other false propositions whose falsehood is counter-factually independent of my actions) to bring it about that they are false; and this is at best dubious. But here we aren't interested, first of all, in giving an independent account of having the power to bring it about that *p* is false; even if (30) isn't a satisfactory general account of that notion, it may serve acceptably in (29). Incorporating (30), therefore, (29) becomes

(31) *p* is accidentally necessary at *t* if and only if *p* is true at *t* and it is not possible both that *p* is true at *t* and that there exists an agent *S* and an action *A* such that (1) *S* has the power at *t* or later to perform *A*, and (2) if *S* were to perform *A* at *t* or later, then *p* would have been false.[21]

Now, so far as I know, Ockham gave no explicit account or explanation of accidental necessity; nevertheless, it is not implausible to see him as embracing something like (31). On this definition, furthermore, (given common-sense assumptions) many soft facts about the past will not be accidentally necessary: for example

(32) Eighty years ago it was true that Paul would not mow his lawn in 1999.

Even if true, (32) is not accidentally necessary: it is clearly possible

[21] Note that on (31) propositions that are necessary in the broadly logical sense turn out to be accidentally necessary. If this is considered a defect, it can be remedied by adding an appropriate condition to the *definiens*. Similar comments apply to (39), (42), and (44) below.

that Paul have the power, in 1999, to mow his lawn; but if he were to do so, then (32) would have been false. The same goes for

(33) God believed eighty years ago that Paul would mow his lawn in 1999

if God is essentially omniscient; for then it is a necessary truth that if Paul were to refrain from mowing his lawn during 1999, God would not have believed, eighty years ago, that he would mow then. (32) and (33), therefore, are not accidentally necessary.

Since (32) and (33) are not hard facts about the past, Ockham would have welcomed this consequence. But our account of accidental necessity has other consequences—consequences Ockham might have found less to his liking. Let's suppose that a colony of carpenter ants moved into Paul's yard last Saturday. Since this colony hasn't yet had a chance to get properly established, its new home is still a bit fragile. In particular, if the ants were to remain and Paul were to mow his lawn this afternoon, the colony would be destroyed. Although nothing remarkable about these ants is visible to the naked eye, God for reasons of his own, intends that the colony be preserved. Now as a matter of fact, Paul will not mow his lawn this afternoon. God, who is essentially omniscient, knew in advance, of course, that Paul will not mow his lawn this afternoon; but if he had foreknown instead that Paul *would* mow this afternoon, then he would have prevented the ants from moving in. The facts of the matter, therefore, are these: if Paul were to mow his lawn this afternoon, then God would have foreknown that Paul would mow his lawn this afternoon; and if God had foreknown that Paul would mow this afternoon, then God would have prevented the ants from moving in. So if Paul were to mow his lawn this afternoon, then the ants would not have moved in last Saturday. But it is within Paul's power to mow this afternoon. There is therefore an action he can perform such that if he were to perform it, then the proposition

(34) That colony of carpenter ants moved into Paul's yard last Saturday

would have been false. But what I have called 'the facts of the matter' certainly seem to be possible; it is therefore possible that there be an agent who has the power to perform an action which is such that, if he were to perform it, then (34) would have been false—in which case it is not accidentally necessary. But (34), obviously enough, is strictly about the past; in so far as we have any grasp at all of this notion, (34) is about as good a candidate for being an exemplification of it as any we can easily think of. So, contrary to what Ockham supposed, not all true propositions strictly about the past—not all hard facts—are accidentally necessary—not, at any rate, in the sense of (31).

Another example: a few years ago Robert Nozick called our attention to *Newcomb's Paradox*. You are confronted with two opaque boxes, box A and box B. You know that box B contains $1,000 and that box A contains either $1,000,000 or nothing at all. You can choose to take both boxes or to take just box A; no other action is possible. You know, furthermore, that the money was put there eighty years ago by an extremely knowledgeable agent according to the following plan: if she believed that you would take both boxes, she put $1,000 in box B and nothing in box A; if on the other hand, she believed that you would exercise a decent restraint and take only box A, she put $1,000 in box B and $1,000,000 in box A. You know, finally, that this being has an amazing track record. Many other people have been in just your situation and in at least a vast majority of such cases, if the person in question took both boxes, he found box A empty; but if he took just box A, he found it to contain $1,000,000. Your problem is: given your depleted coffers and acquisitive nature, what should you do? Should you take both boxes, or just box A? And the puzzle is that there seem to be strong arguments on both sides. First, there seems good reason to take just box A. For if you were to take just box A, then the being in question would have known that you would take just box A, in which case she would have put $1,000,000 in it. So if you were to take just box A, you would get $1,000,000. If you were to take both boxes, on the other hand, then the being in question would have known that you would take both, in which case she would have put nothing in box A and $1,000 in box B. If you were to take both boxes, therefore, you would get $1,000. So if you were to take just box A you would get $1,000,000, and if you were to take both boxes you would get $1,000. Obviously, then, you ought to take just box A.

But there seems an equally plausible argument on the other side. For the money in the boxes has been there for a long time—eighty years, let's say. So if in fact there is $1,001,000 in those boxes, then there is nothing you can do now to alter that fact. So if there is $1,001,000 there, then if you were to take both boxes, you'd get $1,001,000. On the other hand, if there is $1,001,000 there, then if you were to take just box A, you would get only $1,000,000, thus missing out on the extra $1,000. So if there is $1,001,000 there, you would get more if you took both boxes than if you took only one. But a similar argument shows that the same holds if there is just $1,000 there; in that case you'd get $1,000 if you took both boxes but nothing at all if you took just box A. The only prudent course, then, is to take both boxes.

Now the fact is, as I think, that neither of these arguments is conclusive; each takes as a premiss a proposition not obviously true and not entailed by the puzzle conditions. Thus the 'two-boxer' appears to argue that if there is $1,001,000 there, then it follows that if you were to take both boxes, there (still) would have been $1,001,000 there. But of course that doesn't follow; the argument form '*A*: therefore, if *P* were true *A* would be true' is invalid. Or perhaps he argues that, since it is true that if there were $1,001,000 there and you were to take both boxes, you would get $1,001,000, it follows that if there were $1,001,000 there, then if you were to take both boxes, you would get $1,001,000. But that doesn't follow either; exportation doesn't hold for counter-factuals. The one-boxer, I think, has a better time of it. He does claim, however, that if you were to take both boxes, then the being in question would have known that you'd take both boxes; but of course this isn't entailed by the puzzle conditions. The best we can say is that it is *probable*, relative to the puzzle conditions, that if you were to take both, then she would have known that you would take both. This is the best we can say; but can we say even as much as that? How does one determine the probability of such a counter-factual on the basis of such evidence as the puzzle conditions provide?

But suppose we strengthen the puzzle conditions. Suppose it isn't just some knowledgeable being with a splendid track record that puts the money in the boxes, but God. Suppose furthermore, that God is omniscient; and add one of the following further conditions (in order of decreasing strength): God is essentially omniscient; God is omniscient in every world in which you exist; God is omniscient both in the worlds in which you take just box A and the worlds in which you take both; God's being omniscient is counter-factually independent of your decision, so that God would have been omniscient if you were to take box A and would have been omniscient if you were to take both boxes. Add also that the other puzzle conditions are counter-factually independent of your actions. Then there is a knock-down drag-out argument for taking just box A (and no decent argument at all for taking both). For then both

(35) If you were to take both boxes, then God would have believed that you would take both boxes

and

(36) If you were to take both boxes and God had believed that you would take both boxes, then God would have put nothing in box A

follow from the puzzle conditions; from (35) and (36) it follows by counter-factual logic that

(37) If you were to take both boxes, then God would have put nothing in box A;

and from (37) (together with the puzzle conditions) it follows that, if you were to take both boxes, then you'd get only $1,000. But a precisely similar argument shows that, if you were to take just box A, you'd get $1,000,000. So if you were to take just box A, you would get a lot more money than you would if you were to take both. This argument will be resisted only by those whose intellects are clouded by unseemly greed.

But something further follows. The puzzle conditions, thus strengthened, seem possible. But they entail that there is a true proposition *p* strictly about the past and an action you can perform such that, if you were to perform it, then *p* would have been false. For suppose in fact that you will take both boxes, so that in fact

(38) There was only $1,000 there eighty years ago

is true. According to the puzzle conditions, it is within your power to take just box A; but they also entail that, if you were to take just box A, then (38) would have been false. (38), however, is strictly about the past; hence there is a proposition strictly about the past that is not necessary *per accidens*.

So here are a couple of propositions—(34) and (38)—that are hard facts about the past, but are not accidentally necessary. Of course there will be many more. It is possible (though no doubt unlikely) that there is something you can do such that if you were to do it, then Abraham would never have existed. For perhaps you will be confronted with a decision of great importance—so important that one of the alternatives is such that if you were to choose *it*, then the course of human history would have been quite different from what in fact it is. Furthermore, it is possible that if God had foreseen that you would choose *that* alternative, he would have acted very differently. Perhaps he would have created different persons; perhaps, indeed, he would not have created Abraham. So it is possible that there is an action such that it is within your power to perform it and such that if you were to perform it, then God would not have created Abraham. But if indeed that *is* possible, then not even the proposition *Abraham once existed* is accidentally necessary in the sense of (31). By the same sort of reasoning we can see that it is possible (though no doubt monumentally unlikely) that there is something you can do such that if you were to do it, then Caesar would not have crossed the Rubicon and the Peloponnesian War would never have occurred.

It follows, then, that even such hard facts about the past as that Abraham once existed, and that there was once a war between the Spartans and Athenians, are not accidentally necessary in the sense of (31). Indeed, it is not easy to think of *any* contingent facts about the past that are accidentally necessary in that sense. Of course, there are limits to the sorts of propositions such that it is possibly within my power so to act that they would have been false. It is not possible, for example, for there to be an action I can perform such that, if I were to do so, then I would never have existed.[22] But even if it is necessarily not within *my* power so to act that I would not have existed, the same does not go for *you*; perhaps there is an action you can take which is such that, if you were to take it, then I would not have existed. (I should therefore like to ask you to tread softly.) Neither of us (nor anyone else) could have the power so to act that there should never have been any (contingently existing) agents; clearly it is not possible that there be an action *A* some (contingently existing) person could perform such that if he were to do so, then there would never have been any contingent agents. So the proposition 'There have been (contingent) agents' is accidentally necessary; but it is hard indeed to find any stronger propositions that are both logically contingent and accidentally necessary.

IV POWER OVER THE PAST

The notion of accidental necessity explained as in (31) is, I think, a relevant notion for the discussion of the arguments for theological determinism from the necessity of the past; for the question at issue is often, indeed ordinarily, put as the question which propositions about the past are such that their truth entails that it is not within anyone's power so to act that they would have been false. Accidental necessity as thus explained, however, does little to illumine our deep intuitive beliefs about the asymmetry of past and future—the fact that the future is within our control in a way in which the past is not; for far too few propositions turn out to be accidentally necessary.[23] What is the root of these beliefs, and

[22] Every action is necessarily such that, if I were to perform it, I would have existed; so if there were such an action, it would be such that, if I were to perform it, then I would have both existed and not existed.

[23] We might be inclined to broaden (31) as follows:

(31*) *P* is accidentally necessary at *t* if and only if *p* is true at *t* and there is no action *A* and person *S* such that if *S* were to perform *A*, then *p* would have been false.

(31*) is indeed broader than (31). First, it is clearly necessary that any proposition satisfying the *definiens* of (31) also satisfies the *definiens* of (31*). Second, it seems possible that there be a true proposition *p* such that, while indeed it is *possible* that there be a person *S* and an action *A* such that *S* can perform *A* and such that if *S* were to perform *A*, then *p* would have been true, as a matter of fact there is no such person and action. It is therefore possible that there be a proposition that is

what is the relevant asymmetry between past and future? Is it just that the scope of our power with respect to the past is vastly more limited than that of our power with respect to the future? That is, is it just that there are far fewer propositions about the past than about the future which are such that I can so act that they would have been false? I doubt that this is an important part of the story, simply because we really know very little about how far our power with respect to either past or future extends. With few exceptions, I do not know which true propositions about the past are such that I can so act that they would have been false; and the same goes for true propositions about the future.

So suppose we look in a different direction. Possibly there is something I can do such that, if I were to do it, then Abraham would not have existed; but it is not possible—is it?—that I now *cause* Abraham not to have existed. While it may be within Paul's power so to act that the colony of ants would not have moved in last Saturday, surely it is not within his power now—or for that matter within God's power now—to *cause* it to be true that the colony did not move in. Perhaps we should revise our definition of accidental necessity to say that a proposition is (now) accidentally necessary if it is true, and also such that its truth entails that it is not (now) within anyone's power (not even God's) to cause it to be false. And perhaps we could then see the relevant asymmetry between past and future as the fact that true propositions strictly about the past—unlike their counterparts about the future—are accidentally necessary in this new sense.

The right answer, I suspect, lies in this direction; but the suggestion involves a number of profound perplexities—about agent causation, the analysis of causation, whether backwards causation is possible, the relation between causation and counterfactuals—that I cannot explore here. Let us instead briefly explore a related suggestion. In our first sense of accidental necessity, a proposition p is accidentally necessary if and only if p is true and such that it is not possible that p be true and there be an agent and

accidentally necessary in the sense of (31*) but not in the sense of (31). The problem with (31*), however, is a close relative of the problem with (31); under (31*) there will be far too few (contingent) propositions such that *we have any reason to think* them accidentally necessary.

an action such that (1) the agent is now or will in the future be able to perform the action and (2) if he were to do so, the *p* would have been false. Then such propositions as 'Abraham existed in 1995 BC' turn out not to be accidentally necessary because of the possibility of divine foreknowledge and, so to speak, divine fore-co-operation. Perhaps, if I were to do *A*, then God would have foreseen that I would do *A* and would not have created Abraham. My doing *A*, however, is not by *itself* sufficient for Abraham's not existing; it requires God's previous co-operation. So suppose we strengthen the counter-factual involved in the above definition; suppose we say:

(39) *p* is accidentally necessary at *t* if and only if *p* is true at *t* and it is not possible both that *p* is true at *t* and that there exists an action *A* and an agent *S* such that (1) *S* has the power at *t* or later to perform *A*, and (2) *necessarily* if *S* were to perform *A* at *t* or later, then *p* would have been false.

While it may be within Paul's power to do something—namely, mow his lawn—such that, if he were to do so, then that colony of ants would not have moved in, his performing that action does not *entail* the falsehood of the proposition that the ants did move in; and it looks as if there is nothing he or anyone can do that does entail its falsehood.

Permit me a couple of comments on this definition. First, although it involves the idea of a proposition's being true at a time, it is easily revised (as are (42) and (44) below) so as to accommodate our atemporalist friends. Second, I am thinking of the notion of an *agent*, as it enters into the definition, broadly, in such a way as to include agents of all sorts; in particular it is to include God. Third, propositions that are necessary in the broadly logical sense turn out accidentally necessary. Fourth, accidental necessity thus characterized is closed under entailment but not under conjunction. Fifth, many contingent propositions about the past turn out to be accidentally necessary, but so do some contingent propositions about the future. And finally, Ockham's claim that necessity *per accidens* is connected with what is strictly about the past seems to be vindicated on (39); barring a couple of complications, it looks as if a logically contingent proposition about the past is accidentally necessary in the sense of (39) if and only if it is true and strictly about the past. So, for example,

(40) Eighty years ago, the sentence 'Paul will mow his lawn in 1995' expressed the proposition 'Paul will mow his lawn in 1995' and expressed a truth

is true (let's suppose), but not strictly about the past. Here there is indeed something someone can do that entails its falsehood: Paul can mow his lawn in 1985. But it is not possible that there be an action Paul (or anyone) can or will be able to perform such that his performing it entails that

(41) Paul didn't mow his lawn in 1984

is false. We may thus say, with Ockham, that propositions strictly about the past are accidentally necessary; and the relevant asymmetry between past and future is just that contingent propositions strictly about the past are accidentally necessary, while their colleagues about the future typically are not.

Unfortunately, there is a residual perplexity. For what shall we count, here, as *actions*? Suppose it is in fact within Paul's power so to act that the ants would not have moved in; isn't there such an action as *bringing it about that the ants would not have moved in* or *so acting that the ants would not have moved in*? If there is (and why not?) then it is both an action he can perform and one such that his performing it entails that the ants did not move in; but then 'The ants moved in' is not accidentally necessary after all. Here what we need, clearly enough, is the idea of a *basic* action, what an agent can in some sense do *directly*. *Moving my arm*, perhaps, would be such an action; starting a world war, or so acting that the ants would not have moved in, would not. Let's say that an action is one I can *directly* perform if it is one I can perform without having to perform some other action in order to perform it. Starting a war would not be an action I can directly perform; I cannot start a war without doing something like pushing a button, pulling a trigger, or making a declaration. According to Roderick Chisholm, the only actions I can directly perform are *undertakings*.[24]

[24] Roderick Chisholm, *Person and Object* (LaSalle, 1976), p. 85. Chisholm's powerful discussion of agency (pp. 53–88 and 159–74) should be required reading

I can't, for example, raise my arm without trying or endeavouring or undertaking to do so; more exactly (as Chisholm points out[25]), I can't raise it without undertaking to do *something*—scratch my ear, for example. I am inclined to think he is right: more generally, I can't perform an action which is not itself an undertaking, without undertaking some action or other. (What I say below, however, does not depend on this claim.) But he is also right in thinking that undertakings are not undertaken. If so, however, it will follow that the only actions I can directly perform are undertakings.

Now some actions I can perform are such that my undertaking to perform them and my body's being in normal conditions are together causally sufficient for my performing them; raising my hand and moving my feet would be an example. 'Normal conditions' here, includes, among other things, the absence of pathological conditions, as well as the absence of such external hindrances as being locked in a steamer trunk or having my hands tied behind my back. Of course more should be said here, but this will have to suffice for now. Let us say, then, that an action *A* is a basic action for a person *S* if and only if there is an action *A** that meets two conditions: first, *S* can directly perform *A**, and secondly, *S*'s being in normal conditions and his directly performing *A** is causally sufficient for his performing *A*. Then we may revise (39) by appropriately inserting '*A* is basic for *S*':

(42) *p* is accidentally necessary at *t* if and only if *p* is true at *t* and it is not possible both that *p* is true at *t* and that there exists an agent *S* and an action *A* such that (1) *A* is basic for *S*, (2) *S* has the power at *t* or later to perform *A*, and (3) necessarily if *S* were to perform *A* at *t* or later, then *p* would have been false.

There is one more complication.[26]

for anyone interested in that topic. (Chisholm does not use the term 'directly perform', and I am not here using the term 'basic action' in just the way he does.)

[25] Ibid., p. 57.

[26] Called to my attention by Edward Wierenga, to whom I am especially grateful for penetrating comments on an ancestor of this paper. I am grateful for similar favours to many others, including Lawrence Powers, Alfred Freddoso, Mark

(43) God foreknew that Smith and Jones will not freely co-operate in mowing the lawn

should not turn out to be accidentally necessary; but on (42) it does. The problem is that (42) does not properly accommodate co-operative ventures freely undertaken; it must be generalized to take account of multiple agency. This is easily enough accomplished:

(44) *p* is accidentally necessary at *t* if and only if *p* is true at *t* and it is not possible both that *p* is true at *t* and that there exist agents $S_1. \ldots, S_n$ and actions $A_1, \ldots, A_n$ such that (1) A_i is basic for S_i, (2) S_i has the power at *t* or later to perform A_i, and (3) necessarily, if every S_i were to perform A_i at *t* or later, then *p* would have been false.[27]

And now we may say perhaps, that the way in which the future but not the past is within our control is that contingent propositions strictly about the past are accidentally necessary, while those about the future typically are not.

By way of summary and conclusion, then: the two main arguments for the incompatibility of divine foreknowledge with

Heller, Peter van Inwagen, William Alston, David Vriend, the members of the Calvin College Tuesday Colloquium, and especially Nelson Pike.

[27] Again, (44) can obviously be recast so as to accommodate our atemporalist colleagues. What I claim for (44) is that propositions strictly about the past are accidentally necessary in the sense of (44), while their colleagues about the future typically are not; I do not claim that (44) is a satisfactory general analysis of our pre-analytic notion of accidental necessity. So taken, it is subject to counter-examples of various kinds, incuding propositions of the form *PVQ*, where *P* is a false contingent proposition strictly about the past and *Q* is a future proposition to the effect that some free agent *A* will perform some action (an action that is within *A*'s power). I think we do indeed *have* a general pre-analytic notion of accidental necessity, although there are some hard puzzle cases, and the issues get complicated. Allow me to venture the following as a first approximation: say that *p* is *past* accidentally necessary if and only if *p* is a proposition about the past (not necessarily strictly about the past) and *p* is accidentally necessary in the sense of (44); and let *P* be a conjunction of the past necessary propositions.
Then

(44*) *p* is accidentally necessary *simpliciter* if and only if *p* is true and it is not possible that both (*a*) *P* but no proposition properly entailing *P* is past accidentally necessary, and (*b*) there is a past accidentally necessary proposition *q*, an agent *S* and an action *A* such that (1) *A* is basic for *S*, (2) *S* can perform *A* at *t* or later, and (3) necessarily, if *q* is true and *S* were to perform *A*, then *p* would have been false.

human freedom are both failures. The Ockhamite claim that not all propositions about the past are hard facts about the past seems correct; among those that are not hard facts would be propositions specifying God's (past) foreknowledge of future human actions, as well as propositions specifying God's ((past) foreknowledge of future human actions, as well as propositions specifying God's) past beliefs about future human actions, if God is essentially omniscient. Only hard facts about the past, however, are plausibly thought to be accidentally necessary; hence neither God's foreknowledge nor God's forebelief poses a threat to human freedom. Accidental necessity is a difficult notion, but can be explained in terms of the power of agents. The initially plausible account of accidental necessity ((31)) is defective as an account of the intuitively obvious asymmetry between past and future; for far too few propositions turn out to be accidentally necessary on that account. (44), however, is more satisfying.

10

ON THE COMPOSSIBILITY OF THE DIVINE ATTRIBUTES

DAVID BLUMENFELD

Credo quia ineptum
TERTULLIAN

RECENT proponents of the ontological argument have learned an important lesson from Leibniz: the argument requires the assumption, or premiss, that God is possible. In one form or another this premiss appears in the versions of the argument endorsed by Hartshorne, Malcolm, and Plantinga.[1] But Leibniz's lesson has not been taken fully to heart by his modern followers. He thinks that to bring the argument to a triumphant conclusion one needs to *prove* that God is possible. For without this proof, we have no assurance that the idea of God is noncontradictory.[2] So Leibniz struggled—vainly I think—to produce two proofs of the possibility of God.[3] His modern followers, however, have on the whole simply assumed the truth of the critical premiss.[4] The fact that there has been relatively little effort to show that the concept of God is not coherent probably contributes to whatever plausibility

Reprinted with permission from, *Philosophical Studies*, Vol. 34, No. 1, July 1978, pp. 91–103, copyright © 1978 by D. Reidel Publishing Company.

[1] Charles Hartshorne, *Man's Vision of God* (Chicago, 1941), ch. 9; Norman Malcolm, 'Anselm's Ontological Arguments', *Philosophical Review* 69 (1960), pp. 41–62; Alvin Plantinga, *The Nature of Necessity* (Oxford, 1974), ch. 10.

[2] E.g. *New Essays Concerning Human Understanding*, tr. A. G. Langley (LaSalle, 1949), p. 504; and *The Philosophical Works of Leibniz*, tr. G. M. Duncan (New Haven, 1890), pp. 50–1, 140–5.

[3] *New Essays Concerning Human Understanding*, p. 714; and *Philosophical Works*, pp. 145–6.

[4] This is true of Malcolm and Plantinga, but not of Hartshorne, who has given an elaborate defence of the coherence of his own conception of God. His notion of deity differs from the one attacked in this essay, however. References listed in note 1 above.

this procedure has.[5] But, plausible or not, the procedure is mistaken. The concept of God is contradictory—as I shall argue shortly. Establishing this would have consequences that go beyond the ontological argument: the entire edifice of orthodox natural theology would fall at a stroke.[6]

In arguing that the idea of God is contradictory, it is important to be clear about *what* idea of God I have in mind. My target is the standard Judaeo-Christian theological conception of divinity, a being who is by definition absolutely perfect. 'Absolute perfection' is to be taken in a sense strong enough to involve the properties of omniscience, omnipotence, and complete moral goodness. The idea of an absolutely perfect being is that of one who knows all things, has unrestricted power, possesses the maximum amount of virtue, and is free of any sort of defect or limitation. There have been other accounts of deity, and the argument I am going to propose does not apply to all of them. One cannot refute, with a single argument, the existence of such diverse Gods as have been conceived. God has, for example, sometimes been said to be limited in his power, or finite in some other way. Those who are content with such a deity need not be concerned with the present argument. God has also sometimes been identified with the universe (or at other times with 'being itself'). But it is, of course, not my aim to show that the idea of the universe contains a contradiction. My argument concerns nothing less than the greatest deity which has ever been conceived, and my purpose is to show that this deity has not been conceived coherently.

It will be instructive to ask, initially, what would be required if one were trying to prove the *possibility* of God. To accomplish this one would need to do two things. First, one would have to show that each perfection has an intrinsic maximum. It is supposed to be essential to divinity to be unsurpassably great. Therefore, to establish God's possibility one would need to show that there is no

[5] Some exceptions should be noted. For example, see N. J. Findlay, 'Can God's Existence Be Disproved?', *Mind*, vol. 57 (1948), pp. 108–18; and Norman Kretzmann, 'Omniscience and Immutability', *Journal of Philosophy* 53 (1966), pp. 409–21. Charles Hartshorne has also argued at numerous places that the classical conception of God is contradictory.

[6] The qualification 'orthodox' is important here. Heterodox natural theology—including variants of the ontological argument—would remain possible.

great-making characteristic which is such that, for any amount of it one possessed, it would be logically possible to possess more. Second, one who sought to prove the possibility of God would have to show that all of the perfections—in their maximum—are compossible. Not only must there *be* a maximum of knowledge, power, goodness, and so on; there must be no contradiction in the idea of a single being's possessing these properties at once. These requirements suggest two corresponding avenues for proving the impossibility of God. One could show that there is some perfection which has no intrinsic maximum, or he could prove that there are perfections which could not be possessed, in the ultimate degree, by a single being. It is the latter strategy which I shall employ. I shall argue that maximal knowledge and power are not compossible. Since a critical point in the argument turns on the elucidation of the idea of omniscience, let me begin there.

I

Knowledge is a good thing, a perfection. There is no state of knowledge, which, *qua* knowledge, is bad or merely neutral in value. This is a thesis that has been held by most theological writers, and it is one which makes great sense. Apart from being intuitively appealing, however, it is a view which is basic to the traditional conception of God, and it cannot be given up without relinquishing that concept. If knowledge as such were not a good thing, it would not follow from the nature of God as absolutely perfect being that he is omniscient. But what is an omniscient being? It is one who has unsurpassable knowledge. To have this degree of knowledge, one would have to have an utter and complete comprehension of the meaning of every significant proposition. If there were any significant proposition, any part of the meaning of which a being did not comprehend, his knowledge clearly could be greater. To enjoy a state of omniscience, however, one would have to know considerably more than just this. To be *all*-knowing, one would have to know of every true proposition that it is true and of every false proposition that it is false. If a being fully understood the meaning of every proposition, but failed to know the truth value of even one of these propositions, his knowledge, again, clearly could be greater. But if there were a being who fully comprehended the meaning of every significant proposition and who also knew of the true that it is true, and the false that it is false, this being would surely possess an understanding unlimited in its scope. He would be omniscient.

The first step in my argument is to show that there are certain concepts, a full and complete comprehension of which requires experience. I shall then go on to argue that, in the case of at least some of these concepts, the experience which is required is of a type which an omnipotent being could not possibly have. Since a being who did not fully comprehend the meaning of every significant proposition would not be omniscient, it will follow that omniscience and omnipotence are not properties which are compossible.

Now it is evident that there are concepts which one could not understand *completely* if one had never had experience of an instance or exemplification of the concept in question. This is a thesis which is sometimes labelled 'concept empiricism', and it is important to see that I am going to rely on it in an extremely restricted form. The doctrine has been put forward in a variety of different degrees of strength and I believe that all but the most restricted is false. For example, one would be a concept empiricist if one held the following view: for every concept, in order to comprehend it, one must have experienced an instance or exemplification of it. This doctrine is palpably false. One can surely understand the concept *aardvark* without having had the pleasure of the acquaintance of the beast. A considerably more plausible version of concept empiricism is this: for every concept, in order to comprehend it, one must have experienced an instance or exemplification of each of its 'elements'. The idea behind this view is familiar. To have the concept *aardvark*, without being acquainted with an actual aardvark, it would be enough to have experienced (separately) something mammalian, something with an extensile tongue, something with sharp claws, a heavy tail, etc. Or, it would do to have had the experience, not of these things, but of their elements. From the elements one could construct the concept *aardvark* by appropriate mental operations. Now, I am inclined to think that this theory is mistaken too. But if anyone believes it is correct, that is so much the better for my argument, which requires a view that is considerably weaker than this one.

The thesis I rely on is this: for *some* concepts, in order *fully* to comprehend them, one must have had the experience of an instance or exemplification of them. This version of concept empiricism seems to me to be as obviously true as it is obvious that the very strong version of it is false. There is a host of concepts which require experience for their complete comprehension. Take the concept of the sensation of red. Surely one could not fully grasp this notion if one had never had an experience of redness. I do not say that one needs to experience a red *object*. One might come to understand the concept by pushing one's eyeball and getting the appropriate sensation in that way. But I do say that without any acquaintance with redness, one could not fully comprehend *the sensation of red*. The reason for this is that part of the meaning of the concept consists of a certain subjective experience. One who failed to understand fully what this experience is like would thus lack a perfect grasp of its concept. But there is only one way of fully understanding what an experience of redness is like and that is to have it. There is in principle no access which allows a complete comprehension of an experience except having the experience itself. It is, therefore, a necessary truth that if someone had never experienced redness, there would be at least one concept whose meaning he did not fully understand.

I am not denying that such a person could know a large number of true propositions about the sensation of red. He could know, for example, that it is produced under conditions *Q*, *R*, and *S*, that it is correlated with (or, on some views contingently identical to) brain states of types *X*, *Y*, and *Z*, and so on. Perhaps it could be said that this information would give him a partial grasp of *the sensation of red*. But he could not have an *absolutely complete* grasp of this concept without having had the sensation itself.

Many philosophers would maintain that God does not know by experience, and that he does not have an acquaintance with sensuous contents such as red. One argument that has been offered is that God's perfection entails that he is immutable and that, as such, he is not subject to the changes involved in the process of experience. This thesis may be correct, and though many have held it, few have been willing to draw from it the conclusion that God is not omniscient.[7] Yet this conclusion does follow from the thesis. For if it is true that God cannot have any experiences, then there are concepts (viz., those that *require* experience) whose full comprehension he is barred from having. But this line of argument would need considerable defence, and I shall not rest my case upon it. I use the example of the sensation of red merely to support weak concept empiricism. For my purposes, it can be allowed that God can have this experience, and hence that he can also have a full understanding of its concept.

Granting this, however, there are without doubt *some* experiences which God is precluded from having. For certain experiences are possible only if the subject believes that he is limited in power. Since these experiences are required for a full grasp of a number of concepts, it follows that a being who is omnipotent cannot also be omniscient. To make this out, let us first consider some experiences which God could not have. Fear, frustration, and despair are a few examples. The reason I offer for denying that God ever could be subject to these states is not simply that they are experiences. It is rather that their occurrence depends logically on the subject's believing in the limitation of his power. It is important to observe that none of these states is a mere sensation (like an itch or a stinging pain), which could occur in the absence of certain special beliefs that one had. To experience fear, a person would have to believe that he was in danger, that he might somehow be harmed. If he did not in any sense believe this, then no sensation he was having—no cold chill, no sinking feeling in the pit of the stomach—would count as fear. One's experiences would be mere sensations—and nothing more. Without the belief in danger, these states would have to be described in terms other than those which imply that the person is afraid. A similar account can be given of frustration and of despair. There could be no experience of frustration without the belief that one had been (was being, or might be) thwarted. There could be no sense of despair unless a person faced a situation he took to be dire, and for which he

[7] Kretzmann, 'Omniscience and Immutability', does draw this conclusion, though his reasons are quite different from the ones offered here.

believed he was very unlikely to find a remedy. Furthermore, a person who has not undergone these states would not know what it is like to experience them. Consequently he would not have a full understanding of *fear*, *frustration*, and *despair*. A man who had never experienced fear, for example, would lack a complete comprehension of *fear*, just as a man who was blind from birth would lack a full grasp of *the sensation of red*.

My point should now be clear. For what has an omnipotent being to fear? There is no destruction, no harm, nor the slightest diminution of his power that could possibly befall him. In this case (since he knows the extent of his power) he could not believe himself to be endangered, and thus could not have the experience of fear. But if he could not have this experience, he lacks a full appreciation of *fear*. Any proposition involving this concept will be one, at least a part of whose meaning he does not comprehend. He is therefore not omniscient.

Similarly, how could an absolutely perfect and omnipotent being experience frustration? He is all-powerful, and so there is no conceivable obstacle to his will. Whatever he wills, he accomplishes. There is nothing which could conceivably thwart him, or interfere with his divine plan. Since he knows this, there is nothing which could provide him with the occasion to feel frustration. But then he lacks a full comprehension of *frustration*, and so once again fails to be omniscient.

The same can be said of despair. He who is incapable of being thwarted, and who possesses the power to remedy any situation, is of necessity beyond the experience of despair. And for this reason again there is something he cannot fully understand, something he cannot know.

The concepts I have mentioned are only a few in a large family of notions which an omnipotent being could not entirely understand. In general, for every experience whose occurrence presupposes a person's belief that he is lacking in power there is a concept of which God cannot have complete comprehension. *Embarrassment*, *apprehensiveness*, *forlornness*, and *regret* are all further notions of this type. In view of this there appears to be a great deal that an omnipotent being could not understand.

II

There are three possible strategies for attempting to refute my argument. First, one might deny that the kind of experience which God is barred from having is required for knowledge of the concepts I have mentioned. Second, one might concede that this experience is required, but deny that God must have a full grasp of every concept in order to be absolutely perfect. Third, one might give reasons for supposing God *can* have the kind of experience (and consequently the knowledge) which I have said is not open to him. I will take up each of these strategies in turn.

Let us look at the possibilities for developing the first one. If it were not necessary to have the experience of fear, frustration, and despair to have a full comprehension of the concepts of these states my argument would fail. But, as I have already tried to show, the experience *is* required. One who had never felt afraid would necessarily lack what might be called an 'existential appreciation' of fear. Yet there is one venerable doctrine which denies that any such existential appreciation is even a partial component of knowledge: Platonism. For the Platonist, knowledge is purely intellectual (and not sensuous) apprehension. Whatever is known is known by grasping abstract ideas or forms. Experience may stimulate us to recollect these forms, but that is all. It is in no way essential to knowledge.

I concede that if Platonism were true, this would destroy my position. But Platonism (or at any rate the extreme version of it required here) is false. Because this theory has long since been reduced to a totally antique system of thought, I shall not treat it as a live option. Should anyone think that it is wrong to dismiss this view so cursorily, I cannot attempt to satisfy him now. Ultimately, I should have to repeat arguments which have already been repeated for centuries, and which would be out of place to review in this context.

Not every doctrine which would undercut my position is antique, however. Modern philosophical behaviourism is at odds with it too. According to this theory there is no such thing as the *experience* of fear, frustration, and despair over and above a set of complex dispositions to behave in certain ways. But to comprehend fully a disposition to behave, one need not have had this disposition oneself. So, to comprehend fully fear, God need not be afraid. Nor need he ever be frustrated or despairing in order to understand the concepts of these states. If the behaviourist account is correct, one can have a purely intellectual understanding of all psychological concepts.

Now I grant that the behaviourist will not be impressed by my proof of the impossibility of God. But this fact can be of no comfort to the theist, since behaviourism itself provides a proof of the impossibility of God. If this theory were true, then to have any thoughts, or other mental states, God would have to have a body. On the behaviourist view, the notion of a pure spirit is every bit as much an absurdity as the idea of a purely subjective experience. In accepting behaviourism, then, one surrenders the right to believe in the immateriality of God. As traditionally conceived, however, the absolute perfection of God requires that he be immaterial. For God's perfection is taken to exclude even the logically possibility of deterioration—a feature which is essential to material things. Thus behaviourism provides a way of denying a premiss of my argument, but not of evading its conclusion. It is not a theory which leaves the concept of God intact.[8]

Another way of trying to get around my argument is through the doctrine of analogy. This theory cautions us not to suppose that God possesses the traits of knowledge, power, and goodness in the same sense as we do. Since God has these traits only in an analogical sense, there is no licence to infer that his knowledge has such and such features from the fact that knowledge as we commonly understand it has these features. Yet did I not make just this sort of inference? I said that, in order to understand *despair*, God would have to be despairing. And I based this on the claim that we humans cannot fully comprehend this concept in any other way.

In fact, however, this rebuttal misrepresents my argument. I did not make an inference from the limits of our knowledge to the

[8] It is of interest to note that the Platonist and the behaviourist reject my position for opposite reasons. For the behaviourist, subjective experience is too ethereal to be real. For the Platonist, it is insufficiently ethereal to be *fully* real, or to constitute any part of true knowledge.

limits of God's knowledge. I argued, rather, that it is in principle impossible for anyone—human or divine—fully to grasp *despair* without having had an experience of despair. And, I tried to show that God could not have this experience, since he is precluded from having the beliefs on which it is predicated. The theist cannot counter this merely by asserting that God knows things in a way which is different from, but analogous to, ours. To refute my argument he must explicate the analogy, making clear how God can fully appreciate *despair*, etc. without ever being despairing.

The first suggestion that comes to mind is that God gains this appreciation by having an experience which is analogous to the ones we are discussing. As we have seen, however, the experience of despair requires the belief that one faces a situation that one cannot remedy. Is it the case that God comprehends *despair* by having a belief which is analogous to this one? What would such a belief be? If it were of the same sort as ours, it would be false: God can remedy any situation. In that case, we seem forced to conclude that God has a belief which is analogous to a false one. Yet it is not clear that any sense can be attached to this idea. For what would a belief be which did not have the property, *being false*, but instead had the property, *being analogous to being false*?

Perhaps this is not the correct way of constructing the analogy. Possibly the idea is that God is in a state which is like despair but which involves no beliefs. The concept of despair, however, is so intimately tied to a belief in the hopelessness of one's situation that it is not obvious what to make of this suggestion either. And, even if we could make sense of it, the problem would remain that the experience of despair is a sign of imperfection. We should then apparently have to suppose that God knows *despair* by being in a condition analogous to something imperfect. Yet only pure perfections can be attributed to God, and so it is not evident how this would be possible.

Another alternative is that God does not know *despair* through an experience, but through something analogous to an experience. This suggestion, however, is no easier to understand than the ones that have preceded it. It is altogether obscure how an experience could be analogous to a non-experience. Although further problems could be enumerated, I think the ones already at hand strongly suggest the unlikelihood of our constructing a clear analogy here at all.

III

The second strategy is to argue that although the experience of states like fear is necessary for a comprehension of their correlative concepts, it is not required that God have the concepts in order to be absolutely perfect. An argument on behalf of this thesis is as follows. I have claimed that one who knows that he is all-powerful cannot be afraid, and for that reason cannot have a full grasp of concepts such as *fear*. If this argument is correct, however, it follows that anyone who has a full grasp of *fear*, etc. is less than absolutely perfect. But then, it seems, the possession of such concepts cannot be a necessary condition of one's being absolutely perfect. For surely it cannot be a necessary condition of one's *being perfect* that one be in a state which would guarantee that one is less than perfect. Consequently, there is no reason to suppose that God must have a full grasp of the concepts on which I have based my case.

The problem with this argument is that it begs the question. To infer that God need not possess certain concepts from the fact that their possession signifies a defect assumes that their possession could not also be required for absolute perfection. It assumes, in other words, that God is possible. After all, if the lack of these concepts signified a defect too, then God would be imperfect in either case. And this is precisely what the argument I gave was designed to show: imperfection of one kind or another follows whether God has concepts like *fear* or lacks them.

What would have to be established to make the present line of response work is that, while God's possession of the critical concepts would imply a defect in him, his failure to possess them would not. Within the limits of the current strategy, however, there is no way to argue this effectively. The second strategy—unlike the first—concedes that experience of a sort which God cannot have is required for the full possession of certain concepts. But if knowledge *per se* is a perfection, then anything less than full comprehension of every concept constitutes an epistemic defect in a being.

Of course, it might conceivably be denied that knowledge *per se* is a perfection. This would allow one to maintain that a perfect being need not have a complete grasp of every concept, and on this basis one might argue that God's perfection does not require that he fully understand the notions which are in dispute. As I noted earlier, however, this would have the undesirable consequence of robbing God of his essential omniscience. If knowledge *per se* were not a perfection, God's total and complete knowledge would not follow from his definition as absolutely perfect being.[9]

A remaining option is to argue that a being is *better*, all in all, if he is omnipotent, and thus lacks certain concepts, than he would be if he had a full grasp of every concept, but were to some extent impotent. This might be thought to show that the most perfect being does not need to have a full understanding of every concept. Now I do not know what good reason could be offered for ranking power over knowledge in the scale of perfection. But in any case it is clear that this particular ploy is flawed in the same way as the last. Even if power were better than knowledge, the manoeuvre would divest God of his omniscience, thus leaving us without the traditional notion of deity.

IV

The third way of attacking my position is to argue that God actually can have the sorts of experiences which I have said are precluded by his perfect nature. The reason that I offered for thinking that God could not have the experience of fear, etc., is that his power is absolute, and knowing this, he would be incapable of having the beliefs on which this experience is founded. One might hope to undo my argument by showing that God is capable of having the requisite beliefs after all. The problem, however, is that the presence of these beliefs is itself

[9] This manoeuvre would also place the theist in the following embarrassing position: it would force him to admit that in creating this world—which contains abundant amounts of fear, frustration, and the like—God did not fully understand what he was doing.

indicative of imperfection; if God is omnipotent, the beliefs are *false*. So there seems to be no way of imagining God's having these beliefs without being tainted by the imperfection that accompanies them.

It might seem more promising to attack the contention that a belief in one's own vulnerability or weakness is required for experiences like fear, frustration, and despair. Perhaps it will be said that, although these experiences are normally accompanied by such beliefs, the beliefs are not logically presupposed by the experiences. Fear might be thought to be a good case in point. Normally one feels afraid only if one believes oneself to be in danger. But occasionally, it seems, one experiences fear even when one does not believe oneself to be in danger—when, in fact, one knows one is completely safe. For example, I may be terribly afraid when I ride the ferris wheel, though I know perfectly well that there is no real danger. Or, sometimes when I am alone at night, I may feel a sudden uneasiness, a sense of fear without any apparent reason. I know that I am not in danger, for I am at home snug in bed. The doors are bolted and the neighbourhood is a very safe one. I am aware that no harm is imminent, and yet I am afraid. These examples seem to indicate that we can on occasion be afraid without believing in the existence of danger. If this is possible in our case, then an omnipotent being should also be able to experience fear without being subject to the false belief that he is in danger.

I do not think this objection is correct. Consider again the examples that were offered in support of the idea that there can be fear without belief in danger. In both of these the suggestion was made that, since I know that I am not in danger, and yet experience fear, there can be fear without a belief in danger. The reasoning is that it follows from the fact that I know that I am not in danger that I believe that I am not in danger. This much is correct. But it does not follow from the fact that I believe that I am not in danger that I do not *also* believe (in some way, or at some level) that I *am* in danger. If someone who rides with me on the ferris wheel tries to calm me with the assurance that there is no danger, I would be very likely to respond, 'I know I won't be hurt, but I just can't shake the idea that I might fall'. Similarly, my belief in the safety of my home does not rule out the possibility of my having a concurrent belief in my endangered position. Indeed, in both cases, if we do not make the assumption that I harbour such a belief, we will be left without the necessary grounds for describing my experience as fear. My belief in danger may not be my 'official' belief, or one which I would take to be well founded. It may not be one which I can easily discern or readily avow. But it is one I must have, if I am to be afraid.

The answer to the objection, then, is this: we can be afraid even though we know we are in no danger because it is possible for us to have inconsistent beliefs. But obviously there is no similar option for explaining how God can be afraid. A being with an absolutely perfect intellect must be incapable of having any false beliefs. *A fortiori*, he must be incapable of having inconsistent beliefs.

Another reply to my argument is that an infinite being can experience all of the states which I deny. He has only to become finite, as God did in Christ. Through the Incarnation God achieved a full grasp of all the concepts involving finitude. This reply, however, presupposes the coherence of faith and does not supply an argument in its behalf. Judged as an answer rather than as a defiant expression of belief, it has no merit. If God is incapable of limitation, then he cannot become finite. To suggest that he *has* done so, without any explanation of the possibility of the miraculous act, is not to advance the case in any way.[10] In response it is sometimes said that, while we cannot comprehend how the infinite makes itself finite, we can comprehend that there is no contradiction involved in the idea. But this, again, is assertion without substantiation. Is it the very same being who is at once both finite and infinite, limited in his powers and infinite? Or is it a different being? If it is a different being, the problem is not resolved. If it is the same being, the contradiction is apparent. It is sometimes said that there is no contradiction in the same being's (i.e., substance's) having two natures or essences. Perhaps not, provided that these two natures are logically compatible. But where the natures are such that one entails that the substance is

[10] The present strategy also involves the theist in heresy. If God can only fully comprehend *fear*, etc. by becoming finite, then the Incarnation was not an act of grace. It was logically required to secure divine omniscience.

omnipotent and infinite, while the other entails that it is limited in its power and finite, the situation is altogether different.

It seems to me, then, that there is a very strong case for supposing that the traditional concept of God is contradictory. Unless someone can show that there is something wrong with the argument I have given, I think it is fair to say that orthodox theists have a rather serious problem on their hands.[11]

[11] This paper is an offshoot of a project for which the research was supported by a fellowship from the National Endowment for the Humanities. For helpful discussions of the issues dealt with here, I wish to thank Louis Mackey, Laurence BonJour, Jean Beer Blumenfeld, and Charles Hartshorne.

VI

ETERNITY, IMMUTABILITY, AND DIVINE SIMPLICITY

II

ETERNITY

ELEONORE STUMP AND NORMAN KRETZMANN

THE concept of eternity makes a significant difference in the consideration of a variety of issues in the philosophy of religion, including, for instance, the apparent incompatibility of divine omniscience with human freedom, of divine immutability with the efficacy of petitionary prayer, and of divine omniscience with divine immutability; but, because it has been misunderstood or cursorily dismissed as incoherent, it has not received the attention it deserves from contemporary philosophers of religion.[1] In this paper we expound the concept as it is presented by Boethius (whose definition of eternity was the *locus classicus* for medieval discussions of the concept), analyse implications of the concept, examine reasons for considering it incoherent, and sample the results of bringing it to bear on issues in the philosophy of religion.

Eternality—the condition of having eternity as one's mode of existence—is misunderstood most often in either of two ways.

Reprinted from, *The Journal of Philosophy*, Vol. LXXVIII, No. 8 (August 1981), pp. 429–458, by permission of the authors and the Managing Editor.

[1] At least one contemporary philosopher of religion has recently turned his attention to the concept of divine eternality in order to reject it as incompatible with biblical theology and, in particular, with the doctrine of divine redemption. 'God the Redeemer cannot be a God eternal. This is so because God the Redeemer is a God who changes' (Nicholas Wolterstorff, 'God Everlasting', in Clifton J. Orlebeke and Lewis B. Smedes (eds.), *God and the Good* (Grand Rapids, Mich., 1975), pp. 181–203, p. 182). (We are grateful to Kenneth Konyndyk for having supplied us with copies of this article, which is obviously highly relevant to our purposes in this paper. The work we are presenting here was substantially complete by the time we had access to Professor Wolterstorff's work.) Although it is no part of our purposes here to discuss Wolterstorff's arguments, it will become clear that we think he is mistaken in his assessment of the logical relationship between the doctrine of divine eternality and other doctrines of orthodox Christianity, including the doctrine of redemption, even in their Biblical formulations. Passages that have been or might be offered in evidence of a Biblical conception of divine eternality include Malachi 3: 6; John 8: 58; James 1: 17.

Sometimes it is confused with limitless duration in time—sempiternality—and sometimes it is construed simply as atemporality, eternity being understood in that case as roughly analogous to an isolated, static instance. The second misunderstanding of eternality is not so far off the mark as the first; but a consideration of the views of the philosophers who contributed most to the development of the concept shows that atemporality alone does not exhaust eternality as they conceived of it, and that the picture of eternity as a frozen instant is a radical distortion of the classic concept.

I BOETHIUS'S DEFINITION

Boethius discusses eternity in two places: *The Consolation of Philosophy*, book 5, prose 6, and *De Trinitate*, chapter 4.[2] The immediately relevant passages are these:

CP:

That God is eternal, then, is the common judgment of all who live by reason. Let us therefore consider what eternity is, for this makes plain to us both the divine nature and knowledge. Eternity, then, is the complete possession all at once of illimitable life. This becomes clearer by comparison with temporal things. For whatever lives in time proceeds as something present from the past into the future, and there is nothing placed in time that can embrace the whole extent of its life equally. Indeed, on the contrary, it does not yet grasp tomorrow but yesterday it has already lost; and even in the life of today you live no more fully than in a mobile, transitory moment. . . . Therefore, whatever includes and possesses the whole fullness of illimitable life at once and is such that nothing future is absent from it and nothing past has flowed away, this is rightly judged to be eternal, and of this it is necessary both that being in full possession of itself it be always present to itself and that it have the infinity of mobile time present [to it]. (*CP*, 422.5–424.31)

DT:

What is said of God, [namely, that] he is always, indeed signifies a unity, as if he had been in all the past, is in all the present—however that might be—[and] will be in all the future. That can be said, according to the philosophers, of the heaven and of the imperishable bodies; but it cannot

[2] Ed. E. K. Rand, in H. F. Stewart, E. K. Rand, and S. J. Tester, *Boethius: The Theological Tractates and The Consolation of Philosophy* (London and Cambridge, Mass., 1973).

be said of God in the same way. For he is always in that for him *always* has to do with present time. And there is this great difference between the present of our affairs, which is *now*, and that of the divine: our now makes time and sempiternity, as if it were running along; but the divine now, remaining, and not moving, and standing still, makes eternity. If you add '*semper*' to 'eternity', you get sempiternity, the perpetual running resulting from the flowing, tireless now. (*DT*, 20.64–22.77)[3]

The definition Boethius presents and explains in *CP* and elucidates in the earlier *DT* is not original with him,[4] nor does he argue for it in those passages.[5] Similarly, we mean to do no more in this section of our paper than to present and explain a concept that has been important in Christian and pre-Christian theology and metaphysics. We will not argue here, for instance, that there is an eternal entity, or even that God must be eternal if he exists. It is a matter of fact that many ancient and medieval philosophers and theologians were committed to the doctrine of God's eternality in the form in which Boethius presents it, and our purpose in this section of the paper is simply to elucidate the doctrine they held.

Boethius's definition is this: *Eternity is the complete possession all at once of illimitable life.*[6]

[3] There are at least two misleading features of this passage. In the first place, Boethius says that God's eternality *always* has to do with present *time*. In the second place, Boethius's etymology of 'sempiternity' is mistaken. '*Sempiternitas*' is an abstract noun constructed directly on '*semper*', somewhat as we might construct 'alwaysness'. His etymology is not only false but misleading, associating 'sempiternity' with 'eternity' in a context in which he has been distinguishing between sempiternity and eternity.

[4] Its elements stem from Parmenides via Plato, and Plotinus had already framed a definition of eternity on which Boethius's seems to have been based. See note 6 below. Cf. Romano Amerio, 'Probabile fonte della nozione boeziana di eternità', *Filosofia* 1 (1950), pp. 365–73.

[5] The argument that is concluded in the last sentence of passage *CP* is based on premisses about God's eternality and omniscience, and is not an argument in support of the definition.

[6] '*Aeternitas igitur est interminabilis vitae tota simul et perfecta possessio*', *De Trinitate*, p. 422.9–11. This definition closely parallels the definition developed by Plotinus in *Enneads* iii 7: 'The life, then, which belongs to that which exists and is in being, all together and full, completely without-extension-or-interval, is what we are looking for, eternity' (A. H. Armstrong (ed.), *Plotinus* (London and Cambridge, Mass., 1967), vol. 3, p. 304.37–39). The way in which Boethius introduces eternity suggests that he considers himself to be presenting a familiar philosophical concept associated with a recognized definition. The parallel between the Plotinian and Boethian definitions is closest in their middle elements: '*zōē*

We want to call attention to four ingredients in this definition. It is clear, first of all, that anything that is eternal has life. In this sense of 'eternal', then, it will not do to say that a number, a truth, or the world is eternal, although one might want to say of the first two that they are atemporal and of the third that it is sempiternal —that it has beginningless, endless temporal existence.[7]

The second and equally explicit element in the definition is illimitability: the life of an eternal being cannot be limited; it is impossible that there be a beginning or an end to it. The natural understanding of such a claim is that the existence in question is infinite duration, unlimited in either 'direction'. But there is another interpretation that must be considered in this context despite its apparent unnaturalness. Conceivably, the existence of an eternal entity is said to be illimitable in the way in which a point or an instant may be said to be illimitable: what cannot be extended cannot be limited in its extent. There are passages that can be read as suggesting that this second interpretation is what Boethius intends. In *CP* eternal existence is expressly contrasted with temporal existence described as extending from the past through the present into the future, and what is eternal is described contrastingly as possessing its entire life *at once*. Boethius's insistence in *DT* that the eternal now is unlike the temporal now in being fixed and unchanging strengthens that hint with the suggestion that the eternal present is to be understood in terms of the present instant 'standing still'. Nevertheless, there are

homou pasa kai plērēs'/'*vitae tota simul et perfecta*'. Plotinus describes the possessor of this life, and Boethius does not; but, in view of the fact that Boethius is talking about God, he, too, would surely describe the possessor of eternality as 'that which exists and is in being'. The most interesting difference between the two definitions is that the Plotinian has 'completely without-extension-or-interval' and the Boethian has 'illimitable', which suggests that Boethius takes eternity to include duration but Plotinus does not. In the rest of *Enneads* iii 7, however, Plotinus goes on to derive duration from his definition and to stress its importance in the concept. For an excellent presentation and discussion of Plotinus on eternity and time, see Werner Beierwaltes, *Plotin über Ewigkeit und Zeit* (*Enneade* iii 7) (Frankfurt am Main, 1967).

[7] The many medieval discussions of the possibility that the world is 'eternal' really concern the possibility that it is sempiternal, and most often their concern is only with the possibility that the world had no beginning in time. Thomas Aquinas provides an important summary and critique of such discussions in *Summa Contra Gentiles*, bk. ii, chs. 32–8.

good reasons, in these passages themselves and in the history of the concept of eternity before and after Boethius, for rejecting this less natural interpretation. In the first place, some of the terminology Boethius uses would be inappropriate to eternity if eternity were to be conceived as illimitable in virtue of being unextended. He speaks in *CP* more than once of the *fullness* of eternal life. In *DT*, and in *The Consolation of Philosophy* immediately following our passage *CP*, he speaks of the eternal present or an eternal entity as *remaining* and *enduring*.[8] And he claims in *DT* that it is correct to say of God that he is *always*, explaining the use of 'always' in reference to God in such a way that he can scarcely have had in mind a life illimitable in virtue of being essentially durationless. The more natural reading of 'illimitable', then, also provides the more natural reading of these texts. In the second place, the weight of tradition both before and after Boethius strongly favours interpreting illimitable life as involving infinite duration, beginningless as well as endless. Boethius throughout the *Consolation*, and especially in passage *CP*, is plainly working in the Platonic tradition, and both Plato and Plotinus understand eternal existence in that sense.[9] Medieval philosophers after Boethius, who depend on him for their conception of eternity, also clearly understand 'illimitable' in this way.[10] So, for both these sets of reasons, we understand this part of Boethius's definition to mean that the life of an eternal entity is characterized by beginningless, endless, infinite duration.

The concept of duration that emerges in the interpretation of 'illimitable life' is the third ingredient we mean to call attention to. Illimitable life entails duration of a special sort, as we have just seen, but it would be reasonable to think that any mode of existence that could be called a life must involve duration, and so there may seem to be no point in explicitly listing duration as an

[8] See, e.g., p. 424.51–56.

[9] See Plato, *Timaeus* 37D–38C; Plotinus, *Enneads* iii 7 (and cf. note 6 above).

[10] See, e.g., Thomas Aquinas, *Summa Theologiae*, pt. i, q. 10. Augustine, who is an earlier and in general an even more important source for medieval philosophy and theology than Boethius and who is even more clearly in the Platonist tradition, understands and uses this classic concept of eternity (see, e.g., *Confessions*, bk. xi, ch. 11; *The City of God*, bk. xi, ch. 21); but his influence on the medieval discussion of eternity seems not to have been so direct or important as Boethius's.

ingredient in Boethius's concept of eternality. We call attention to it here, however, because of its importance as part of the background against which the fourth ingredient must be viewed. The fourth ingredient is presented in the only phrase of the definition still to be considered: 'The complete possession all at once'. As Boethius's explanation of the definition in *CP* makes clear, he conceives of an eternal entity as atemporal, and he thinks of its atemporality as conveyed by just that phrase in the definition. What he says shows that something like the following line of thought leads to his use of those words. A living temporal entity may be said to possess a life, but, since the events constituting the life of any temporal entity occur sequentially, some later than others, it cannot be said to possess all its life *at once*. And since everything in the life of a temporal entity that is not present is either past and so no longer in its possession or future and so not yet in its possession, it cannot be said to have the *complete* possession of its life.[11] So whatever has the complete possession of all its life at once cannot be temporal. The life that is the mode of an eternal entity's existence is thus characterized not only by duration but also by atemporality.

With the possible exception of Parmenides, none of the ancients or medievals who accepted eternity as a real, atemporal mode of existence meant thereby to deny the reality of time or to suggest that all temporal experiences are illusory. In introducing the concept of eternity, such philosophers, and Boethius in particular, were proposing two separate modes of real existence. Eternity is a mode of existence that is, on Boethius's view, neither reducible to time nor incompatible with the reality of time.

In the next two sections of this paper, we will investigate the apparent incoherence of this concept of eternity. We will begin with a consideration of the meaning of atemporality in this connection, including an examination of the relationship between eternity and time; and we will go on to consider the apparent incoherence generated by combining atemporality with duration and with life.

[11] Notice that these characteristics of a temporal entity's possession of its life apply not just to finite temporal lives but even to a temporal life of beginningless, endless duration—a sempiternal life.

II THE ATEMPORALITY OF AN ETERNAL ENTITY: PRESENTNESS AND SIMULTANEITY

Because an eternal entity is atemporal, there is no past or future, no earlier or later, *within* its life; that is, the events constituting its life cannot be ordered sequentially from the standpoint of eternity. But, in addition, no temporal entity or event can be earlier or later than or past or future with respect to the whole life of an eternal entity, because otherwise such an eternal life or entity would itself be part of a temporal series. Here it should be evident that, although the stipulation that an eternal entity completely possesses its life all at once entails that it is not part of any sequence, it does not rule out the attribution of presentness or simultaneity to the life and relationships of such an entity, nor should it. In so far as an entity *is*, or *has*, life, completely or otherwise, it is appropriate to say that it has present existence in some sense of 'present'; and unless its life consists in only one event or it is impossible to relate an event in its life to any temporal entity or event, we need to be able to consider an eternal entity or event as one of the *relata* in a simultaneity relationship. We will consider briefly the applicability of presentness to something eternal and then consider in some detail the applicability of simultaneity.

If anything exists eternally, it exists. But the existing of an eternal entity is a duration without succession, and, because eternity excludes succession, no eternal entity has existed or will exist; it *only* exists. It is in this sense that an eternal entity is said to have present existence. But since that present is not flanked by past and future, it is obviously not the temporal present. And, furthermore, the eternal, pastless, futureless present is not instantaneous but extended, because eternity entails duration. The temporal present is a durationless instant, a present that cannot be extended conceptually without falling apart entirely into past and future intervals. The eternal present, on the other hand, is by definition an infinitely extended, pastless, futureless duration.

Simultaneity is of course generally and unreflectively taken to mean existence or occurrence at one and the same time. But to attribute to an eternal entity or event simultaneity with anything we need a coherent characterization of simultaneity that does not make it altogether temporal. It is easy to provide a coherent characterization of a simultaneity relationship that is not temporal in case both the *relata* are eternal entities or events. Suppose we designate the ordinary understanding of temporal simultaneity *T-simultaneity*:

(T) T-simultaneity = existence or occurrence at one and the same time.

Then we can easily enough construct a second species of simultaneity, a relationship obtaining between two eternal entities or events:

(E) E-simultaneity = existence or occurrence at one and the same eternal present.

What really interests us among species of simultaneity, however, and what we need for our present purposes, is not E-simultaneity so much as a simultaneity relationship between two *relata* of which one is eternal and the other temporal. We have to be able to characterize such a relationship coherently if we are to be able to claim that there is any connection between an eternal and a temporal entity or event. An eternal entity or event cannot be earlier or later than, or past or future with respect to, any temporal entity or event. If there is to be any relationship between what is eternal and what is temporal, then, it must be some species of simultaneity.

Now in forming the species T-simultaneity and E-simultaneity, we have in effect been taking the genus of those species to be something like this:

(G) Simultaneity = existence or occurrence at once (i.e., together).

And we have formed those two species by giving specific content to the broad expression 'at once'. In each case, we have spelled out 'at once' as meaning at one and the same *something*—time, in the case of T-simultaneity; eternal present, in the case of E-simultaneity. In other words, the *relata* for T-simultaneity occur together at the same time, and the *relata* for E-simultaneity occur together at the same eternal present. What we want now is a species of simultaneity—call it *ET-simultaneity* (for eternal–temporal simultaneity)—that can obtain between what is eternal and what is temporal. It is only natural to try to construct a definition for ET-simultaneity as we did for the two preceding species of simultaneity, by making the broad 'at once' in (G) more precise. Doing so requires starting with the phrase 'at one and the same ____' and filling in the blank appropriately. To fill in that blank appropriately, however, would be to specify a single mode of existence in which the two *relata* exist or occur together, as the *relata* for T-simultaneity coexist (or co-occur) in time and the *relata* for E-simultaneity coexist (or co-occur) in eternity.[12] But, on the view we are explaining and defending, it is theoretically impossible to specify a single mode of existence for two *relata* of which one is eternal and the other temporal. To do so would be to reduce what is temporal to what is eternal (thus making time illusory), or what is eternal to what is temporal (thus making eternity illusory), or both what is temporal and what is eternal to some *third* mode of existence; and all three of these alternatives are ruled out. The medieval adherents of the concept of eternity held that both time and eternity are real and that there is no mode of existence besides those two.[13]

Against this background, then, it is not conceptually possible to construct a definition for ET-simultaneity analogous to the definitions for the other two species of simultaneity, by spelling out 'at once' as 'at one and the same ____' and filling in the blank appropriately. What is temporal and what is eternal can coexist, on the view we are adopting and defending, but not within the same mode of existence; and there is no single mode of existence that can be referred to in filling in the blank in such a definition of ET-simultaneity.

The significance of this difficulty and its implications for a working definition of ET-simultaneity can be better appreciated by returning to the definition of T-simultaneity for a closer look.

[12] In the interest of simplicity and brevity, we will for the most part speak only of coexistence in what follows, taking it as covering co-occurrence too.

[13] The medieval concept of the *aevum* or of *aeviternitas* seems to us to be not the concept of a third mode of existence, on a par with time and eternity. See, e.g., Thomas Aquinas, *Summa Theologiae*, pt. i, q. 10, arts. 5 and 6.

Philosophers of physics, explaining the special theory of relativity, have taught us to be cautious even about the notion of temporal simultaneity; in fact, the claim that temporal simultaneity is relative rather than absolute is fundamental to the special theory of relativity.

For all ordinary practical purposes, and also for our theoretical purposes in this paper, time can be thought of as absolute, along Newtonian lines. But, simply in order to set the stage for our characterization of ET-simultaneity, it will be helpful to look at a standard philosophical presentation of temporal simultaneity along Einsteinian lines.[14] Imagine a train travelling *very* fast, at six-tenths the speed of light. One observer (the 'ground observer') is stationed on the embankment beside the track; another observer (the 'train observer') is stationed on the train. Suppose that two lightning bolts strike the train, one at each end, and suppose that the ground observer sees those two lightning bolts simultaneously. The train observer also sees the two lightning bolts, but, since he is travelling toward the light ray emanating from the bolt that strikes the front of the train and away from the bolt that strikes the rear of the train, he will see the lightning bolt strike the front of the train before he sees the other strike the rear of the train. 'This, then, is the fundamental result: events occurring at different places which are simultaneous in one frame of reference will not be simultaneous in another frame of reference which is moving with respect to the first. This is known as *the relativity of simultaneity*'.[15]

We want to leave to one side the philosophical issues raised by this example and simply accept it for our present purposes as a standard example illustrating Einstein's notion of the relativity of temporal simultaneity. According to this example, the very same two lightning flashes are simultaneous (with respect to the reference frame of the ground observer) and not simultaneous (with respect to the reference frame of the train observer). If we interpret 'simultaneous' here in accordance with our definition of

[14] Our adaptation of this example is a simplified version of Wesley C. Salmon's presentation of it in his *Space, Time, and Motion* (Encino, Cal., 1975), pp. 73–81. We mean to do little more here than cite the example. An understanding of its significance for relativity theory requires a consideration of a presentation as full (and clear) as Salmon's.

[15] Salmon, *Space, Time, and Motion*, p. 76.

T-simultaneity, we will have to say that the same two lightning flashes occur at the same time and do not occur at the same time; that is, it will be both true and false that these two lightning flashes occur at the same time. The incoherence of this result is generated by filling in the blank for the definition of T-simultaneity with a reference to one and the same time, where time is understood as one single uniform mode of existence. The special theory of relativity takes time itself to be relative and so calls for a more complicated definition of temporal simultaneity than the common, unreflective definition given in (T), such as this relativized version of temporal simultaneity:

(RT) RT-simultaneity = existence or occurrence at the same time within the reference frame of a given observer.

This relativizing of time to the reference frame of a given observer resolves the apparent incoherence in saying that the same two lightning flashes occur and do not occur at one and the same time. They occur at the same time in the reference frame of one observer and do not occur at the same time in the reference frame of a different observer.[16]

Once this is understood, we can see that, if we persist in asking whether or not the two lightning bolts are *really* simultaneous, we are asking an incoherent question, one that cannot be answered. The question is asked about what is assumed to be a feature of reality, although in fact there is no such feature of reality; such a question is on a par with 'Is Uris Library *really* to the left of Morrill Hall?' There is no absolute state of being temporally simultaneous with, any more than there is an absolute state of being to the left of. We determine the obtaining of the one relationship as we determine the obtaining of the other, by reference to an observer and the observer's point of view. The two lightning flashes, then, are RT-simultaneous in virtue of occurring at the same time within the reference frame of the ground observer and not RT-simultaneous

[16] It is important to understand that by 'observer' we mean only that thing, animate or inanimate, with respect to which the reference frame is picked out and with respect to which the simultaneity of events within the reference frame is determined. In the train example we have two human observers, but the example could have been set up just as well if the observers had been nothing more than devices, primitive or sophisticated, for recording flashes of light.

in virtue of occurring at different times within the reference frame of the train observer. And, Einstein's theory argues, there is no privileged observer (or reference frame) such that with respect to it we can determine whether the two events are *really* simultaneous; simultaneity is irreducibly relative to observers and their reference frames, and so is time itself. Consequently, it would be a mistake to think that there is one single uniform mode of existence that can be referred to in specifying 'at once' in (G) in order to derive a definition of temporal simultaneity.

These difficulties in spelling out even a very crude acceptable definition for temporal simultaneity in the light of relativity theory foreshadow and are analogous to the difficulties in spelling out an acceptable definition of ET-simultaneity. More significantly, they demonstrate that the difficulties defenders of the concept of eternity encounter in formulating such a definition are by no means unique to their undertaking, and cannot be assumed to be difficulties in the concepts of ET-simultaneity or of eternity themselves. Finally, and most importantly, the way in which we cope with such difficulties in working out a definition for RT-simultaneity suggests the sort of definition needed for ET-simultaneity. Because one of the *relata* for ET-simultaneity is eternal, the definition for this relationship, like that for E-simultaneity, must refer to one and the same present rather than to one and the same time. And because in ET-simultaneity we are dealing with two equally real modes of existence, neither of which is reducible to any other mode of existence, the definition must be constructed in terms of *two* reference frames and *two* observers. So we can characterize ET-simultaneity in this way. Let '*x*' and '*y*' range over entities and events. Then:

(ET) for every *x* and for every *y*, *x* and *y* are ET-simultaneous iff
- (i) either *x* is eternal and *y* is temporal, or vice versa; and
- (ii) for some observer, *A*, in the unique eternal reference frame, *x* and *y* are both present—i.e., either *x* is eternally present and *y* is observed as temporally present, or vice versa; and
- (iii) for some observer, *B*, in one of the infinitely many

temporal reference frames, *x* and *y* are both present —i.e., either *x* is observed as eternally present and *y* is temporally present, or vice versa.

Given the concept of eternity, condition (ii) provides that a temporal entity or event observed as temporally present by some eternal observer *A* is ET-simultaneous with every eternal entity or event; and condition (iii) provides that an eternal entity or event observed as eternally present (or simply as eternal) by some temporal observer *B* is ET-simultaneous with every temporal entity or event.

On our definition, if *x* and *y* are ET-simultaneous, then *x* is neither earlier nor later than, neither past nor future with respect to, *y*—a feature essential to any relationship that can be considered a species of simultaneity. Further, if *x* and *y* are ET-simultaneous, *x* and *y* are not temporally simultaneous; since either *x* or *y* must be eternal, it cannot be the case that *x* and *y* both exist *at one and the same time* within a given observer's reference frame. ET-simultaneity is symmetric, of course; but, since no temporal or eternal entity or event is ET-simultaneous with itself, the relationship is not reflexive; and the fact that there are different domains for its *relata* means that it is not transitive. The propositions

(1) *x* is ET-simultaneous with *y*.

and

(2) *y* is ET-simultaneous with *z*.

do not entail

(3) *x* is ET-simultaneous with *z*.

And even if we conjoin with (1) and (2)

(4) *x* and *z* are temporal.

(1), (2), and (4) together do not entail

(5) *x* and *z* are temporally simultaneous.

(RT) and the Einsteinian conception of time as relative have served the only purpose we have for them in this paper, now that they have provided an introductory analogue for our characterization of ET-simultaneity, and we can now revert to a Newtonian conception of time, which will simplify the discussion without involving any relevant loss of precision. In the first place, at least one of the theological issues we are going to be discussing—the problem of omniscience and immutability—depends on the concept of an absolute present, a concept that is often thought to be dependent on a Newtonian conception of absolute time. But the concept of an absolute present which is essential to our discussion is not discredited by relativity theory.[17] Every conscious temporal observer has an undeniable, indispensable sense of the absolute present, *now*, and that thoroughly pervasive feature of temporal consciousness is all we need. We do not need and we will not try to provide a philosophical justification for the concept of an absolute present; we will simply assume it for our present purposes. And if it must be said that the absolute present is absolute only within a given observer's reference frame, that will not affect our use of the concept here. In the second place, in ordinary human circumstances, all human observers may be said—*should* be said—to share one and the same reference frame, and distinguishing individual reference frames for our discussion of time in the rest of this paper would be as inappropriate as taking an Einsteinian view of time in a discussion of historical chronology.

III IMPLICATIONS OF ET-SIMULTANEITY

If *x* and *z* are temporal entities, they coexist if and only if there is some time during which both *x* and *z* exist. But if anything exists eternally, its existence, although infinitely extended, is fully realized, all present at once. Thus the entire life of any eternal entity is coexistent with any temporal entity at any time at which that temporal entity exists.[18] From a temporal standpoint, the

[17] On this issue see William Godfrey Smith, 'Special Relativity and the Present', *Philosophical Studies*, 36(3) (Oct. 1979), pp. 233–44.

[18] Since no eternal entity or event can itself be an element in a temporal series, no temporal entity or event can be earlier or later than the whole life or than any part of the life of an eternal entity. It is not clear that it makes sense to think in terms of parts of atemporal duration (cf. Aquinas, *Summa Theologiae*, pt. i, q. 10,

present is ET-simultaneous with the whole infinite extent of an eternal entity's life. From the standpoint of eternity, every time is present, co-occurrent with the whole of infinite atemporal duration.[19]

We can show the implications of this account of ET-simultaneity by considering the relationship between an eternal entity and a future contingent event. Suppose that Richard Nixon will die at noon on 9 August 1990, precisely sixteen years after he resigned the Presidency. Nixon's death some years from now *will be* present

art. 1, ad. 3); but even if it does, it cannot make sense to think of any such part as earlier or later than anything temporal. If the Battle of Waterloo were earlier than some part of atemporal duration, it would be uniquely simultaneous with one other part of atemporal duration, in which case one part of atemporal duration would be earlier than another, which is impossible.

[19] In the development of the classic concept of eternity, geometric models were sometimes introduced in an attempt to clarify the relationship we are calling ET-simultaneity. There is a passage in Boethius, for instance (*Consolation*, bk. iv, prose 6; *De trinitate*, pp. 364.78–366.82), which suggests that he took the relationship between time and eternity to be analogous to that between the circumference and the centre of a circle. Aquinas developed this sort of analogy in connection with an account of an eternal entity's apprehension of temporal events: 'Furthermore, God's understanding, just like his being, does not have succession; it is, therefore, always enduring all at once, which belongs to the nature of eternity. The duration of time, on the other hand, is extended in the succession of before and after. Thus the relationship of eternity to the whole duration of time is like the relationship of an indivisible to a continuum—not indeed of an indivisible that is a limit of the continuum, which is not present to each part of the continuum (an instant of time bears a likeness to that), but of the indivisible that is outside the continuum and nevertheless coexists with each part of the continuum or with a designated point in the continuum. For, since time does not extend beyond change, eternity, which is entirely beyond change, is nothing belonging to time; on the other hand, since the being of what is eternal is never lacking, eternity in its presentness is present to each time or instant of time. A sort of example of this can be seen in a circle. For a designated point on the circumference, although it is an indivisible, does not coexist together with another point as regards position since it is the order of position that produces the continuity of the circumference. But the centre, which is outside the circumference, is directly opposite any designated point on the circumference. In this way, whatever is in any part of time coexists with what is eternal as being present to it even though past or future with respect to another part of time. But nothing can coexist with what is eternal in its presentness except as a whole, for it does not have the duration of succession. And so in its eternity the divine understanding perceives as present whatever takes place during the whole course of time. It is not the case, however, that what takes place in a certain part of time has been existent always. It remains, therefore, that God has knowledge of those things that, as regards the course of time, are not yet' (*Summa Contra Gentiles*, bk. i, ch. 66).

to those who will be at his death-bed, but it *is* present to an eternal entity. It cannot be that an eternal entity has a vision of Nixon's death before it occurs; in that case an eternal event would be earlier than a temporal event. Instead, the actual occasion of Nixon's dying is present to an eternal entity. It is not that the future pre-exists somehow, so that it can be inspected by an entity that is outside time, but rather that an eternal entity that is wholly ET-simultaneous with 9 August 1974, and with today, is wholly ET-simultaneous with 9 August 1990, as well. It is *now* true to say 'The whole of eternity is ET-simultaneous with the present'; and of course it was true to say just the same at noon of 9 August 1974, and it will be true to say it at noon of 9 August 1990. But since it is one and the same eternal present that is ET-simultaneous with each of those times, there is a sense in which it is now true to say that Nixon at the hour of his death is present to an eternal entity; and in that same sense it is now true to say that Nixon's resigning of the Presidency is present to an eternal entity. If we are considering an eternal entity that is omniscient, it is true to say that that entity is *at once* aware of Nixon resigning the Presidency and of Nixon on his death-bed (although of course an omniscient entity understands that those events occur sequentially and knows the sequence and the dating of them); and it is true to say also that for such an entity both those events are present at once.[20]

Such an account of ET-simultaneity suggests at least a radical epistemological or even metaphysical relativism, and perhaps plain incoherence. We *know* that Nixon is now alive. An omniscient eternal entity *knows* that Nixon is now dead. Still worse, an omniscient eternal entity also *knows* that Nixon is now alive, and so Nixon is apparently both alive and dead at once in the eternal present.

These absurdities appear to be entailed partly because the full implications of the concept of eternity have not been taken into account. We have said enough to induce caution regarding

[20] In *The Consolation of Philosophy* Boethius introduces and develops the concept of eternity primarily in order to argue that divine omniscience is compatible with human freedom, and he does so by demonstrating that omniscience on the part of an eternal entity need not, cannot, involve *fore*knowledge. See also section VI below.

'present' and 'simultaneous', but it is not difficult to overlook the concomitant ambiguity in such expressions as 'now' and 'at once'. To say that we know that Nixon is now alive although an eternal entity knows that Nixon is now dead does not mean that an eternal entity knows the opposite of what we know. What we know is that:

(6) Nixon is alive in the temporal present.

What an eternal entity knows is that

(7) Nixon is dead in the eternal present.

and (6) is not incompatible with (7). Still, this simple observation does nothing to dispel the appearance of incompatibility between (7) and

(8) Nixon is alive in the eternal present.

and, on the basis of what has been said so far, both (7) and (8) are true. But Nixon is temporal, not eternal, and so are his life and death. The conjunction of (7) and (8), then, cannot be taken to mean that the temporal entity Nixon exists in eternity, where he is simultaneously alive and dead, but rather something more nearly like this. One and the same eternal present is ET-simultaneous with Nixon's being alive and is also ET-simultaneous with Nixon's dying; so Nixon's life is ET-simultaneous with and hence present to an eternal entity, and Nixon's death is ET-simultaneous with and hence present to an eternal entity, although Nixon's life and Nixon's death are themselves neither eternal nor simultaneous.

These considerations also explain the appearance of metaphysical relativism inherent in the claim that Nixon's death is really future for us and really present for an eternal entity. It is not that there are two objective realities, in one of which Nixon's death is really future and in the other of which Nixon's death and life are really present; that *would* be incoherent. What the concept of eternity implies instead is that there is one objective reality that contains two modes of real existence in which two different sorts of duration are measured by two irreducibly different sorts of measure: time and eternity. Given the relations between time and eternity spelled out in section II of this paper, Nixon's death is really future or not depending on which sort of entity, temporal or eternal, it is being related to. An eternal entity's mode of existence is such that its whole life is ET-simultaneous with each and every temporal entity or event, and so Nixon's death, like every other event involving Nixon, is really ET-simultaneous with the life of an eternal entity. But when Nixon's death is being related to *us*, today, then, given our location in the temporal continuum, Nixon's death is not simultaneous (temporally or in any other way) with respect to us, but really future.[21]

IV ATEMPORAL DURATION AND ATEMPORAL LIFE

With this understanding of the atemporality of an eternal entity's existence, we want to consider now the apparent incoherence generated by combining atemporality with duration and with life in the definition of eternity.

The notion of atemporal duration is the heart of the concept of eternity and, in our view, the original motivation for its development. The most efficient way in which to dispel the apparent incoherence of the notion of atemporal duration is to consider, even if only very briefly, the development of the concept of eternity. The concept can be found in Parmenides, we think,[22] but it finds its first detailed formulation in Plato, who makes use of it in working out the distinction between the realms of being and becoming; and it receives its fullest exposition in pagan antiquity in the work of Plotinus.[23] The thought that originally stimulated

[21] The claim that Nixon's death is really future rests on the assumption around which we all organize our lives, the view that the temporal present is absolute, that the expressions 'the present', 'the past', and 'the future' are uniquely (and differently) referring expressions on each occasion of their use, that 'now' is an essential indexical. On the notion of an essential indexical see John Perry, 'The Problem of the Essential Indexical', *Noûs* 13(1) (March 1979), pp. 3–21. We are grateful to Marilyn Adams for letting us see some of her unpublished work which brings out the importance of the notion of the absolute present in discussions of this sort, particularly in the discussion we will take up in section VI below, and for calling our attention to Perry's article.

[22] Most clearly in fr. 8, as we read it. For excellent examples of both sides of the controversy over the presence of the concept of eternity in Parmenides, see G. E. L. Owen, 'Plato and Parmenides on the Timeless Present', *Monist* L (3) (July 1966), pp. 317–340; and Malcolm Schofield, 'Did Parmenides Discover Eternity?', *Archiv für Geschichte der Philosophie* 52 (1970), pp. 113–35.

[23] See notes 6 and 9 above.

this Greek development of the concept of eternity was apparently something like this. Our *experience* of temporal duration gives us an impression of permanence and persistence which an analysis of time convinces us is an illusion or at least a distortion. Reflection shows us that, contrary to our familiar but superficial impression, temporal duration is only apparent duration, just what one would expect to find in the realm of becoming. The existence of a typical existent temporal entity, such as a human being, is spread over years of the past, through the present, and into years of the future; but the past is not, the future is not, and the present must be understood as no time at all, a durationless instant, a mere point at which the past is continuous with the future.[24] Such radically evanescent existence cannot be the foundation of existence. Being, the persistent, permanent, utterly immutable actuality that seems required as the bedrock underlying the evanescence of becoming, must be characterized by genuine duration, of which temporal duration is only the flickering image. Genuine duration is fully realized duration—not only extended existence (even *that* is theoretically impossible in time) but also existence *none* of which is already gone and *none* of which is yet to come—and such fully realized duration must be atemporal duration. Whatever has atemporal duration as its mode of existence is 'such that nothing future is absent from it and nothing past has flowed away', whereas of everything that has temporal duration it may be said that from it *everything* future is absent and *everything* past has flowed away. What has temporal duration 'does not yet grasp tomorrow but yesterday it has already lost'; even today it exists only 'in a mobile, transitory moment', the present instant. To say of something that it is future is to say that it is not (yet), and to say of something that it is past is to say that it is not (any longer). Atemporal duration is duration none of which is not—none of which is absent (and hence future) or flowed away (and hence past). Eternity, not time, is the mode of existence that admits of fully realized duration.

[24] For some discussion of this analysis of time in Aristotle and Augustine, see Fred Miller, 'Aristotle on the Reality of Time', *Archiv für Geschichte der Philosophie* 61 (1974), pp. 132–55; and Norman Kretzmann, 'Time Exists—But Hardly, or Obscurely (*Physics* iv, 10; 217b29–218a33)', *Aristotelian Society Supplementary Volume* 1 (1976), pp. 91–114.

The ancient Greek philosophers who developed the concept of eternity were using the word '*aiōn*', which corresponds in its original sense to our word 'duration', in a way that departed from ordinary usage in order to introduce a notion which, however counter-intuitive it may be, can reasonably be said to preserve and even to enhance the original sense of the word. It would not be out of keeping with the tradition that runs through Parmenides, Plato, and Plotinus into Augustine, Boethius, and Aquinas to claim that it is only the discovery of eternity that enables us to make genuinely literal use of words for duration, words such as 'permanence' and 'persistence', which in their ordinary, temporal application turn out to have been unintended metaphors. 'Atemporal duration', like the ancient technical use of '*aiōn*' itself, violates established usage; but an attempt to convey a new philosophical or scientific concept by adapting familiar expressions is not to be rejected on the basis of its violation of ordinary usage. The apparent incoherence in the concept is primarily a consequence of continuing to think of duration only as 'persistence *through time*'.

Since a life is a kind of duration, some of the apparent incoherence in the notion of an atemporal life may be dispelled in rendering the notion of atemporal duration less readily dismissible. But life is in addition ordinarily associated with processes of various sorts, and processes are essentially temporal, and so the notion of an atemporal entity that has life seems incoherent.[25] Now what Aquinas, for example, is thinking of when he attributes life to eternal God is the doctrine that God is a mind. (Obviously what is atemporal cannot consist of physical matter; we assume for the sake of the argument that there is nothing incoherent in the notion of a wholly immaterial, independently existent mind.) Since God is atemporal, the mind that is God must be different in important ways from a temporal, human mind. Considered as an atemporal mind, God cannot deliberate, anticipate, remember, or plan

[25] William Kneale has taken this notion to be genuinely incoherent and among the most important reasons for rejecting the classic concept of eternity. See his 'Time and Eternity in Theology', *Proceedings of the Aristotelian Society* 61 (1960), pp. 87–108; also his article 'Eternity' in Paul Edwards (ed.), *The Encyclopedia of Philosophy* (New York, 1967), vol. 3, pp. 63–6. Cf. Martha Kneale, 'Eternity and Sempiternity', *Proceedings of the Aristotelian Society*, 69 (1968–9), pp. 223–38.

ahead, for instance; all these mental activities essentially involve time, either in taking time to be performed (like deliberation) or in requiring a temporal viewpoint as a prerequisite to performance (like remembering). But it is clear that there are other mental activities that do not require a temporal interval or viewpoint. Knowing seems to be the paradigm case; learning, reasoning, inferring take time, as knowing does not. In reply to the question 'What have you been doing for the past two hours?' it makes sense to say 'Studying logic' or 'Proving theorems', but not 'Knowing logic'. Similarly, it makes sense to say 'I'm learning logic', but not 'I'm knowing logic'. And knowing is not the only mental activity requiring neither a temporal interval nor a temporal viewpoint. Willing, for example, unlike wishing or desiring, seems to be another. Perceiving is impossible in any literal sense for a mind that is disembodied, but nothing in the nature of incorporeality or atemporality seems to rule out the possibility of awareness. And though *feeling* angry is impossible for an atemporal entity—if feelings of anger are essentially associated, as they seem to be, with bodily states—we do not see that anything prevents such an entity from *being* angry, a state the components of which might be, for instance, being aware of an injustice, disapproving of it, and willing its punishment. It seems, then, that the notion of an atemporal mind is not incoherent, but that, on the contrary, it is possible that such a mind might have a variety of faculties or activities. Our informal, incomplete consideration of that possibility is not even the beginning of an argument for such a conclusion, but it is enough for our purposes here to suggest the line along which such an argument might develop. The notion of an atemporal mind is not *prima facie* absurd, and so neither is the notion of an atemporal life absurd; for any entity that has or is a mind must be considered to be *ipso facto* alive, whatever characteristics of other living beings it may lack.

V THE NOTION OF AN ETERNAL ENTITY'S ACTING IN TIME

The difficulties we have considered so far are difficulties in the concept of eternity itself. We have by no means dealt explicitly with all the objections to the concept which have been raised in contemporary discussions; but many of those objections involve difficulties over simultaneity, and such objections can, we think, be dealt with adequately in the light of our previous discussion of ET-simultaneity. We hope, for instance, to have revealed the misunderstanding underlying such attempted reductions of the concept to absurdity as this one:

> But, on St Thomas' view, my typing of this paper is simultaneous with the whole of eternity. Again, on his view, the great fire of Rome is simultaneous with the whole of eternity. Therefore, while I type these very words, Nero fiddles heartlessly on.[26]

We want now to turn to fundamental difficulties in theological applications of the concept, particularly those which arise in considering the possibility of interaction between eternal and temporal entities.

There are several reasons for thinking that an eternal entity, as we have characterized it, could not affect or respond to temporal entities, events, or state of affairs. Just as an eternal entity cannot exist in time, so, we might suppose, (I) an eternal entity cannot act in time. It might seem, furthermore, that (II) the nature of a temporal action is such that the agent itself must be temporal. Nelson Pike provides the following case in point:

> Let us suppose that yesterday a mountain, 17,000 feet high, came into existence on the flatlands of Illinois. One of the local theists explains this occurrence by reference to divine creative action. He claims that God produced (created, brought about) the mountain. Of course, if God is timeless, He could not have produced the mountain *yesterday*. This would require that God's creative-activity and thus the individual whose activity it is have position in time. The theist's claim is that God *timelessly* brought it about that yesterday, a 17,000 feet high mountain came into existence on the flatlands of Illinois. . . . [But] The claim that God *timelessly* produced a temporal object (such as the mountain) is absurd.[27]

On this basis Pike denies that God, considered as atemporal, could

[26] Anthony Kenny, 'Divine Foreknowledge and Human Freedom', in Kenny (ed.), *Aquinas: A Collection of Critical Essays* (Garden City, NY, 1969), pp. 255–70, 264.

[27] Nelson Pike, *God and Timelessness* (London, 1970), pp. 104–5.

produce or create anything; whatever is produced or created begins to exist and so has a position in time. And it might be argued along similar lines that (III) an atemporal entity could not preserve anything temporal in existence because to do so would require temporal duration on the part of the preserver.

If God is taken to be eternal, considerations I, II, and III are incompatible with some doctrines central to most versions of theism, such as the divine creation and preservation of the world, and divine response to petitionary prayer. More specifically, they militate against the central doctrine of Christianity, since the Incarnation of Christ entails that the second person of the Trinity has a temporal nature and performs temporal actions during a certain period of time.

We think all three of these considerations are confused. In connection with consideration I, a distinction must be drawn between (*a*) acting in such a way that the action itself can be located in time and (*b*) acting in such a way that the effect of the action can be located in time. For temporal agents the distinction between (*a*) and (*b*) is generally nugatory; for an atemporal entity, however, (*a*) is impossible. An agent's action is an event in the agent's life, and there can be no temporal event in the atemporal life of God. But such an observation does not tell against (*b*). If an eternal God is also omnipotent, he can do anything it is not logically impossible for him to do. Even though his actions cannot be located in time, he can bring about effects in time unless doing so is logically impossible for him.

Considerations II and III may be construed as providing reasons for thinking that it is indeed logically impossible for an atemporal entity to produce temporal effects. Pike's version of consideration II, however, involves a confusion like the confusion just sorted out for consideration I. He says:

(9) '[I]f God is timeless, He could not have produced the mountain *yesterday*.'

(10) 'The claim that God *timelessly* produced a temporal object (such as the mountain) is absurd.'

Both these propositions are ambiguous because of the possibility of assigning different scopes to 'yesterday' and to 'timelessly' (or 'atemporally'), and the ambiguities can be sorted out in this way:

(9)(*a*) If God is atemporal, he cannot yesterday have brought it about that a temporal object came into existence.

(9)(*b*) If God is atemporal, he cannot (atemporally) bring it about that a temporal object came into existence yesterday.

(10)(*a*) It is absurd to claim that God atemporally brings it about that a temporal object came into existence.

(10)(*b*) It is absurd to claim that God brings it about that a temporal object came into existence atemporally.[28]

Apparently without taking account of the ambiguity of propositions (9) and (10), Pike understands them as (9)(*a*) and (10)(*b*) respectively. Propositions (9)(*a*) and (10)(*b*) are indeed true, but they do not support Pike's inference that an atemporal God cannot produce a temporal object. In drawing that inference, Pike seems to be relying on an assumption about a temporal relationship that must hold between an action and its effect. The assumption is not entirely clear; in some passages of his *God and Timelessness* it looks as if Pike thinks that an action and its effect must be simultaneous, an assumption that is plainly false in general regarding actions and their effects as ordinarily conceived of. But if we do adopt co-occurrence as a theoretically justifiable condition on causal connection between an action and its effect, we can point out that any and every action of an eternal entity is ET-simultaneous with any temporal effect ascribed to it. And, since it would simply beg the question to insist that only *temporal* simultaneity between an action and its effect can satisfy this necessary condition of causal connection, we see no reason for denying of an eternal, omnipotent entity that its atemporal act of willing could bring it about that a mountain came into existence on [yesterday's date]. Consequently, we can see no reason for thinking it absurd to claim that a divine action resulting in the

[28] These ambiguities, like the two interpretations provided for consideration I above, are of the sort extensively investigated by medieval logicians under their distinction between the compounded and divided senses of propositions. Thus (9)(*a*) and (10)(*a*) present the compounded senses of propositions (9) and (10), whereas (9)(*b*) and (10)(*b*) present their divided senses.

existence of a temporal entity is an atemporal action. In other words, we think that propositions (9)(*b*) and (10)(*a*) are false, although they are legitimate senses of the ambiguous propositions (9) and (10). And so we reject consideration II as well as I.

Our reasons for rejecting these first two considerations apply as well, *mutatis mutandis*, to consideration III. If it is not impossible for an omnipotent, eternal entity to act in eternity (by atemporally willing) in such a way as to bring it about that a temporal entity begins to exist at a particular time, it is not impossible for an omnipotent, eternal entity to act in eternity (by atemporally willing) in such a way that that temporal entity continues to exist during a particular temporal interval.

A different sort of difficulty arises in connection with answering prayers or punishing injustice, for instance, since in such cases it seems necessary that the eternal action occur later than the temporal action; and so our reasons for rejecting considerations I, II, and III, based on the ET-simultaneity of eternal actions with temporal events, seem inapplicable. The problem of answering prayers is typical of difficulties of this sort. An answer to a prayer must be later than the prayer, it seems, just because

(11) Something constitutes an answer to a prayer only if it is done because of the prayer.

and

(12) Something is done because of a prayer only if it is done later than the praying of the prayer.

We think that (11) is true; (12), on the other hand, seems doubtful even as applied to temporal entities. If at 3 o'clock a mother prepares a snack for her little boy because she believes that when he gets home at 3.30 he will ask for one, it does not seem unreasonable to describe her as preparing the food because of the child's request, even though in this case the response is earlier than the request. Whatever may be true regarding temporal entities, however, if (12) is true, it obviously rules out the possibility of an eternal entity's responding to prayers. But consider the case of Hannah's praying on a certain day to have a child and her conceiving several days afterward.[29] Both the day of her prayer and the day of her conceiving are ET-simultaneous with the life of an eternal entity. If such an entity atemporally wills that Hannah conceive on a certain day after the day of her prayer, then such an entity's bringing it about that Hannah conceives on that day is clearly a response to her prayer, even though the willing is ET-simultaneous with the prayer rather than later than it. If ET-simultaneity is a sufficient condition for the possibility of a causal connection in the case of God's bringing about the existence of temporal entity, it is likewise sufficient for the possibility of his acting because of a prayer prayed at a particular time.[30]

The principal difficulty in the doctrine of the Incarnation seems intractable to considerations of the sort with which we have been trying to alleviate difficulties associated with an eternal entity's willing to bring about a temporal event, because according to the doctrine of the Incarnation an eternal entity itself entered time. If we take the essence of the doctrine to be expressed in

(13) 'When the fulness of the time was come, God sent forth his Son, born of a woman' (Galatians 4: 4).

it is not difficult to see, in the light of our discussion so far, how to provide an interpretation that shows that, as regards God's sending his Son, the doctrine is compatible with God's eternality:

(13′) God atemporally wills that his Son be born of a woman at the appointed time.

But the possibility of making sense of an eternal action with a temporal effect does not settle this issue, because the principal difficulty here does not lie in the nature of the relationship between an eternal agent and a temporal effect. The difficulty here is rather that an eternal entity is also a *component* of the temporal effect—an effect which is, to put it simplistically, an eternal entity's having become temporal without having ceased (*per impossibile*) to exist eternally. Formulating the difficulty in the

[29] I Samuel 1: 9–20.

[30] For a discussion of other philosophical problems associated with petitionary prayer see Eleonore Stump, 'Petitionary Prayer', *American Philosophical Quarterly*, 16(1) (Jan. 1979), pp. 81–91.

doctrine of the Incarnation simplistically, however, simply exacerbates it. And whereas this formulation of it may present an insuperable difficulty for one or more of the heresies of the Patristic period that took the person of Christ to be only divine or only human, it is ineffective against the orthodox doctrines of the Trinity and the dual nature of Christ. A full treatment of those philosophically intricate doctrines lies outside the scope of this paper, but we will consider them very briefly on the basis of our limited understanding of them in order to suggest some reasons for supposing that the doctrine of the Incarnation is not incompatible with the doctrine of God's eternality.

The doctrine of the Trinity maintains that God, although one substance, consists in three persons, the second of which is God the Son. The doctrine of the dual nature maintains that the second person of the Trinity has not merely one essence or nature, like every other person divine or human, but two: one the divine nature common to all the persons of the Trinity, the other the human nature of the Incarnation. One of the explicitly intended consequences of the doctrine of the dual nature is that any statement predicating something of Christ is ambiguous unless it contains a phrase specifying one or the other or both of his two natures. That is, the proposition

(14) Christ died.

is ambiguous among these three readings:

(14)(*a*) Christ with respect to his divine nature (or *qua* God) died.
(14)(*b*) Christ with respect to his human nature (or *qua* man) died.
(14)(*c*) Christ with respect to his divine and human natures (or *qua* both God and man) died.

From the standpoint of orthodox Christianity (14)(*a*) and (14)(*c*) are false, and (14)(*b*) is true. (14)(*b*) is not to be interpreted as denying that God died, however—such a denial forms the basis of at least one Christian heresy—but to deny that God, the second person of the Trinity, died with respect to his divine nature. Such an account is loaded with at least apparent paradox, and it is not part of our purpose here even to sketch an analysis of it; but, whatever its internal difficulties may be, the doctrine of the dual nature provides *prima facie* grounds for denying the incompatibility of God's eternality and God's becoming man.

A Boethian account of the compatibility of divine eternality and the Incarnation might be developed along these lines, we think.[31] The divine nature of the second person of the Trinity, like the divine nature of either of the other persons of the Trinity, cannot become temporal; nor could the second person at some time acquire a human nature he does not eternally have. Instead, the second person eternally has two natures; and at some temporal instants, all of which are ET-simultaneous with both these natures in their entirety, the human nature of the second person has been temporally actual. At those times and only in that nature the second person directly participates in temporal events. We need no theologian to tell us how rudimentary this outline is, and no other philosopher to tell us how paradoxical it looks; but we are not now willing or able or required by our main purpose in this paper to undertake an analysis or defence of the role of the doctrine of the dual nature in establishing the compatibility of divine eternality and the Incarnation. We hope simply to have pointed out that the doctrine of the Incarnation cannot be reduced to the belief that God became temporal and that, if it is understood as including the doctrine of the dual nature, it can be seen to have been constructed in just such a way as to avoid being reduced to that simple belief. And those observations are all we need for now in order to allay the suspicion that eternality must be incompatible with the central doctrine of orthodox Christianity.

It seems to us, then, that the concept of eternity is coherent and that there is no logical impossibility in the notion of an eternal being's acting in time, provided that acting in time is understood as we have explained it here.

[31] Although Boethius treats of the Incarnation and the dual nature of Christ in his theological tractates, especially in his *Contra Eutychen et Nestorium* (in Stewart, Rand, and Tester, *Boethius*), he does not apply his concept of eternity in those discussions as we think it ought to be applied.

VI OMNISCIENCE AND IMMUTABILITY

The doctrine that God is eternal is obviously of critical importance in the consideration of any issue involving the relationship of God to temporal entities or events. We will conclude our exploration of the concept of eternity by sampling its effect on three such issues concerning either God's knowledge or God's power in connection with the future, the past, and the present, respectively.

First, the short answer to the question whether God can foreknow contingent events is no. It is impossible that any event occur later than an eternal entity's present state of awareness, since every temporal event is ET-simultaneous with that state, and so an eternal entity cannot *fore*know anything. Instead, such an entity considered as omniscient knows—is aware of—all temporal events, including those which are future with respect to our current temporal viewpoint; but, because the times at which those future events will be present events are ET-simultaneous with the whole of eternity, an omniscient eternal entity is aware of them as they are present.[32]

Second, the short answer to the question whether God can change the past is no. But it is misleading to say, with Agathon, that not even God can change the past.[33] God *in particular* cannot change the past. The impossibility of *God's* changing the past is a consequence, not of the fact that what is past is over and done with, but rather of the fact that the past is solely a feature of the experience of temporal entities. It is just because no event can be past with respect to an eternal entity that an eternal entity cannot alter a *past* event.[34] An omnipotent, omniscient, eternal entity can affect temporal events, but it can affect events only as they are

[32] What we present here is essentially Boethius's line against the suggestion that divine omniscience and human freedom are incompatible, a line in which he was followed by many medievals, especially Aquinas. On Aquinas's use of the Boethian solution, see Kenny, 'Divine Foreknowledge and Human Freedom'; see also note 18 above.

[33] Aristotle, *Nicomachean Ethics*, vi, 2.

[34] Although the concept of *the* past, dependent on the concept of the absolute temporal present, has no application for an eternal entity, for an omniscient eternal entity there is the awareness of your past, your present, your future as of 1 January 1970, and of your past, your present, your future as of 1 January 1980, and so on for every temporal entity as of any date in its duration.

actually occurring. As for a past event, the time at which it was actually occurring is the time at which it is present to such an entity; and so the battle of Waterloo is present to God, and God can affect the battle. Suppose that he does so. God can bring it about that Napoleon wins, though we know that he does not do so, because whatever God does at Waterloo is over and done with as we see it. So God cannot alter the past, but he can alter the course of the battle of Waterloo.[35]

Third, the short answer to the question whether God can know what time it is is yes. There is a published attempt to prove that, although for orthodox Christianity God is necessarily both omniscient and immutable, omniscience and immutability are in fact incompatible characteristics.[36] The proof reads as follows:

[35] These observations regarding God's relationship to the past might suggest further issues regarding petitionary prayer. It is obviously absurd to pray in 1980 that Napoleon win at Waterloo when one knows what God does not bring about at Waterloo, but it might not seem absurd—at least not in the same way—to pray in 1980 that Napoleon lose at Waterloo. After all, your prayer and the battle are alike present to God; why should your prayer not be efficacious in bringing about Napoleon's defeat? But, as a petition addressed to the will of God, a prayer is also an expression of the will of the one who prays it, and any temporal entity who prays in 1980, 'Let Napoleon lose at Waterloo', is to that extent pretending to have atemporal knowledge and an atemporal will. The only appropriate version of that prayer is 'Let Napoleon have lost at Waterloo', and for one who knows the outcome of the battle more than a hundred and fifty years ago, that prayer is pointless and in that sense absurd. But a prayer prayed in ignorance of the outcome of a past event is not pointless in that way. (We are thus disagreeing with Peter Geach, when he claims that 'A prayer for something to have happened is simply an absurdity, regardless of the utterer's knowledge or ignorance of how things went' (*God and the Soul* (London, 1969), p. 90); but we find much else to admire in his chapter 'Praying for Things to Happen'.) On the hypothesis that there is an eternal, omniscient, omnipotent God, the praying of such a prayer would indeed qualify as 'the only instance of behaviour, on the part of ordinary people whose mental processes we can understand, designed to affect the past and coming quite naturally to us' (Michael Dummett, 'Bringing About the Past', *Philosophical Review* 73(3) (July 1964), p. 341). We are grateful to members of the Sage School of Philosophy at Cornell for pointing out the relevance of Dummett's discussion. Dummett does not draw on the concept of divine eternality, but, if it is acceptable in its own right, its introduction would lead to a modification and strengthening of some of the claims he makes—e.g., 'I am not asking God that, even if my son has drowned, He should *now* make him not to have drowned; I am asking that, at the time of the disaster, He should then have made my son not to drown at that time' (p. 342).

[36] Kretzmann, 'Omniscience and Immutability', *Journal of Philosophy* 63(14) (July 1966), pp. 409–21. This article has been discussed and criticized by a number of writers, including Hector-Neri Castañeda, 'Omniscience and Indexical Reference',

(1) A perfect being is not subject to change.
(2) A perfect being knows everything.
(3) A being that knows everything always knows what time it is.
(4) A being that always knows what time it is is subject to change.
∴(5) A perfect being is subject to change.
∴(6) A perfect being is not a perfect being.
∴(7) There is no perfect being.

Steps (1) and (2) are the immutability and omniscience claims. Step (3) is intended as the claim that an omniscient being knows what time it is *now* in the absolute present, what part of history is neither past nor future but presently occurring. In explaining (4) the author takes 'It is now t_n' as the form of propositions that say what time it is. Thus a being that always knows what time it is knows first that it is now t_1 (and not t_2), then that it is now t_2 (and not t_1), and so on; and in that way such a being's knowledge is constantly changing. And, if a being's knowledge is changing in such a way that it no longer knows what it once knew, then that being itself is also changing.

But God's eternality is as much a part of orthodox Christian doctrine as are God's omniscience and immutability;[37] and, when not only time is taken into account but also eternity, as the mode of God's existence,then, as we have seen, such expressions as 'now' and 'present' are equivocal. Given the way in which the concept of eternity affects the interpretation of such expressions, it is clear that the weak point in the proof is premiss (3), which contains two implicit references to the present. The first of these is

Journal of Philosophy 64(7) (April 1967), pp. 203–9; Richard Swinburne, *The Coherence of Theism* (Oxford, 1977); Anthony Kenny, *The God of the Philosophers* (Oxford, 1979), esp. ch. 6, 'Omniscience, Eternity, and Time'. We are grateful for having been shown two as yet unpublished discussions: Marilyn McCord Adams, 'Can God Know What Time It Is?' and Walter Horn, 'God and Current Events'. None of the criticisms of the argument in 'Omniscience and Immutability' which we have seen takes the line we take in the rest of this discussion; none of the defences we have seen is effective against our line of attack.

[37] In this connection it is interesting to note that Aquinas bases his attribution of eternality to God in *Summa Theologiae*, pt. i, q. 10, on his attribution of immutability to God in q. 9.

in the tense of 'is', since the point of the premiss is that an omniscient being always knows what time it is *now*; the second is in the tense of the second occurrence of 'knows', since part of the idea underlying the proof is that knowledge of what time it is must be present knowledge or knowledge one has at the present time.

If we analyse (3) to bring out the equivocations at those two points, we produce the following four possible interpretations:

(3)(*a*) A being that knows everything always knows in the temporal present what time it is in the temporal present.
(3)(*b*) A being that knows everything always knows in the eternal present what time it is in the temporal present.
(3)(*c*) A being that knows everything always knows in the temporal present what time it is in the eternal present.
(3)(*d*) A being that knows everything always knows in the eternal present what time it is in the eternal present.

Interpretations (3)(*c*) and (3)(*d*) can be dismissed at once as incoherent in virtue of the expression 'what time it is in the eternal present'. (3)(*a*) is obviously the intended sense of premiss (3); but (3)(*a*) is true just in case only a temporal entity can be omniscient, since an omniscient atemporal entity cannot be said to know in the temporal present, and it begs the question at issue to assume that no atemporal entity can be omniscient. The evaluation of the proof, then, depends on the evaluation of (3)(*b*).

(3)(*b*) is hard to evaluate because it is hard to interpret. What exactly is being picked out as the temporal present? If it is the time at which you are reading these words, then (3)(*b*) may be taken to be true, for it is true that

(3)(*b′*) For any time experienced as present by a temporal entity, an omniscient eternal entity knows all the events actually occurring at that time (as well as the dating of that time and its being experienced as present by a temporal entity).

But if premiss (3) is interpreted as (3)(*b′*), it will not contribute as it is designed to do to the support of sub-conclusion (5) in the proof; a being that always knows what time it is in the way laid out in (3)(*b′*) is not a being subject to change in virtue of its always knowing what time it is. If premiss (3) is read as (3)(*b′*), then (3) is true but (4) is false.

The defender of the proof we are criticizing may feel that (3)(*b′*) rests on a notion of the temporal present as merely relative. He may well want to insist that some things have actually happened, some things are actually going to happen, and some things are actually happening; and what he wants to know is whether God knows *what is actually happening as it is happening.* The answer to that question, too, is yes. The whole of eternity is ET-simultaneous with each temporal event as it is actually happening; the only way in which an eternal entity can be aware of any temporal event is to be aware of it as it is actually happening. And from the eternal viewpoint every temporal event is actually happening. There is no single temporal viewpoint; even when the temporal present is taken to be absolute, the temporal viewpoint that is correctly designated as *now* is incessantly changing. (3)(*b′*) has already expressed what we have to say about an eternal being's epistemic relationship to temporal nows, but perhaps our analysis of premiss (3) will be clearer if we provide a simpler version of that interpretation alongside an interpretation involving the single eternal now.

(3)(*b″*) For every temporal now, God knows which temporal events are actually happening now.

(3)(*b‴*) For the unique eternal now, God knows which temporal events are actually happening now.

The temporal events picked out in (3)(*b″*) are, for instance, those which are temporally simultaneous with your reading these words; the temporal events picked out in (3)(*b‴*) are all of them. Taken together, (3)(*b″*) and (3)(*b‴*) ascribe to God all there is to be known regarding the actual occurrence of temporal events, and there is no further sense in which to press the question whether God knows what time it is.

The proof we have been criticizing may be said to succeed in showing the incoherence of the concept of an omniscient, immutable, temporal entity; but that is not the concept of the perfect being that has been identified as God in orthodox Christian theology, which takes God to be eternal.[38]

[38] We benefited a great deal from criticisms and suggestions offered by several people who read or listened to earlier drafts of this paper. We cannot mention them all, but we are especially grateful for thoughtful comments, in some cases very extensive, from William Alston, John Bennett, Richard Creel, John Crossett, Anthony Kenny, William Rowe, Judith Slein, Richard Sorabji, and Richard Swinburne.

12

SIMPLICITY AND IMMUTABILITY IN GOD

WILLIAM E. MANN

I am God; I change not.

MALACHI 3: 6

STEADFASTNESS is a virtue we prize in persons. All other things being equal, we disapprove of those who break their promises, forsake their covenants, or change their minds capriciously. We regard as childish those who are easily deflected from the pursuit of their goals. We pity those who suffer radical transformations of character. It is not surprising, then, that many theists believe that no such fickle flickerings of human inconstancy could characterize God.[1] Many theists—especially those infected with a bit of philosophy—carry these speculations a step further. God is supremely steadfast, but he is also insusceptible to ceasing to be the being he is. A steadfast mortal is still mortal. If it be true that we are immortal, perhaps that is only because God's sustaining activity will not let death be ultimately proud. In contrast, nothing could possibly prevail against his nature. If he is essentially omnipotent, for example, then there is no time at which his power could possibly falter. For many theists, then, God is both supremely steadfast and essentially indomitable.

Many orthodox theologians and philosophers have taken yet a further step. For example, the great medieval philosophers argued that God is utterly and completely immutable, that no change of

Reprinted with permission from, *International Philosophical Quarterly*, Vol. 23, No. 3, Sept. 1983, 267–276.

[1] Genesis 6: 5–7 can easily be read as recording a change of mind in God. Such a reading receives a vigorous denial both by Philo (*Quod Deus Immutabilis Sit*, 20–32) and St Augustine (*De Civitate Dei*, xv, 24–5). See also Numbers 23: 19 and I Samuel 15: 11, 15: 29.

any kind can befall him.[2] He does not get better; he does not get worse. He does not learn, nor does he forget. He does not become wrathful or sorrowful. The activities of his creatures do not stir him to respond, for to respond is to change. It is this doctrine—the Doctrine of Divine Immutability (DDI)—which I wish to examine and defend.

In recent years the DDI has drawn fire from virtually every philosopher who has considered it. Perhaps the most fundamental objection to it is that an immutable being could not be a *personal* being, a being who intervenes in history, who cares for his creatures, who is aware of our sins and works for our redemption, who hears and answers our prayers, who consoles us in our grief, who inspires us in our joy. An immutable God would be a completely impassive God, uncomfortably akin to the textbook caricature of Aristotle's narcissistic unmoved mover.[3] Moreover, once we overcome our fears about change—caused, in large part, by our trying to rebuild the timeless temples of Elea and Athens in Jerusalem—we can see that God changes in all sorts of ways which redound to his credit. Here is but one example, which I describe in such a way as to emphasize the changes which apparently occur in God. At such-and-such a time, t_1, God willed that the Egyptians should suffer a hailstorm, and after that, as a result of God's perceiving at t_2 the Pharaoh's continued intransigence and as a reaction to it, he willed that the Egyptians be visited with a plague of locusts at t_3. At t_3 he could not still have been willing the hailstorm, for if he had, given that God's will is unimpedable, it would still have been hailing at t_3.

One may be excused for wondering, however, whether the dispute between medievals and moderns has really been joined. For in addition to arguing for God's immutability, the medievals argued strenuously that God is perfectly *active*, with no trace of

[2] Particularly strong and influential statements of the thesis can be found in St Augustine, *De Trinitate*, v, 2, 3; xv, 5, 7–8; St Anselm, *Monologion*, 25; St Thomas Aquinas, *Summa Theologiae*, pt. i, q. 9.

[3] See, for example, W. Kneale, 'Time and Eternity in Theology', *Proceedings of the Aristotelian Society* 61 (1960–1), pp. 87–108, esp. pp. 99–101; Nicholas Wolterstorff, 'God Everlasting', in Clifton J. Orlebeke and Lewis B. Smedes (eds.), *God and the Good* (Grand Rapids, 1975), pp. 181–203; and Richard Swinburne, *The Coherence of Theism* (Oxford, 1977), pp. 211–22.

passivity.[4] Yet these two characteristics seem to pull in opposite directions: how can a being be both immutable and active? I suggest that the answer lies in a relatively neglected doctrine which the medievals thought entailed both characteristics, and which illuminates the present issues. The Doctrine of Divine Simplicity (DDS) maintains that God has no 'parts' or components whatsoever. He has no properties, neither essential nor accidental. He has no spatial extension. Nor does he have any temporal extension: there is no division of his life into past or future stages, for that would imply temporal compositeness.[5] The DDS in turn is motivated by the consideration that God is a perfect being, and that *qua* perfect, he must be independent from all other things for his being the being he is, and he must be sovereign over all other things. If God himself were composite, then he would be dependent upon his components for his being what he is, whereas they would not be dependent upon him for their being what they are.[6]

Speaking strictly, then, an adherent of the DDS cannot say that omnipotence is an *attribute* of God, for the DDS maintains that in the case of God, the metaphysical distinction between a substance and its attributes does not apply. As Aquinas put it, God *is* his omnipotence, where the 'is' here expresses a necessary identity. In similar fashion, if God is omniscient, then God is the omniscience of God. It follows, of course, that the omniscience of God is the omnipotence of God.

To be sure, these are strange-sounding sayings. I think,

[4] See, for example, Aquinas, *Summa Contra Gentiles*, i, 16; *Summa Theologiae*, pt. i, qs. 1–2.

[5] See, for example, St Anselm, *Monologion*, 21; *Proslogion*, 20. Dennis C. Holt, following a claim made by A. N. Prior and others, has argued that things and persons have no temporal parts; only their lives or histories do. The claim is then applied to the *Monologion* in an attempt to show that Anselm's arguments for the eternality of God are misguided. God indeed has no temporal location or extension, but then neither do we, and so there is no crucial difference in that respect between God and us. See Holt's 'Timelessness and the Metaphysics of Temporal Existence', *American Philosophical Quarterly* 18 (1981), 149–56. Although I cannot argue the point in detail here, I see no compelling reason to accept Holt's thesis.

[6] See, for example, St Anselm, *Monologion*, 17; *Proslogion*, 18; Aquinas, *Summa Contra Gentiles*, i, 18; *Summa Theologiae*, pt. i, q. 3, a. 7; Alvin Plantinga, *Does God Have a Nature?* (Milwaukee, 1980), pp. 28–37.

however, that philosophical sense can be made of them if one can defend the intelligibility of the following theses:

(1) The thesis that all the divine attributes are necessarily coextensive. According to this thesis, it would be impossible for any being to instantiate the attribute *being omniscient*, say, without also instantiating the attribute *being omnipotent*, and vice versa.

(2) The thesis that necessarily coextensive attributes are necessarily identical.

Of these two theses, (1) surely requires more defence. Notice that (1) and (2) are jointly sufficient to underwrite such identities as that the omniscience of God = the omnipotence of God.

(3) The thesis that if God exists, then he is an instance of an attribute, the attribute of *being a Godhead*, which attribute is identical, by theses (1) and (2), to *being omniscient*, etc. (3) is itself an entailment of a more general thesis, namely, that any individual thing is an instance of a *rich property*, the conjunctive property formed from all and only those essential and accidental properties which truly characterize the individual in question. In the case of God, a defender of the DDS will insist on three provisions with respect to thesis (3). (*a*) God's rich property is not multiply instantiable: there cannot be two Gods. (*b*) God's rich property contains only one conjunct. (*c*) God's rich property contains no accidental properties. Thesis (3) implies that God is his own Godhead, and thus his own omniscience, and so on.

I shall not here directly defend the DDS, as defined by theses (1)–(3).[7] Instead I shall offer an indirect defence, showing how the DDS enables us to understand the DDI, and in particular, the notion of an immutable person.

The DDS implies that there are no temporally successive stages to God's existence. It is thus incompatible with God's being sempiternal. In fact, the DDS implies that God is eternal in Boethius' sense, i.e., that God enjoys 'the complete possession all at once of illimitable life'.[8] 'Complete possession all at once',

[7] I have defended theses (2) and (3) elsewhere. See my 'Divine Simplicity', *Religious Studies* 18 (1982), pp. 451–71.

[8] Boethius, *De Consolatione Philosophiae*, v, prose 6. The translation is from

because there are no past or future stages in a simple being's life; 'illimitable life', because a simple being, *qua* perfect, must be supremely active, and activity presupposes life. Now it is clear that if God is eternal, he is immutable: if there are not even two stages in his life, then *a fortiori* there are no two stages in his life such that something in the one stage is different from something in the other. Thus the DDS implies that God is eternal, which in turn implies the DDI.

But how can an eternal, immutable being be a person? Well, what is it to be a person? Daniel Dennett has pointed out that there have been at least six different notions of personhood put forth in the philosophical tradition, each offered as an individually necessary if not sufficient condition of personhood.[9] A is a person only if:

(1) A is a rational being.
(2) A is a being to which states of consciousness can be attributed.
(3) Others regard or can regard A as a being to which states of consciousness can be attributed.
(4) A is capable of regarding others as beings to which states of consciousness can be attributed.
(5) A is capable of verbal communication.
(6) A is self-conscious; i.e., A is capable of regarding him/her/itself as a subject of states of consciousness.

Suppose we take the high road and insist that, in order to be a person, A must satisfy *all* of conditions (1)–(6). Our question then becomes this: can an eternal, immutable being satisfy (1)–(6), thus not precluding its being a person?

Let us consider conditions (2), (3), (4), and (6) first. In an obvious way, they all require that certain kinds of states of consciousness be properly ascribed to A. (2) and (3) require only

Eleonore Stump and Norman Kretzmann, 'Eternity', *Journal of Philosophy*, 78 (1981), pp. 429–58, esp. 430; reprinted as Ch. XI in this volume.

[9] Daniel Dennett, 'Conditions of Personhood', in Amelie Oksenberg Rorty (ed.), *The Identities of Persons* (Berkeley, 1976), pp. 175–96. Dennett explores the connections between the six conditions. I shall reluctantly suppress discussion of those issues.

the ascription of first-order states (e.g., perhaps, that A believes that *p*), while (4) and (6) require the ascription of some second-order states (such as, perhaps, that A believes that B desires that *p*). Now there are some sorts of mental states or activities which by their very nature either take time themselves or imply past or future mental states or activities in the same agent. *Growing resentful* is an example of the former kind; *forgetting the date of the Battle of Stamford Bridge* and *anticipating the joy of getting to the end of this paper* are examples of the latter. It is clear that an eternal, immutable being cannot be the subject of any such mental states or activity. But there are other kinds of mental activity whose correct ascription to an agent implies no necessary temporal spread. It takes time to grow resentful, but it need not take any time at all to *know* something. Of course one can know something for a period of years, but the point is that knowing is not a process whose fulfilment takes time, or an activity which entails the existence of earlier or later stages in the mental life of the knowing agent. Similar remarks hold for *willing*. The concept of an instantaneous intention, whose objective is realized simultaneously with its formulation, may tax one's credulity, but there is no absurdity in the idea of a volition whose object is simultaneously realized: '"Fiat lux". Et facta est lux'. Finally, there are analogous observations to be made concerning second-order states and activities. My expectation that I will learn all about recursive function theory by the end of the year is a coherent expectation only if I am in time. But A's awareness that A knows that *p* does not in itself imply that A is in time. So although an eternal, immutable being cannot wax wroth, remember, forget, calculate, or fall in love, such a being can know, will, love, and know that it knows, and thus be the subject of certain kinds of states or activities of consciousness.[10] The repertoire of kinds of states of consciousness available to an eternal, immutable being may thus be somewhat restricted: there is no reason, however, to think that the curtailed repertoire threatens the candidacy for personhood of such a being.

Condition (1) requires that persons be rational beings. Once

[10] This point is made admirably clearly in Stump and Kretzmann, 'Eternity', pp. 446–7.

again, there are some elements of human rationality which could not characterize an immutable being. An eternal, immutable being could not make inductive inferences based on past experience, nor (it seems to me) infer 'B' from '(A → B)' and 'A'. Nevertheless, such a being could *understand* that 'B' is a consequence of '(A → B)' and 'A' and understand that evidence *e* is good evidence for hypothesis *h*. Rationality in action requires a certain fit between an agent's beliefs, desires, and actions. We now have reason to believe that believing and desiring need not imply temporality, and I now want to suggest how God, *qua* eternal, immutable being, can be said to act.

Let us return to the hailstorm–plague of locusts example, and see how the DDI, buttressed by the DDS, can cope with it. According to Aquinas, the power of God is the substance of God and the power of God is the activity of God,[11] whence it follows that the substance of God is the activity of God, i.e., God's essence *is* his activity, and this in turn just *is* God. Since God is his activity and his activity can have no stages, processes, or compositeness to it, it must be that the activity by which he wills the hail storm at t_1 is the activity by which he wills the plague of locusts at t_3. That is, one and the same divine, eternal activity has as two of its effects (1) that the Egyptians experience a hailstorm at t_1 and (2) that the Egyptians suffer a plague of locusts at t_3. There is surely nothing unusual about one and the same cause having distinct and non-simultaneous effects. A particular sun storm may be the cause of certain thermal phenomena in the vicinity of the sun and, some eight minutes later, certain radio phenomena on earth. Of course the case is not perfectly analogous to God's activity, since the radio phenomena are a more indirect effect of the sun storm than the thermal phenomena, whereas the plague of locusts is not a more indirect effect of God's activity than the hailstorm: God's activity is equally present to both t_1 and t_3. Moreover, the sun storm is a datable event with temporal duration, while in the hailstorm–plague of locusts case, God's activity is not, even though the effects of it are. I do not see, then, any absurdity in ascribing rational activity to an immutable being.

[11] Aquinas, *Summa Contra Gentiles*, ii, 8–9.

Condition (5) requires that persons be capable of verbal communication. The account sketched in the previous paragraph provides the wherewithal to see how an eternal, immutable being could have such a capacity. In 'speaking' to Moses, God brought it about that Moses heard certain statements. Moses' hearing the statements is a temporal process which took place during a certain interval, but it does not follow from that fact that God's bringing it about is a temporal process, or even that it happened at a certain time.[12] A defender of the DDI must be careful with a question like 'When did God will the hailstorm?' The apparently obvious answer, 'at t_1', misleads. The sentence, 'God wills that there be a hailstorm at t_1', is to be distinguished, depending on how we interpret the scope of the temporal modifier, 'at t_1'. If it is interpreted *in sensu composito* the sentence expresses the proposition

(P1) At t_1, God wills that there be a hailstorm.

Interpreted *in sensu diviso*, the sentence expresses the proposition

(P2) God wills that-there-be-a-hailstorm-at-t_1.

A defender of the DDI will brand (P1) as false, but (P2) can be accepted as true, provided that the verb 'wills' is understood as being tenseless. In similar fashion, the question, 'When did God will the hailstorm?', is amphibolous between these two questions:

(P3) When in God's career did he will that the hailstorm occur?
(P4) When did the hailstorm, which God wills, occur?

The answer to (P4) is a straightforward 'at t_1', but the DDI defender should greet (P3) with stony silence.

I have been arguing that there is no absurdity to the notion of an immutable yet active personal God, and I have helped myself to the DDS in order to make my argument. In the remainder of this paper I want to examine four objections to my enterprise. The first one questions the necessity of the DDS for the DDI; the other three allege that the DDS itself generates various kinds of unacceptable consequences.[13]

[12] On this latter point, see Stump and Kretzmann, 'Eternity'.

[13] I owe the first and the fourth objections to Eleonore Stump, who commented on an earlier and shorter version of this paper at the American Philosophical

Objection 1

'The doctrine of God's eternality is sufficient by itself to establish the DDI. That is, if God is eternal (in Boethius's sense) then he is immutable. Thus we do not need the DDS to secure the DDI, and if we do not need it, why should we use it?'

Consider the following analogy. 'The fact that light rays bend in the vicinity of the Sun is implied by the thesis that space is curved. The General Theory of Relativity implies that space has curvature, but we do not need the General Theory of Relativity to establish the fact that light rays bend in the vicinity of the Sun; the thesis that space is curved is sufficient by itself.' The point to be made in reply here is that without the General Theory of Relativity we have no good antecedent reason to accept the thesis that space is curved. By itself the thesis is unmotivated and *ad hoc* to the case of bending light rays. The General Theory of Relativity serves to justify the thesis that space is curved by showing how it fits into a more comprehensive theory about the physical world.

The moral of the story should be clear with respect to the first objection. Entailment is not justification. The doctrine of God's eternality does indeed entail the DDI, but that fact alone provides no reason for accepting either it or the DDI. The explanatory necessity of the DDS emerges when we ask why we should accept the doctrine of God's eternality. The DDS highlights the fact that both the doctrine of God's eternality and the DDI are embedded in a more comprehensive theory about God's nature. If God were not eternal and immutable he would not be simple, and if he were not simple, he would not be perfect. It is ultimately the 'logic of perfection' which gives us the DDS and the DDI.

Objection 2

'Abbreviate the proposition that the Pharaoh is intransigent at t_2 by '*P*' and the proposition that the Egyptians suffer a plague of locusts at t_3 by '*L*'. If he is omniscient, God knows that *P* and *L* are logically independent propositions. Now consider the following dilemma. Either God's knowledge that *P* is identical with his knowledge that *L* or it is distinct. If it is distinct, then the DDS is

Association Eastern Division meeting in 1981. I am happy to acknowledge my debt to her, but not confident that I will have overcome her scepticism about the DDS.

false. But the notion that God's knowledge that *P* is identical to his knowledge that *L* is unintelligible. Your knowledge that *P* is a different item of knowledge from your knowledge that *L* simply because *P* and *L* are independent propositions. The same must be true of God. Therefore, if God is simple, he can know at most one thing, and so he is not omniscient.'

Solution: The DDS maintains that, necessarily, the activity by which God knows that $P =$ the activity by which God knows that L. It does not thereby imply that $P = L$, nor does the fact that $P \neq L$ imply that an agent's knowing that *P* requires an act of cognition different from that agent's knowing that *L*. A being of extremely limited cognitive capacities may not be able to walk and chew gum at the same time, but we humans can know different propositions in one act of cognition. Acts of cognition are not individuated by their atomic propositional objects, or at least there is no good reason to think that that is so. One and the same act of cognition may reveal to me that a window is closed *and* freshly painted. By extending this line of reasoning one can see that there is no absurdity in the notion of a being of unlimited cognitive capacities being aware of the truth of an unlimited number of propositions by means of one act of cognition. The *content* of God's knowledge may be unlimited, but the DDS need only insist that the *activity* by which he knows is simple.

Objection 3

'The DDS is incompatible with human freedom, if human freedom involves the possibility of doing otherwise. For the following two features of the DDS preclude there being any contingency in the created world:

(A) Necessarily, the omniscience of God is the essence of God.
(B) Necessarily, God is the essence of God; i.e., it is not possible for God to be other than what he is in any respect; if God were different in any respect, he would not be God.

Now suppose that the Pharaoh's intransigence at t_2 is a specimen of free behaviour. This supposition implies, at a minimum, that the proposition *P* is logically contingent; although true, *P* could have been false. Now the argument, which takes the shape of a *reductio*:

(1) It is possible for *P* to have been false. (Supposition)
(2) If it is possible for *P* to have been false, then it is possible for God not to know that *P*.
(3) If it is possible for God not to know that *P*, then it is possible for God's omniscience to be other than what it is.

Thus:

(4) It is possible for God's omniscience to be other than what it is. (From (1), (2), and (3))

Thus:

(5) It is possible for God's essence to be other than what it is. (From (4) and (A))

Thus:

(6) It is possible for God to be other than what he is. (From (5) and (B))

But (6) clearly contradicts (B). Therefore if the DDS is true, there are no logically contingent propositions and no free actions.'

Note that the argument correctly appeals to God's omniscience, but not to foreknowledge: God has no foreknowledge if he is eternal. Nevertheless, the argument trades on an ambiguity in the phrase 'God's omniscience'. In one sense 'God's omniscience' could have been otherwise, as step (4) maintains. In this sense of 'God's omniscience', *what* God knows or the *content* of God's knowledge would be different from what it in fact is. If the Pharaoh had not been intransigent at t_2, God would know that the Pharaoh is not intransigent at t_2. So step (4) is more perspicuously rendered as

(4′) It is possible for the content of God's omniscience to be other than what it is,

and the defender of the DDS need have no demurral about (4′). But (4′) does not take us to step (5), even with the aid of (A). To do that, (A) would have to be interpreted as

(A′) Necessarily, the content of God's omniscience is the essence of God.

Now the DDS defender need not accept (A′) as a correct gloss of (A). What he/she must accept is (A*):

(A*) Necessarily, the power or activity by which God knows all things is the essence of God.

And, to complete the story, the combination of (4′) and (A*) does not yield (5).

Objection 4

'The DDS logically precludes *God's* freedom of will. Let us suppose that he wills that-there-be-a-hail-storm-at-t_1, and let us abbreviate the hyphenated material as 'that-*H*'. We are supposing, then, that

(1) God wills that-*H*.

Does he have it in his power not to will that-*H*?[14] To suppose that he does is to suppose, at a minimum,

(2) It is possible that God not will that-*H*.

But (2) flies in the face of three principles implied by the DDS. One is principle (B), mentioned in objection 3. The others are these:

(C) Necessarily, the essence of God is the will of God.
(D) Necessarily, the will of God contains no parts, stages, or complexity of any kind.

(D) implies that God's willing that-*H* is not a *part* of God's will; it necessarily *is* God's will. That is, by (D) we have

[14] Do not confuse this question with another one—'Does he have it in his power to will that-not-*H*?' The second question asks whether God can will some outcome other than what he in fact wills, while the first one asks whether he can refrain from willing a certain outcome which he in fact wills. Of course, if we assume (*a*) that the two outcomes are logically incompatible and (*b*) that God does not will logically incompatible outcomes, then it follows that if he wills that-not-*H*, then he does not will that-*H*. (Assumptions (*a*) and (*b*) are not enough to establish the converse.) In other words, given assumptions (*a*) and (*b*), God's not willing that-*H* is a necessary condition for his willing that-not-*H*.

(3) Necessarily, if God wills that-*H*, then God's will is God's willing that-*H*.

(3) and (C) yield

(4) Necessarily, if God wills that-*H*, then God's essence is God's willing that-*H*.

But (1) allows us to detach from (4)

(5) God's essence is God's willing that-*H*.

Now if we accept (2), then (2) and (5) imply

(6) It is possible that God's essence be other than what it is.

But since God is his essence, according to (B), (6) and (B) imply

(7) It is possible that God be other than what he is.

(7), however, contradicts (B). So if the DDS is true, then (1) and (2) cannot both be true, and in general, God cannot do other than what he in fact does.'

The argument fails, for a reason similar to the reason the argument in objection 3 failed. 'The will of God', as it appears in (C) and (D), is ambiguous. It can mean God's willing power or activity on the one hand or, on the other, what God wills, i.e., the results, outcomes, or contents of God's willing activity; compare 'the will of God always achieves the good' with 'your present happiness is the will of God'. Bearing this ambiguity in mind, we can consider two versions each of (C) and (D):

(C′) Necessarily, the essence of God is what God wills.
(C*) Necessarily, the essence of God is the power or activity by which God wills all things.
(D′) Necessarily, what God wills contains no parts, stages, or complexity.
(D*) Necessarily, the power or activity by which God wills all things contains no parts, stages, or complexity.

The DDS is not committed either to (C′) or (D′), and that is a good thing, for on a straightforward interpretation of them, they are false. The DDS is committed to (C*) and (D*). But (D*) does not imply (3); the closest it gets us to (3) is

(3′) Necessarily, if God wills that-*H*, then the power or activity by which God wills all things is the power or activity by which God wills that-*H*.

In turn, (3′) and (C*) give us not (4) but

(4′) Necessarily, if God wills that-*H*, then God's essence is the power or activity by which God wills that-*H*.

(1) and (4′) imply

(5′) God's essence is the power or activity by which God wills that-*H*.

However, (5′) and (2), the assumption that it is possible that God not will that-*H*, simply do not imply (6). Instead of (2), one would need, in conjunction with (5′), something like

(2′) It is possible that the power or activity by which God wills that-*H* be other than what it is.

There is a world of difference between (2) and (2′). In particular, (2) can be true while (2′) is false. Thus, a defender of the DDS can accept (2) and reject (2′).

To see the difference between (2) and (2′) it is crucial to distinguish between a power or activity and its manifestation. Consider Smith, who has the power to lift any object whose weight is less than or equal to 150 pounds, and who does not have the power to lift any object which weighs more than 150 pounds. In the world as it actually is, Smith can lift some objects but not others. Let us now consider two different counter-factual situations. One is a world, W_1, in which there are no objects which weigh over 150 pounds; the other a world, W_2, in which every object weighs over 150 pounds. (Such worlds may have different physical laws from the actual world.) In these two cases it is perfectly coherent to suppose that Smith's lifting power remains invariant, even though its manifestations are quite different: in W_1 Smith can lift every object; in W_2 he can lift none.[15] The point to be seen here is

[15] Extreme verificationists might quarrel over the intelligibility of the attribution to Smith in W_2 of the power in question, since in that world, there would be no way to distinguish Smith's power from that of a person who could only lift objects weighing less than 149 pounds, or less than 148 pounds, and so on.

that the manifestations of Smith's invariant power will typically change as the counter-factual situations change.

Think now of God, who according to the DDS, is his own power or activity, and who, according to traditional theism, is supremely powerful and active. The manifestation of that power in different counter-factual situations can or will vary just because the situations are different. In a situation in which the Pharaoh relents at t_2 and lets Moses' people go, it is reasonable to think that the manifestation of God's activity at t_3 will be different: the Egyptians will not suffer a plague of locusts. But this supposition provides no reason to think that God's power or activity would somehow be different in that counter-factual situation from what it is in the actual situation in which the Pharaoh did not relent. Thus it seems to me that a defender of the DDS can maintain simultaneously that God can will other than when he does will and that God's willing power or activity cannot be other than what it is.

There may be other, fatal objections to the DDI and the DDS, but if so, I have not seen them. My provisional conclusion, then, is that the doctrines are surprisingly resilient, and worth more serious attention than they have recently received.

NOTES ON CONTRIBUTORS

ROBERT MERRIHEW ADAMS is Professor of Philosophy at the University of California, Los Angeles.

WILLIAM P. ALSTON is Professor of Philosophy at Syracuse University.

DAVID BLUMENFELD is Professor of Philosophy at Southwestern University.

THOMAS P. FLINT is Assistant Professor of Philosophy at the University of Notre Dame.

ALFRED J. FREDDOSO is Associate Professor of Philosophy at the University of Notre Dame.

ANTHONY KENNY is Master of Balliol College, Oxford.

NORMAN KRETZMANN is Susan Linn Sage Professor of Philosophy at Cornell University.

WILLIAM E. MANN is Professor of Philosophy at the University of Vermont.

THOMAS V. MORRIS is Assistant Professor of Philosophy at the University of Notre Dame.

ROBERT OAKES is Professor of Philosophy at the University of Missouri.

ALVIN PLANTINGA is O'Brien Professor of Philosophy at the University of Notre Dame.

ELEONORE STUMP is Professor of Philosophy at Virginia Polytechnic Institute and State University.

WILLIAM J. WAINWRIGHT is Professor of Philosophy at the University of Wisconsin–Milwaukee.

SELECT BIBLIOGRAPHY

This bibliography contains only a selected list of books and articles which have appeared since 1960. No separate mention is made of many of the papers to be found in the anthologies listed below. More complete bibliographical information relevant to the topics of this book is to be found in Cahn and Shatz, and in Dore. The most extensive bibliography available is W. J. Wainwright, *Philosophy of Religion: An Annotated Bibliography of Twentieth Century Writings in English* (New York, 1978).

BOOKS

Brody, B., *Readings in the Philosophy of Religion: An Analytic Approach* (Englewood Cliffs, New Jersey, 1974).

Cahn, S. and Shatz, D. (eds.), *Contemporary Philosophy of Religion* (Oxford, 1982).

Creel, R., *Divine Impassibility* (Cambridge, 1985).

Davis, S., *Logic and the Nature of God* (London, 1983).

Dore, C., *Theism* (Dordrecht, 1984).

Durrant, M., *The Logical Status of 'God'* (London, 1973).

Freddoso, A. (ed.), *The Existence and Nature of God* (Notre Dame, 1983).

Geach, P., *Providence and Evil* (Cambridge, 1977).

Helm, P., *Divine Commands and Morality* (Oxford, 1981).

Jantzen, G., *God's World, God's Body* (Philadelphia, 1984).

Kenny, A., *The God of the Philosophers* (Oxford, 1979).

Kvanvig, J., *The Possibility of an All-Knowing God* (London, 1986).

Morris, T., *Anselmian Explorations* (Notre Dame, 1987).

Pike, N., *God and Timelessness* (New York, 1970).

Plantinga, A., *Does God Have a Nature?* (Milwaukee, 1980).

Ross, J., *Philosophical Theology*, second edition (Indianapolis, 1980).

Swinburne, R., *The Coherence of Theism* (Oxford, 1977).

Urban, L. and Walton, D. (eds.), *The Power of God: Readings on Omnipotence and Evil* (Oxford, 1978).

Ward, H., *Rational Theology and the Creativity of God* (Oxford, 1982).

JOURNAL ARTICLES

Adams, R. M., 'Middle Knowledge and the Problem of Evil', *American Philosophical Quarterly* 14 (1977), 109–17.

Burrell, D., 'God's Eternity', *Faith and Philosophy* 1 (1984), 389–406.

Dore, C., 'The Possibility of God', *Faith and Philosophy* 1 (1984), 303–15.

Fitzgerald, P., 'Stump and Kretzmann on Time and Eternity', *Journal of Philosophy* 82 (1985), 260–9.

Fischer, J., 'Freedom and Foreknowledge', *Philosophical Review* 92 (1983), 69–79.

——, 'Ockhamism', *Philosophical Review* 94 (1985), 81–100.

Flint, T., 'The Problem of Divine Freedom', *American Philosophical Quarterly* 20 (1983), 255–64.

Gellman, J., 'Omnipotence and Impeccability', *New Scholasticism* 51 (1977), 21–37.

Grim, P., 'Some Neglected Problems of Omniscience', *American Philosophical Quarterly* 20 (1983), 265–76.

—— 'Against Omniscience: The Case from Essential Indexicals', *Noûs* 19 (1985), 151–280.

Guleserian, T., 'God and Possible Worlds: The Modal Problem of Evil', *Noûs* 17 (1983), 221–38.

——, 'Can Moral Perfection be an Essential Attribute?', *Philosophy and Phenomenological Research* 46 (1985), 219–41.

Hasker, W., 'Concerning the Intelligibility of "God is Timeless"', *New Scholasticism* 57 (1983), 170–95.

—— 'Foreknowledge and Necessity', *Faith and Philosophy* 2 (1985), 121–57.

Hoffman, J., 'Can God Do Evil?', *Southern Journal of Philosophy* 17 (1979), 213–20.

Hoffman, J. and Rosenkranz, G., 'What an Omnipotent Agent Can Do', *International Journal for Philosophy of Religion* 11 (1980), 1–19.

—— ——, 'Hard and Soft Facts', *Philosophical Review* 93 (1984), 419–34.

Hunt, M., 'Some Remarks About the Embodiment of God', *Religious Studies* 17 (1981), 105–8.

Jantzen, G., 'On Worshipping an Embodied God', *Canadian Journal of Philosophy* 8 (1978), 511–19.

Kneale, W., 'Time and Eternity in Theology', *Proceedings of the Aristotelian Society* 61 (1960–1), 87–108.

Kretzmann, N. and Stump, E., 'Absolute Simplicity', *Faith and Philosophy* 2 (1985), 353–82.

Kvanvig, J. 'Divine Transcendence', *Religious Studies* 20 (1984), 377–87.

La Croix, R., 'Omniprescience and Divine Determinism', *Religious Studies* 12 (1976), 365–81.

——, 'Aquinas on God's Omnipresence and Timelessness', *Philosophy and Phenomenological Research* 42 (1982), 391–9.

Lazerowitz, M., 'On a Property of a Perfect Being', *Mind* 92 (1983), 257–63.

Mann, W., 'The Divine Attributes', *American Philosophical Quarterly* 12 (1975), 151–9.

——, 'Divine Simplicity', *Religious Studies* 18 (1982), 451–71.

Morriston, W., 'Is God "Significantly Free"?', *Faith and Philosophy* 2 (1985), 257–64.

Oakes, R., 'Classical Theism and Pantheism: A Reply to Professor Quinn', *Religious Studies* 16 (1980), 353–6.

——, 'Classical Theism and Pantheism: A Victory for Process Theism?' *Religious Studies* 13 (1977), 167–73.

Pike, N., 'Divine Omniscience and Voluntary Action', *Philosophical Review* 74 (1965), 27–46; reprinted in Cahn and Shatz, 61–76.

——, 'Omnipotence and God's Ability to Sin', *American Philosophical Quarterly* 6 (1969), 208–16; reprinted in Helm, 67–82.

——, 'Fischer on Freedom and Foreknowledge', *Philosophical Review* 93 (1984), 599–614.

Quinn, P., 'Divine Conservation and Spinozistic Pantheism', *Religious Studies* 15 (1979), 289–302.

——, 'Metaphysical Necessity and Modal Logics', *Monist* 65 (1982), 444–55.

——, 'God, Moral Perfection, and Possible Worlds', in Sontag, F. and Bryant, M., *God: The Contemporary Discussion* (New York, 1982), 197–215.

Reichenbach, B., 'Must God Create the Best Possible World?', *International Philosophical Quarterly* 19 (1979), 203–12.

Stump, E. and Kretzmann, N., 'Absolute Simplicity', *Faith and Philosophy* 2 (1985), 353–82.

Sutherland, S. 'God, Time, and Eternity', *Proceedings of the Aristotelian Society* 79 (1978), 103–21.

Wierenga, E., 'Intrinsic Maxima and Omnibenevolence', *International Journal for Philosophy of Religion* 10 (1979), 41–50.

——, 'Omnipotence Defined', *Philosophy and Phenomenological Research* 43 (1983), 363–75.

Wolterstorff, N., 'God Everlasting', in Orlebeke, C. and Smedes, L. (eds.), *God and the Good: Essays in Honor of Henry Stob* (Grand Rapids, 1975); reprinted in Cahn and Shatz, 77–98.

INDEX OF NAMES